CODES AND CONTRADICTIONS

SUNY series, Power, Social Identity, and Education
Lois Weis, editor

CODES AND CONTRADICTIONS

Race, Gender Identity, and Schooling

JEANNE DRYSDALE WEILER

State University
of New York
Press

Published by
State University of New York Press, Albany

Production by Susan Geraghty
Marketing by Fran Keneston

Printed in the United States of America

For information, address State University of New York
Press, State University Plaza, Albany, N.Y., 12246

Library of Congress Cataloging-in-Publication Data

Weiler, Jeanne.
    Codes and contradictions : race, gender identity, and schooling /
by Jeanne D. Weiler.
        p.   cm. — (SUNY series, power, social identity, and
education)
    Includes bibliographical references and index.
    ISBN 0-7914-4519-4 (alk. paper). — ISBN 0-7914-4520-8 (pbk. : alk.
paper)
        1. Women—Education—Social aspects—United States Case studies.
2. Women—United States—Identity Case studies. 3. Race awareness-
-United States Case studies. 4. Feminism and education—United
States. I. Title. II. Series.
LC1755.W45 2000
    373.1822'09747'1—dc21   99-15651
                                                                         CIP

10 9 8 7 6 5 4 3 2 1

CONTENTS

LIST OF TABLES

PREFACE

> I came to Alternative High School because I wasn't gonna make it in another school. I was a regular truant. They wanted to send me to court to take me away from my mother cause I wasn't going. I had a lot of absences and then they put me in AIDP [attendance improvement dropout prevention] and then I passed and my guidance counselor told me to come here cause if I was to go to a regular high school, I would've dropped out.
>
> —Marlissa, age 15, 1989

In testimony to the success of Alternative High School (A.H.S.)[1] in New York City, Marlissa, once considered a student at risk of not completing high school, graduated in September 1992. Indeed, Alternative High School, a haven for students who have disengaged from traditional schooling, has many similar successes—85 percent of its students graduate with a high school diploma and almost one-half of those students go on to some form of higher education.

"Success," however, is relative. Working-class and low-income students of color, however "successful" they are at graduating from high school, still must enter a race- and sex-segregated labor market with diminishing opportunities for adequate wages and meaningful work. I want to be clear, however, at the beginning of this book, that I believe for working-class and low-income young women, a high school diploma, at the minimum, is absolutely necessary to enhance their chances of avoiding poverty or finding adequate employment to financially sustain themselves or their families. I make this statement based on both New York City and national data, which clearly indicate the relative worth of a high school diploma for young women. For example, in New York City, Rivera-Batiz (1994) has calculated that earnings for women with less than a high school degree have fallen while female high school graduates' earnings have been increasing. National data also provide convincing evidence that young women need to stay in school. Both African American and white women with a high school diploma earn approximately one-fifth as much as those without one (National Center for Education Statistics, 1997). Thus, I refer to Alternative High School's success in graduating students.

The formula for the success of Alternative High School is complex and multifaceted. The administration and faculty have done away with the most overt forms of pedagogical practices generally associated with unequal school outcomes such as tracking, ability grouping, traditional grading practices, Eurocentric and sex-differentiated curricula, and a punitive and authoritarian environment. The school is small (less than five hundred students), the teacher/student ratio is low, intensive counseling as well as other social and emotional supports are provided to students. It is a school that not only affords educationally disenfranchised students with hope that they will graduate, but through its reconfigured infrastructure, provides students the material and psychological supports to do so. I wish the reader to continually bear in mind the uniqueness of this school and its unparalleled success in educating disengaged students who otherwise would have little hope of completing high school.

Alternative High School, designed to prepare students to make reasonable and informed future occupational and educational choices, offered a singular opportunity to research how school processes actually contribute to and shape girls' self-understandings and future expectations, particularly as they relate to wage labor. I wish to emphasize here that although the centerpiece of the school's curriculum is the career education and internship component, the reader should in no way construe A.H.S. as a vocational high school. Rather, the school's career education program is an effort to orient its students toward formulating future career goals at the same time the academic curriculum is preparing them for higher education.

This book is about a group of young women enrolled in the ninth grade at A.H.S., all of whom have experienced past educational failure. I document their experiences within school and speculate on the impact these experiences have in the shaping of their future aspirations and hopes. While many of the participants in the study furnished me with rich information about their day-to-day lives, the main focus of this book is on the processes solely within the school itself. Certainly gender identity is also created and refashioned within other social or cultural spheres such as the family, peer group, community, and workplace.

Many people have had a hand in helping me to conceptualize this study, and complete the data collection, analysis, and writing. I could not have completed such tasks alone.

Most importantly, I owe my greatest thanks to the young women who allowed me to briefly enter their lives and who fill the pages of this book with their energy, insights, optimism, and aspirations. I am also indebted to the administrators and teachers at A.H.S. who spoke candidly about their feelings and observations and provided me with opportunities to learn how their school has become a place that truly challenges the status quo.

Gail Kelly's thoughts and words are woven throughout this book. We spent much time together in her kitchen and on her front porch clarifying the original ideas that shaped this work. I owe tremendous thanks to Lois Weis for generously taking over the guidance of my project after Gail's death. I am especially appreciative of Lois's astute insights, constant encouragement, and mentoring along the way. I also owe many thanks to Michelle Fine for her incisive comments on an earlier draft of this work. Maxine Seller, Catherine Raissiguier, and Angela Calabrese Barton read various versions of the entire manuscript and provided me with many helpful suggestions as did an anonymous reviewer. My friends Kowsar Chowdhury, Olga Drogal, Kate Josephson, Junko Kanamura, Grace Mak, Bonnie Oglensky, Melissa Ragona, Barbara Schollar, and Wendy Schwartz contributed their friendship and perceptive insights.

It would not have been possible to complete such an undertaking without the patience, encouragement, and many forms of support—intellectual, material, and emotional—that I received from my husband, John. I am also grateful to both our families for their unflagging encouragement. I could not have sustained such a long-term effort without the love and support of my parents. My mother Jean Thompson Weiler generously dedicated her time and energy in transcribing interviews and providing much-needed child care. My mother-in-law, Ruby Choonoo, during her long visits, took on many household activities that gave me the time to work uninterrupted.

This book is dedicated to our children, Ruby Jean and Jeffrey.

CHAPTER 1

Introduction

At 20 [years old] how do I picture myself? Married, going to law school, wearing my tight black pants, my hair pouffed out. I want to have a son by then.
                            —Doreen, age 15, Italian American

I want to be successful [in the future]. I do want to get married, but like I want to be successful. First I want a college degree, then a good job. I ain't gonna think about getting married. I could have a boyfriend here and there.
                            —Aurea, age 14, Puerto Rican descent

I'm going straight to college [after high school]. I'll be living in a dorm. Everything will be alright. I'll have my car. I'll be preparing for my career. I won't have no kids.
                            —Saundria, age 14, African American

I think you have to be an example [to your children]. When they grow up you're not gonna be sitting around the house waiting for the husband to bring whatever you want. I'll have a steady job so I could bring home the money and my kids could learn that.
                            —Lucy, age 15, Colombian descent

Above are the voices of young working-class women enrolled in an alternative high school in New York City.[1] This book is about them and their female classmates who made up the entering ninth-grade class at Alternative High School (A.H.S.) in 1988. Since that time, all have entered adulthood, some bearing a high school diploma and entering higher education, and others leaving school prior to graduation to enter an increasingly unequal and contracting urban labor market. The focus of this book is not about why some of the young women graduated from high school while others did not, but rather how in one historical moment in time—a time in which the massive restructuring of the U.S. economy was resulting in profound changes in gender relations as women's labor-market participation increased, and at the same time, exacerbating existing disparities in resources between rich and poor and African Americans and Latinos and whites—young working-class women of different racial/ethnic[2] origins define the possibilities for themselves as adult women.[3] How did these young working-class women at this historical juncture (in which messages about women's economic potential compete with the realities of declining urban markets), understand the possibilities for their future adult lives and how did they construe the use of schooling in attaining those future goals? But most importantly, how are understandings of and possibilities for the future shaped by young women's experiences within various racial/ethnic communities and economic contexts? And, what is the role of their school in shaping and creating those understandings and possibilities?

The answers to these questions and others raised in this book contribute to a small but growing body of knowledge on youth development from which new questions can be generated. For example, how do young adults at the end of the 1990s, especially white working-class and young adults of color, reconcile and understand the disjunction between their teenage aspirations and the realities of declining opportunities in adulthood? Only by documenting the lived experiences of different groups of young working-class women at one unique historical moment can we move forward toward a fuller understanding of how race, ethnicity, and social class shape the particular experiences of women throughout their lifetime.

THE DROPOUT "PROBLEM"

It has been well documented that urban working-class and minority youth drop out of school at disconcertingly high rates. In urban areas, approximately 50 or 60 percent of adolescents leave high school prior to graduation (Fine, 1989). In New York City, the percentage is even higher: youth advocacy organizations estimate that in some African American and Latino communities, up to 80 percent do not graduate from high school.

Much that has been written about the dropout "problem" has attempted to identify background characteristics predicting who will drop out, and to analyze schooling practices contributing to student "push out" before graduation. Very little research, however, has sought to understand either the students' perspective on dropping out or the social forces influencing their decisions to stay or leave.

Ogbu (1978, 1982, 1994) has posited an explanatory framework (discussed later in this chapter) that links students' responses to schooling to larger sociocultural forces outside of school. Ogbu argued that the black students he studied were apt to construct beliefs about their future job opportunities by observing which jobs were held by blacks in their communities. He further maintained that not only the beliefs but also the behavior of black students were dependent upon their perceptions of the opportunity structure, which assumes the character of a "castelike" system for people of color. Thus, the lack of articulation between education and future occupations and earnings leads to disillusionment among black students about the value of schooling, and produces behaviors that ultimately are self-defeating. He did not examine, however, the role of gender in students' perceptions of opportunities available to their group.

The small but growing body of research addressing the effects of race on students' responses to school also suggests that identity formation among young people of color is distinctly different from that among white youth.

Matute-Bianchi (1986) has contributed one such study, comparing successful and unsuccessful students of Mexican and Japanese descent, and arguing that minority status per se does not account for differences in school success or failure. What is most salient is not "[the students'] objective material conditions so much as . . . their perception of themselves and others—and the value of their investment in education." Anticipating their future adult roles, students develop appropriate skills and behaviors to meet those expectations, and respond in terms of their perceived role in their future. The unsuccessful students of Mexican descent (there were no unsuccessful students of Japanese descent) tended to emphasize their collective ethnic identity as a socially disadvantaged group. Matute-Bianchi sees such identification as the "product of historical and structural forces of exclusion and subordination by the dominant group, as well as the vehicle of resistance that the group has made to structural inequality."

Working within a similar framework, Fordham's study (1988) of high-achieving black students suggests that students often develop a strategy of racelessness in order to attain success. Because of a conflict or tension that makes identity a problematic choice between the "indigenous Black American cultural system" and the individualistic cultural system of American society, students frequently find it practical to put social distance between themselves and other members of their group. This is particularly the case among high-achieving black females who, more than males, seem to be "more willing to be closely identified with the values and beliefs of the dominant social system" (p. 67).

By focusing on how students perceive their investment in education, Ogbu, Matute-Bianchi, and Fordham have contributed significantly to a deeper understanding of how minority youth respond to schooling. In other words, young people's consciousness of their group's social status exerts a powerful influence upon their response to schooling and their aspirations for the future. Other influences remain to be investigated and more satisfactorily understood. For example, while the importance of peer culture has long been recognized, especially as a factor in the decision of students to drop out of school, we still know little about what creates and contributes to the identity of the peer group itself. More to the point of my project here, many recent studies either have not differentiated between female and male students or have not taken gender as a central problematic; there has thus been a failure or at best a feeble attempt to address how gender intersects with race or ethnicity and minority status to create different expectations and responses to education among women.

The above studies usefully draw attention to the radical disjunction between pedagogical assumptions and social reality for minority youth. Such disjunctions created contradictions exacerbated by an educational practice that does not adequately recognize and counter the power of students' perceptions of reality in determining their sense of the usefulness of remaining in school. Very little research has been undertaken, however, on how such responses to school may differ between males and females, and, most importantly for my study, how responses to schooling differ among groups of young women with different social and historical locations.

SCHOOL PROCESSES AND IDENTITY FORMATION

In this case study on young working-class Latina, African American, and white women, I explore female gender identity as it is constructed, defined, and maintained within a dropout-prevention program. I focus particularly on how the girls' understandings of themselves relate to their educational, occupational, and adult gender-role expectations and how those expectations are shaped and reinforced by their schooling experiences. Central to this analysis is the role that membership in a racial/ethnic and social-class group plays in how young women construe the possible use of schooling in their futures.

It has been well documented that schools are delineated by race, gender, and class relations that reflect other sectors of society and it is within this context (as well as within other social and cultural spheres) that students' race, class, and gender identities are constructed and reshaped. Yet little is known about exactly how such social forces are "marbled" into schooling processes and how they contribute to the shaping of identity.

I use the concept of identity to denote an individual's understanding, interpretation, and presentation of self as shaped within a complex web of continually changing social relations. Identity formation is a dynamic process in which people actively refashion their social location within a hierarchy of social structures (Davidson, 1996; Raissiquier, 1994). The constitution of identity needs to be understood in part through an examination of the intersection of gender, ethnicity, and class as social relations within the school. What I mean by this is that we must examine the various ways in which ethnicity/race and social class interact and reshape the various dimensions of young women's feminine identities. Young women's identities, the ways in which they present and define themselves in relation to their positioning in the world around them, constantly shift in an ongoing process that is both fragmented and unstable (Irvine, 1994).

In this study, I specifically explore those processes through which female gender identity is constituted, defined, and reinforced for differently located groups of girls. My study challenges the premise inherent in previous research on youth cultural studies—the uniformity of identity formation among girls within particular social-class groupings. I will clearly show just how variable gender identity actually is among girls with similar social-class backgrounds.

This study seeks to press beyond the formal organization of the school as an institution to explore the cultural and social interactions that go on in school life and are implicated in the constitution of identity. As Kessler (1985) and her associates make clear, young peoples' identities and understandings of gender are formed, in part, in relation to a school's "gender regime." This they define as the "pattern of practices that constructs various kinds of femininity and masculinity among staff and students, [and] orders them in terms of prestige and power." And, they argue, through a school's gender regime, dominant versions of femininity and masculinity become hegemonic.

In a similar vein, Arnot (1982), utilizing the Bernsteinian notion of "code" developed the concept of gender code to analyze how messages defining "appropriate" models of masculinity and femininity are embedded within school processes and how these messages are both transmitted to and received by young people.

For example, ethnographic research by Kelly (1993) and Schofield (1995) have highlighted the ways gender codes operate through everyday schooling processes. Kelly's study of two continuation high schools (schools for academically disengaged students) in California documents many ways in which young women's schooling experiences tended to foster and recreate prevailing models of femininity through the formal and informal curriculum. For example, elective courses were strongly sex-segregated (e.g., only girls in home economics and typing and only boys in drafting and wood shop), and future vocational options discussed with students were extremely sex-typed (girls encouraged to pursue jobs in cosmetology, nursing, etc. while boys were steered toward construction, welding, etc.). Kelly also describes gender-differentiated expectations by the staff in terms of boys' and girls' conduct and clean-up tasks assigned to students in the classroom. School staffing patterns also reflected a strong gendered division of labor where men held top administrative positions and taught subjects such as math, science, and wood shop, and women generally supervised social activities and taught subjects such as language, art, and child development.

Similarly, Schofield's (1995) study of computers and schooling, in which she argues that student access to technology is structured by gender (and race) relations within the school, documents a range of school processes that reflected or reinforced "traditional" gender relations. As Kelly found, Schofield documents the tendency of some teachers to encourage narrowly proscribed career choices for girls in explicit discussions with them as well as in jokes and comments in the classroom. Patterns in staffing and course enrollment also reflected the kinds of gendered breakdowns that Kelly found: high-level administrators were all men, although half of the faculty were women, and men tended to teach math and science while women taught English. Course-tracking patterns also steered female students to business classes that taught office and secretarial skills. Schofield also suggests that part of the reason why girls may have been discouraged from enrolling in high-level computer courses was because of a considerable amount of gender stereotyping in computer-science texts. In an interesting analysis of the gendered and raced dynamics of the "gifted" program, Schofield illustrates how young women are marginalized both by boys in the program and other girls outside the program thus creating an atmosphere that discouraged girls from participating in higher level computer classes.

Throughout this study, I examine the school's gender code, that is, the kinds of practices and messages that encourage particular forms of femininity and discourage others. However, as Connell (1985) has pointed out, practices and messages within a school are not always consistent. For example, girls may be encouraged to take courses in mathematics or science, all of which then turn out to be taught by men.

A central contention of this study is that even within a "progressive" educational institution, contradictions exist in the school's gender code. Through various processes, the gender code of the school promotes occasionally contradictory versions of femininity, sometimes emphasizing academic mastery and economic self-sufficiency and at other times condoning "traditional" patterns of gendered cultural and social interaction. It is within this context, in which contradictory messages compete, that the young women of different racial/ethnic backgrounds struggle to construct meaning in acquiring educational credentials.

THE STUDY

I intend this book on young women's identity formation to be a contribution to the tradition and development of feminist research. One of the hallmarks of such research is that "it generates its problematic from the perspective of women's experiences" (Harding, 1987, p. 7). Feminist scholars have argued that what in the past has been deemed worthy of study directly reflected the interests of privileged white men and thus reflected their experience—a truncated or distorted picture of social life. As Stanley and Wise comment:

> Our experience has been named by men, but not even in a language derived from their experience. Even this is too direct and too personal. And so it is removed from experience altogether by being cast in abstract and theoretical terms. We need a women's language, a language of experience. And this must necessarily come from our exploration of the personal, the everyday, and what we experience—women's lived experiences. (1983, p. 146)

The focus on the everyday world can reveal in important ways how larger social and economic forces, both ideological and material, shape the way women experience the world. Dorothy Smith suggests:

> The everyday world, the world where people are located as they live, located bodily and in that organization of their known world as one that begins from their own location in it, is generated in its varieties by an organization of social relations which originate "elsewhere." (1987, p. 176)

In other words, we would do well to conceptualize women's experiences as multifarious and linked to the unequal class, race, and gender social relations of society. Indeed, as Bonnie Thornton Dill (1987) has argued, white bourgeois women not only have been taken as representative of the category "women" but this category itself has been construed as racially and culturally homogenous. Dill argues that an accurate analysis of social reality must include critical accounts of women's situations in every race, class, and culture.

The production of knowledge derived from everyday experiences, however, must "go beyond the microscopic and the anecdotal" (Rais-siguier, 1994, p. 7). Although critics contend that ethnographic case studies are nongeneralizable, as Spindler (1982) has noted:

> "ethnographic inquiry by nature focuses on single cases or at most on a limited setting of action. . . . Ethnographers also usually feel that it is better to have in-depth accurate knowledge of one setting than super-ficial and possibly skewed or misleading information about isolated relationships in many settings. (Cited in Valli, 1986, p. 215)

Furthermore, as Smith points out, in-depth case studies use people's lived experiences as the starting points that then proceed to allow us to "see the 'micro' and 'macro' sociological levels in a determinate rela-tion" (Smith, 1987, p. 99).

With the above in mind, this book is based on a single case study of an alternative high school in which I closely followed and interviewed a group of thirty ninth-grade female students ranging in age from fourteen to sixteen years old.

In my original research design, I had proposed to study a group of young white, Latina, and African American female students enrolled in a drop-out prevention program within a traditional high school in New York City. After a year spent trying to identify schools with such pro-grams and then trying (unsuccessfully) to obtain permission from prin-cipals to conduct my research, I decided to focus only on alternative high schools, which I believed would be more open to having a researcher "hang around" for a year. I was right.

The first alternative school principal I contacted (a woman) met with me in early June. During our meeting I handed her a one-page prospectus outlining the research design. She enthusiastically agreed to allow me to begin my research the next fall and introduced me to a female guidance counselor who was to help me get acclimated, and she in turn introduced me to teachers and students. The only stipulation the principal insisted upon was that I limit my focus to female students who were entering the ninth grade, since the year of my data gathering would be the first year the school admitted ninth-grade students. While I had the approval of the principal, I still needed to get permission from the teachers whose classes I would be visiting. It was also agreed that I would obtain official Board of Education clearance during the course of the school year, as well as parental permission from any student I inter-viewed. That meeting proved to be invaluable. Not only did I finally gain official entry to a school, but the guidance counselor introduced me to a group of six young women with whom I could pretest my interview questions.

Conducting my research in an alternative high school met the specifications of my original proposal. My main criteria for choosing a site were that the program be designed for students with histories of academic failure and poor attendance and who were considered to be potential dropouts, and that the student body be racially and ethnically diverse. Alternative High School met both criteria.

Situating my study within an alternative high school setting allowed a unique opportunity to analyze the various processes that contribute to the transmission and acquisition of gender identities. At the time this study was conducted, the girls had just entered the ninth grade. For the most part, they had experienced past educational failure (including truancy, suspensions, lack of academic achievement, etc.) and were likely to eventually drop out of school. Having been unable to interview the girls prior to their enrollment in the school, I therefore had to assume that their previous lack of success was related, in part, to the lack of articulation between their actual schooling experience and the expectations they had of themselves as adult women.

Alternative High School is unique among regular or alternative high schools in that it functions as a collaborative high school–college program and is housed in one of three buildings that comprise a community college. Throughout the day, students circulate among all three buildings. A.H.S. students are given college IDs and have access to all college facilities; no college areas are off-limits to high school students.

In addition to this collaboration with a community college, A.H.S. is also unique in its offering of a career education internship program. Each student is required to complete a full or part-time internship during three of the four years spent in high school. Students earn academic credit, not money, from these internship positions, which typically entail community service (hospitals, schools, police stations, social service agencies). Each student in internship is assigned a career education supervisor who maintains a close relationship with the student throughout the four years.

Another feature of the school that differentiates it from other high schools, both regular and traditional, is its counseling component. As stated in school documents, a major goal of A.H.S. is to develop in each student a sense of belonging to the school community. All staff members[4] (teachers, counselors, paraprofessionals, administrators, secretaries, and security personnel) are charged with the role of "an adult able to make an impact on the lives of students." A.H.S. is divided into three clusters designed to create a feeling of "institutional caring." Each cluster is divided into "houses" with twenty to twenty-five students, a house teacher, guidance counselor, and a house "mom" (paraprofessional). One third of all students participate in group counseling each day during the school year, designed to help students develop "coping strategies."

Alternative High School boasts a low dropout rate of 5 percent or an institutional retention rate of 85 percent over a ten-year period. Estimates of dropout rates in regular New York City public schools range from 35 to 80 percent. The average daily student attendance rate at A.H.S. is approximately 81 percent compared to 69 percent in other alternative high schools in New York City.

Approximately 40 percent of the incoming students[5] are determined to be more than two years below grade level in reading skills, and about 55 percent are below grade level in mathematics. The school maintains an enrollment of approximately 450 students. According to school records, 60 percent of the students' families are on public assistance and 70 percent of the students come from single-parent homes. Table 1.1 provides the sex and ethnic characteristics of the student population during the 1988–89 school year.

After gaining entree to the school, I spent, on average, three full days (Tuesday, Wednesday, and Thursday) each week at the school during the course of the school year. During the first three months (October, November, and December), I conducted classroom observations. I did no formal interviewing during this time, preferring instead to establish familiarity with students. During the mornings I observed two classrooms back-to-back (9:20–10:30 and 10:40–11:50) and spent lunchtime and early afternoon in the cafeteria. The cafeteria provided a rich source of informal interview and observation data. I also attended school functions such as awards assemblies and basketball games.

Thirty ninth-grade female students ranging in age from fourteen to sixteen years old participated in the study. The following remarks

TABLE 1.1
Composition of A.H.S. Student Body, 1989

Ethnicity/Race	Number	Percent
White*	183	40.9
Hispanic†	151	33.7
African American	102	23.4
Asian	9	2.0
Female	260	58.0
Male	185	42.0

* Includes students of European-American backgrounds.
† Includes students of Puerto Rican, Dominican, and South and Central American descent.

describe the ethnic and racial backgrounds of the young women who comprised the sample. Ten girls were of European American descent. Of these ten young white women, one with a first-generation Irish American mother and a father born in Puerto Rico considers herself Irish American; one was first-generation Rumanian; two were second-generation Italian; and six were mostly third- and fourth-generation white European. Seven girls were of Puerto Rican descent; all were born and raised in New York City, as were most of their mothers and some of their fathers. Three girls were of African American backgrounds, all born in Queens, New York, and all had close relatives in the southern United States. The group of ten immigrant Latinas included four girls of Dominican descent—three born in the Dominican Republic, and one born in the United States; four girls of Colombian descent—three born in Colombia and one born in Miami; and two girls of Ecuadoran descent—both born in their country of origin.

Without exception, the young women who were born outside of the United States immigrated with their parents as young children and spoke English with native proficiency.

Determining the social-class background of many in the group of young women was somewhat difficult since the social class of the male head of household usually determines the social class position of the family. Historically, a family's class status is defined by the husband/father's relationship to the production process (Wright, 1985). However, given the changing social and economic realities in which wives/mothers are often employed or seek paid work when their husbands become unemployed or underemployed, this definition no longer aptly defines a family's "objective" class position (Mirza, 1992). Moreover, as Mirza makes clear, given vastly differing historical, social, cultural, and economic factors among people within a social-class category, traditional definitions of class position no longer hold.

Thus, in determining the social class background of the girls under study, I utilized Mirza's redefinition of class background that she employed in her study on young women in England of West Indian descent. She observed that many West Indian women make reliable and long-term contributions to the family income—that they, in other words, often meet the conditions that determine status according to conventional stratification analysis. These women, therefore, should qualify as principal determinants in the definition of their families' social-class status. The researcher must consequently be prepared to assume that either the mother or the father will direct social classification of the family, each case depending on the researcher assessing who most appropriately satisfies the determinant criteria.

The backgrounds of the young women of white European descent were easily established as working class. All (except one) of these young women had employed fathers who qualified as the main income earners in the family; they all held jobs in which they either lacked significant control over the labor processes involved in their work (as chauffeur, doorman, factory worker, roofer, bartender, etc.) or were self-employed as petty entrepreneurs (as truckdriver, landscaper, etc.). Of this group of girls, three had mothers who were not in the labor market, and seven had mothers who were generally employed (not necessarily fulltime) in office work, babysitting, or the service industry (as waitress, cashier, etc.).

The three African American girls were also considered to belong to the working class. Although none had fathers in the home or who contributed substantially to the family income, all three had mothers who were employed full time (as secretary, post office employee, and municipal traffic officer).

The social-class backgrounds of the group of Latina girls were more difficult to determine. This group showed a great deal of complexity in the employment backgrounds of their parents—a complexity no doubt partly attributed to such factors as immigration status, length of time in the United States, relative fluency in the English language, and so forth. Of the group of seven girls of Puerto Rican descent three had fathers or stepfathers in the home; of those, two fathers worked as hospital aids (one mother worked as a secretary and one mother was not employed), and one father was unemployed (as was the mother). Of the group of ten non–Puerto Rican Latina girls, three had fathers who lived in the home but did not contribute to the family income, while one mother was employed as a factory worker and the other was unemployed. Of the remaining seven girls (without fathers in the home), five had mothers employed in such occupations as nursing, factory work, babysitting, and secretarial work; and two had mothers drawing public assistance. None of the fathers living outside of the girls' homes contributed substantially to the family income. While the above employment and family descriptions of some of the Latinas may suggest families living in poverty or at subsistence level during the time of the interviews, I chose for emphasis the fact that during most of the girls' childhoods, one or the other parent or both parents had held jobs, ones in which they lacked sufficient control over the labor processes at their work (Roman, 1988).

In general, all the mothers of the young women in the study had completed more years of education than the fathers. However, there were important educational differences between the girls' mothers. For example, while almost two thirds of the mothers who were white, African American, or of Puerto Rican descent had completed high school, nearly none of the mothers who had immigrated to the United

States from the Dominican Republic and South America had a high school degree. (One mother of Dominican descent, however, had completed two years of college in the United States.)

In order to gain insight into girls' lives and their future expectations, I decided it would be best to utilize mainly qualitative research methods. These included loosely structured, in-depth formal and informal interviews with individual girls or groups of girls and teachers, and systematic observations in classrooms, hallways, the cafeteria, and the surrounding campus. In addition, I had access to the girls' academic attendance records and other school documents.

I was given permission by two sets of team teachers to observe their classrooms for the year. During my first visit to each classroom, the teachers introduced me as a college student who was doing research on young women. I briefly explained that I was interested in learning about what school was like for ninth-grade girls and that I would be at the school for a year. I was generally greeted by questions from both boys and girls who inquired about my age, whether I attended the college across the street, what my purpose was in the study, and so forth.

Since A.H.S. is housed on an urban community-college campus, I was able to comfortably "pass" as a local college student. Being identified as a student was beneficial to me as a researcher in this setting because I was not perceived as a teacher and thus part of the authority structure. Because I was much older than the girls in the study, however, I did not try to establish myself as part of their peer-group culture either. I believe I was received as a visitor, but clearly sympathetic. I realized this one day as I was sitting in the cafeteria with a group of girls who were cutting (not attending) class and the principal walked in: one girl urgently whispered to me, "Could you pretend you're interviewing us, then she'll leave us alone." (See appendix A for a more detailed description of my research role.)

Aside from being perceived as a college student who attended the "college across the street," I had little else in common with the young women whom I followed and interviewed. As a white middle-class woman of European background, I shared neither social-class background nor racial/ethnic group affiliation with the majority of young women whom I studied. Although I did not feel that my access to the young women or the confidentiality of our interviews was compromised significantly, it does raise important concerns regarding the interpretation and representation of the young women's narratives and experiences. One concern is the question of subjectivity that arises in any qualitative research. Stanley and Wise (1983), however, argue that subjectivity is necessary in the study of women and has been submerged by a quest for "objectivity" (Mirza, 1992, p. 9). Readers must continually bear in mind that the analysis and interpretations presented in this book are derived by me as a member of a privileged racial/ethnic group.

In the next chapter, I present the central arguments and theoretical debates that inform this study on gender identity and schooling. Chapter 3 defines the social, economic, and educational contexts of different groups of women in U.S. society in general and in New York City in particular. In chapters 4, 5 and 6, I outline in detail the kinds of ideas young women of European, African American, Puerto Rican, Dominican, and South American descent project about their lives as adult women, and highlight some aspects of their day-to-day lives that contribute to their understandings of themselves in the future. Chapter 7 explores aspects of the school that appear to redefine the role of school in the lives of young women who have previously experienced school failure. In chapter 8, I provide an analysis of the formal curriculum in use in the ninth-grade classrooms and speculate on the impact it has on young women's identity formations. Next, chapter 9 examines the school's contradictory gender code and how it relates to young women's understandings of themselves in the future. Finally, I summarize the findings, discuss the implications of these findings, and offer recommendations on schooling young women in chapter 10.

In the following chapter, I outline the central arguments within educational research regarding gender and race and feminist theory that have framed the analysis of this study.

CHAPTER 2

Social Class, Race/Ethnicity, Gender, and Schooling: A Theoretical Overview

EDUCATIONAL RESEARCH AND SOCIAL CLASS

In the 1970s, Marxists and structuralist theoreticians began looking at the social and economic structures of society to explain the ways in which schools contributed to the unequal allocation of individuals in society. These theorists (sometimes known as reproduction theorists), examined the processes through which existing social structures maintain and reproduce themselves; they argued that schools actually reproduce the social relations of production in capitalism. For example, Althusser's (1985) influential work on ideology and ideological state apparatuses directly addressed the role of the schools in the reproduction of capitalist society. Equally influential in the development of a social reproduction theory of education specifically addressing the United States was Bowles and Gintis's *Schooling in Capitalist America* (1976). In this work, the authors present schooling as a means in the reproduction of the class structure and as a mechanism for inculcating new recruits to the workforce with values and ideas (ideologies) appropriate to their positioning in the labor market. To Bowles and Gintis, schools function in a directly dependent relationship with the economy: "the organization of education—in particular the correspondence between school structure and jobs structure" (1976, p. 13)—occurs within the realm of social relations.

Although Bowles and Gintis were plainly aware of the presence of racial and gender inequities, their analysis privileged, rather, economic and class relations. Moreover, their work represents the typical youth as male; there is no recognition of the patriarchal relationships in schools nor of the production of gendered subjects either in terms of sexual relations or patriarchal work relations (Arnot, 1982). According to Bowles and Gintis, reproduction of the sexual division of labor occurs primarily in the family.

The early feminist reproduction theorists turned their attention toward the ways in which schooling reproduces gender oppression, in particular how schooling prepares young girls for their roles in production and in the domestic sphere. Early feminist writers such as Barrett (1980) and Wolpe (1978) were interested in how schools create and maintain unequal gender relations within the class structure. Wolpe's analysis emphasized the power of ideology to shape gender relations through the educational system, arguing that school practices were underpinned by an official state ideology that deliberately restricted women's options, circumscribing their futures to unpaid domestic labor and low-paying jobs (Holland and Eisenhart, 1990, p. 29). Schoolgirls themselves internalized the hegemonic male perspective and their own work as insignificant. This gender ideology was not monolithic, however. As Raissiguier (1994) points out, Wolpe's major contribution was to shed light on the contradictory nature of gender ideologies in schools that was rooted in the larger societal conflict between economic imperatives and cultural intransigence—"between the recent economic need for a highly trained labor force and the traditional exclusion of girls from technical commitment due to their primary responsibility within the family" (Raissiguier, 1994, p. 20). But the fundamental questions remained unanswered: how did the girls make sense of these contradictions? and to what extent did they internalize the messages?

In short, these early structuralist accounts of schooling failed to articulate exactly how inequality was actually reproduced within the school. The view of schooling as a "black box" accompanied a simultaneous concern with culture and forms of knowledge through an analysis of school curricula. Known as the "new sociology of education," theories such as those advanced by Bourdieu (1977), Bernstein (1971), and Young (1971) began to address the ways in which certain groups enjoy advantages in school through language, knowledge and patterns of interaction. This attention to the discrimination and privileging of cultures within schools became increasingly influential in both the United States and Great Britain.

While the structural and cultural analyses of education expressed in reproduction theories began to illuminate how and why schools reproduce inequality, there was growing dissatisfaction with the failure to deal with human agency especially with the assumption of the certainty about the outcomes of gender identity. Critics such as Giroux (1983), Apple (1982), and Wexler and Whitson (1982) systematically attacked radical theoretical accounts of schooling, objecting to the portrayal of human action as structurally determined. Instead, they argued that human action is produced through cultural interpretation by people actively attempting to make sense of and respond to their "inherited structural and material conditions of existence" (Willis, 1983, p. 112).

With his *Learning to Labour* (1977), Willis contributed greatly to the concern with the "importance of human agency and the notion of resistance"; he demonstrated how working-class "lads" collude in their own continued subordination in the labor market through their adherence to a subculture that rejects school knowledge and emphasized resistance to the dominant culture in school.

Feminist researchers, however, have faulted Willis's work as presenting an uncritical examination of the patriarchal, sexist, and racist attitudes of the lads (McRobbie, 1980). Willis's exclusive interest in white working-class boys sparked feminist investigations into working-class girls' schooling experiences and subcultures. Feminist scholars on gender and schooling began to incorporate notions of conflict and resistance into their research. For example, Kelly and Nihlen (1982), who examined the reproductive role of schools in the sexual division of labor, sought to ascertain whether girls internalize school messages about "appropriate" definitions of femininity or actively resist or "renegotiate" them. Similarly, Arnot (1982), influenced by social reproduction and Bernstein's theory of cultural reproduction, moved the discussion of girls' resistance further by highlighting the contested nature of the construction of both class and gender identities. She argues that "it would appear . . . that girls become "feminine" without any problems. . . . There has been an overwhelming emphasis upon the pattern of subordination of girls through education with very little emphasis upon patterns of struggle and resistance" (p. 74).

Several important studies focusing on the formation of white working-class girls' antischool subcultures were conducted by feminist researchers in England. McRobbie (1978), who like Willis used a class analysis to explain girls' responses to education, argued from premises about the girls' oppression under capitalism and patriarchy (Weiler, 1988, p. 42). McRobbie suggests that girls' attitudes toward work reflect cultural biases about femininity that emphasize dating, marriage, and motherhood. Girls accept this "pre-existent culture of femininity" as part of the natural order (Miles, 1987) rather than as a social construct under patriarchy. Accepting their position as unpaid workers in the home—in effect, trained *not* to perceive themselves as paid workers—these girls approach the labor market haphazardly, gravitating toward work without promise of long-term commitment or trading off glamour and the possibility of romance against low pay and poor conditions (Mirza, 1992). McRobbie argues that the girls realize that for them schooling will prove of limited value and so, rejecting it as irrelevant, they reconstruct the school as an arena in which they enact their own antischool activities. They reject, in effect, what official middle-class ideology posits as girls' role in school and replace it with their own more feminine and sexual one (Weiler, 1988). Later research by Anyon

(1983), Gaskell (1985), and Valli (1986) has also observed how school-girls' immersion in the culture of femininity becomes a de facto form of resistance to many aspects of the dominant ideology; but in the end, they accommodate themselves to traditional notions of femininity.

Such absorption in a "culture of romance or femininity" leads many young women to fail to identify with or invest themselves in waged labor; instead, they envision futures directed toward marriage and romance (Valli, 1986; McRobbie, 1978; Griffen, 1985; Holland and Eisenhart, 1990). Nevertheless, these studies also reveal that in their construction and reconstruction of gender identity, young women are likely to experience a number of conflicts and contradictions (Griffen, 1984; Lees, 1986; Sharpe, 1987). Having for so long observed the examples of their mothers' and other women's lives, working-class girls are well aware that they will spend a significant portion of their lives in paid employment (due to economic necessity); and at the same time they fully expect to be involved in domesticity and childrearing. As Griffen (1985) shows, this tension is established quite early in life, with girls much more likely than boys to be assigned domestic chores. She postulates that girls learn about their probable future positions in both the home and labor market through such early experiences; and they consequently take for granted that they will have to shape future employment around responsibilities.

Another special problem besetting girls, a problem that Sharpe (1987) acutely identified and illustrated, arises when the pursuit of "femininity" with its multitudinous distractions (fashion, appearance, boyfriends, etc.) produces a decline of interest in academic activities, which ultimately "influences the subsequent nature of their life and work" (p. 140). Similarly, Wolpe (1978) found that girls' sense of their developing gender identity, particularly their sexuality, seems to diminish their commitment to studying. Academic failure then is legitimated (by girls themselves and others) because they are female and they do not have to succeed academically to be feminine. But by accepting this construction of feminine identity, the girls contribute to their own subordination. Importantly, as Holland and Eisenhart (1990) point out, Lees (1986) argues that girls' investment in feminine activities increases as they see their chances for a career decreases.

Sexual reputation poses another peculiar difficulty for girls. Lees's work underscores the centrality of a girl's sexual reputation construed in terms of a false dilemma—a girl is either "decent" or overtly sexual. Little more than a rephrasing of the virgin/whore dichotomy, such categories and characterizations operate to pressure girls into getting steady boyfriends. These assumptions also undermine girls' academic pursuits: conditioned to regard sexual behavior as truly appropriate only within a context of love and marriage, the girls are subtly trained to shift their focus from school and career to marriage.

The above studies suggest that female gender identity is constructed through a variety of processes, and that the constituent elements are not the same for all girls. Work by Connell and his associates (1982), for example, illustrates how girls can resist notions of a "romantic female sexuality" or a particularly "feminine" identity, although "exaggerated" versions of femininity can win out in particular contexts.

Recent work by Weis (1990) has challenged the view that young white working-class girls define themselves primarily as future home-makers, mothers, and part-time laborers. The girls in her study, situated within a rapidly deindustrializing economy, challenge specific cultural notions of femininity, domesticity, and romance; for them, obtaining wage labor is a primary goal (p. 55). Weis's findings point to the changing nature of white working-class girls' construction of a gender identity. She has argued that, given the rapidly changing nature of the labor market, we need to better describe the processes at work in school in terms of identity formation. With the shifts in women's employment and greater economic independence, along with concomitant changes in the power relations within families, the prospects that schools assume for women are far less rigidly circumscribed than in the past. Citing Touraine (1981), Weis suggests that it is no longer appropriate to envisage the struggle between labor and capital as the central pivot in society. Society is better understood as a dynamic set of social movements. Similarly, Wexler (1987) calls for research of the "self-formative role of youth's cultural action (the work of identity formation) in relation to larger social movements" (cited in Raissiguier, 1994, p. 18).

Feminist researchers such as Roman (1988) and Lesko (1988) have argued that work on youth identity formation has been exclusively theorized in relation to one's current or future position in waged labor, thus marginalizing other social forces. These descriptions of class-based identities, formed out of a priori class interests, perpetuate the tendency to construe identity as unitary, homogenous, and fully determined. (Roman, 1988, p. 143). Although advancing our understanding of how individuals negotiate forms of power and make sense of their schooling experience such as the studies previously described, racial dynamics in particular have remained marginal to the more central concern with social class.

THE IMPACT OF RACE/ETHNICITY
ON YOUNG PEOPLE'S SCHOOLING EXPERIENCES

The reproduction paradigm has failed to adequately address the issue of the school's role in the creation and maintenance of racial inequality.

Class-based analyses fail to explain discrepancies in school performance between different racial or ethnic children with similar social-class backgrounds. Moreover, it cannot account for the paradox of both high educational aspirations and low school performance among black students faring poorly in school and in the labor market (Ogbu, 1978, 1982, 1988, 1989).

Ogbu has put forth a powerful argument in which he theorizes that perceptions of and responses to education differ between castelike or nonvoluntary "minorities" (e.g., African Americans, Native Americans) and the dominant societal group of the respective society. Castelike "minorities" differ from other minority groups such as immigrants (voluntary "minorities") in that they have been incorporated into the existing society involuntarily but occupy a permanent place. Generally, they face obstacles to social mobility such as job ceilings, which Ogbu describes as "highly consistent pressure and obstacles which selectively assign minorities to jobs at the lowest level of status, power, dignity, and income, allowing members of the dominant group to compete more easily for more desirable jobs above that ceiling" (1982, p. 270).

Education for both minority groups and the dominant group facilitates social mobility; however, for castelike minorities, education does not nearly correlate with the same rewards and opportunities for economic self-advancement as it does for the dominant group members. Further (given comparable levels of education and family background), large gaps remain in occupational status (i.e., income) between members from both groups. In fact, Ogbu argues that, in the case of blacks, the more education an individual receives, the more unequal the income differential becomes when compared to whites with similar education.

The relative lack of articulation between education, occupation, and income consequently leads to disillusionment among minorities about the value of schooling. Ogbu suggests that such disillusionment encourages the development of alternative strategies for survival ("folk theories of getting ahead") as well as responses to the schooling experience itself. For example, he argues that "black youths know from observing their parents' situation and that of other adults in their communities that their chances of making it through education and mainstream jobs are not very good" (1989, p. 264). They therefore often become increasingly disillusioned as they get older and consequently try less and less to perform schoolwork seriously.

Ogbu did not, however, explore the role gender plays in shaping the realities of male and female black students and how these students understand the opportunities open to their race, social class, and gender groups (Grant and Sleeter, 1986).

In one of the few empirical studies to test Ogbu's hypothesis, Mickelson (1990, 1992) argues that while Ogbu's thesis aptly describes the male experience in education and in the opportunity structure, the situation for women is rather different. She suggests that for working and middle-class African American and white females, the relatively poor occupational return (compared to men of the same race and class background) does not appear to depress either their school performance or their willingness to earn advanced degrees (1992, p. 151). Mickelson posits several hypotheses to explain this achievement paradox, but she concludes that none adequately factors in the class and race differences between the women studied. Mickelson's work takes an important step toward empirically verifying Ogbu's thesis; and her work highlights what reliable information, however scant, is available about what distinguishes differences in females' educational experiences and their motivation in obtaining an education.

Ogbu has contributed to our understanding of how racial stratification operates in schools to recreate and maintain racial disadvantages characteristic of society. However, as Apple and Weis (1983) argue, schools are also stratified by class and gender as well as race. In their critical account of how racial inequality gets "mediated" by school processes, Apple and Weis advance from a "parallelist" position, where race and gender and class are recognized as dynamic processes that constantly interact within other social systems—economic, political, and cultural. This framework moves us away from a purely structural analysis, which focuses on the properties of the economy in order to explain inequality, toward a model that comprehends how the complex relations of race, class, and gender determine unequal school outcomes.

McCarthy (1990) agrees that the parallelist position allows us to understand race as a "vital social process which is integrally linked to other social processes and dynamics operating in education and society" (p. 80). Unfortunately, this model often misleadingly formulates race, class, and gender dynamics in terms of linear additions or separate dimensions that "interact" with each other. McCarthy, therefore, attempts to conceptualize the interconnections between race, class, and gender dynamics within social institutions, such as schools, by adopting what he calls a "nonsynchronous" theory of race relations in schooling. He argues that "the intersection of race, class and gender in the institutional setting of the school is systematically contradictory or nonsynchronous and can lead to the augmentation or diminution of the effectivity of race, or for that matter, any other of these variables operating in the school environment" (p. 9). Thus, for example, students of different race-gender configurations will experience "asynchronies" or differential experiences based on race in the acquisition of gendered identities in school (McCarthy, 1990).

FEMINIST PERSPECTIVES: THE INTERSECTIONS
OF RACE, GENDER AND CLASS

As Apple and Weis, and McCarthy have argued, in order to appreciate the differing educational experiences of women of different racial or ethnic backgrounds, we need to look beyond additive models that formulate race, class, and gender dynamics as independent dimensions of experience. The recent theoretical contributions of feminists of color have been extremely important in bringing to the fore how the intersection of race, gender, class, and sexuality shapes women's various experiences and identities. In this section I discuss briefly the advances in feminist theory that have helped to frame my research questions and shed light on the processes involved in the construction of identity among young women. Next, I present a discussion of several empirical studies that highlight the ways in which race, gender, and class intersect to produce qualitatively different schooling experiences for young women of different racial/ethnic backgrounds.

Since the 1960s, ways of theorizing about gender have changed tremendously. Feminists of color have raised concerns about their exclusion from feminist scholarship and maintained that their experiences have been misrepresented. They have challenged the notion of a shared oppression that unites all women. Indeed, the category of "woman" itself has been problematized; depending on the contexts and circumstances, its meaning can no longer be assumed. As Baca Zinn and Dill (1996) posit, the search for women's universal or essential characteristics is being abandoned, which has led to new understandings of the multiple ways that women experience themselves as raced, classed, and gendered (p. 321).

Feminists of color have taken white women to task not only for privileging patriarchy over issues of race, class, sexual preference, and other forms of oppression, but also for defining patriarchy and the construction of women's experiences in terms that ignore or marginalize the experiences of women of color. Carby (1982) makes the point that what white feminists understand as at issue in patriarchy—the family, dependency, and reproduction—becomes problematic when applied to the experience of black women (Mirza, 1992, p. 24). Similarly bell hooks (1984) has argued that applying the concept of patriarchy as the source of all women's oppression has failed to address the fact that for women of color there are different sites of oppression and struggle. For example, hooks maintains that because the family is a site of resistance against racism for women of color, the family does not have the same degree of significance in accounting for women's oppression as it does for white women.

Criticism of second-wave feminism has also centered on the inattention to the experience of racism. Kimberle Crenshaw (1989, 1991) for example, argues that black women have been excluded from feminist theory because the theory is based on a set of experiences of privileged group members and does not accurately reflect the intersection of race and gender. Invoking the concept of intersectionality, Crenshaw argues that race and gender intersect to shape black women's lives in multiple ways that cannot be understood by looking at the race and gender dynamics of those experiences separately (1991, p. 1244). For example, Crenshaw illustrates how black women are dealt with in antidiscrimination lawsuits; courts either focus on sex discrimination, which fails to take into account the racial dimension of the women's experiences, or vice versa. Crenshaw makes the point that analyzing gender and race dimensions as mutually exclusive categories of experience cannot accurately account for black women's experiences. Black women can experience discrimination in ways that are both similar to and different from those experienced by white women and black men.

The idea that gender is constructed by a range of intersecting inequalities is also at the heart of Patricia Hill Collins's concept of a "matrix of domination" (1990). She suggests that women's lives are influenced by their social location within multiple hierarchies and that women experience race, class, and gender differently depending upon their location within those structures (Baca Zinn and Dill, 1996). Similarly, Baca Zinn and Dill (1996) call for a multiracial feminism that they explain "as an attempt to go beyond analyzing differences among women to understand the importance of race in the social construction of gender" (p. 327).

The focus on the intersection of race, gender, and class points to a need to conceptualize young women's identities as multiple and multifaceted—identities that are socially constructed and respond to changing social, economic, and political relations. I present next a brief overview of the few empirical studies that illustrate how the intersection of race, gender, and class create multiple identities and differing educational experiences among young women of color.

One such early study that looked at young black women in London explored how their responses to work and education and to "traditional" notions of femininity differed from those of young white working-class girls (Fuller, 1983; Griffen, 1985; Riley, 1985). Fuller's study (1983) analyzed how a young person's sex and race or ethnicity can shape academic aspirations and achievements. She described how the black girls created a particular subculture of resistance in which they adopted an antischool posture (pretending to be lazy or apathetic, engaging in truancy, challenging teacher authority, etc.), but were nonetheless deeply, if covertly, committed to education. Fuller believed it was the girls' awareness of their "double subordination"—being black and female—that led to their pursuit of educational credentials. Furthermore, they asserted their independence from West Indian boys and adhered to a strategy of "going it alone," focusing on those aspects of schooling that will provide them with practical occupational credentials (Mirza, 1992).

In another British study, this time examining Asian girls and schooling, Sheila Miles (1987) argues that "if class and gender are held constant, it is the racial dimension that influences [Asian girls'] aspirations for the future." Miles looks at the experience of immigration, attitudes to marriage, work, and education. Contrary to claims that Asian women are entirely dominated by a patriarchal culture that forbids them to work outside the home, substantial numbers of Indian women engage in waged labor, albeit low-paying. Such women also assume primary care of home and family. Miles contends that an awareness of their mothers' hardship or double burden stimulates these girls to seek better jobs and lead richer lives than their mothers had enjoyed. Staying in school represents a crucial step toward this goal. School is perceived as the preeminent means to develop the necessary qualifications to secure a good job or to gain entry to college.

In a recent study on identity formation of young black women in two London high schools, Mirza (1992) found that all were committed to future full-time paid work and a desire for economic independence. Unlike the girls in Fuller's study, they did not foresee future relationships with men as interfering with their right to work. Furthermore, the girls planned to work regardless of domestic and child-rearing responsibilities. Mirza points out that whereas the girls' white peers echoed the dominant ideology that approves of women taking on major economic responsibility only when circumstances prevent men from adequately providing for them, black girls did not consider themselves as an economically marginal resource of last resort (p. 156). They believed the financial security of the household to be a joint responsibility. Moreover, unlike the girls in Fuller's study who embraced a strategy of "going it alone," these girls voiced a "cautious, yet positive approach to marriage and relationships" (p. 158).

Raissiguier's (1994) research on girls of Algerian descent is one of the few that illustrates how the constructions of gender identity and class consciousness are deeply shaped by racial and ethnic forces and how these forces play out within the school. For example, Raissiguier explains how in order to achieve success at the school, young women must conform to a certain kind of femininity and deportment. Girls of Algerian descent compared with their French counterparts found it more difficult to conform to the particular norms and values that are associated with a French middle-class model of femininity and thus found it harder to achieve the school-defined version of success. Raissiguier also found significant differences between young women of Algerian descent and those of French descent in terms of what they believed possible for themselves in the future. Most of the women saw involvement in some form of paid labor as a central goal alongside the pursuit of emotional attachments and domestic arrangements. However, for the French girls, marriage and motherhood were approached with many more mixed feelings than previous studies on white working-class girls have found. Nevertheless, extended interviews revealed they were still pulled into an ideology of romance to a degree that was not visible among girls of Algerian descent (p. 126). Raissiguier found that the girls of Algerian descent both challenged and abided by "traditional" expectations; she states, "while they [Algerian descent girls] are committed to moving away from a future of domesticity and dependence, they are also attached to traditional marital arrangements (p. 119)." Traditional expectations emanating from their communities and families exerted powerful pulls as to what was possible in the future. Algerian descent and French descent girls also differed in the significance they attached to getting an education. While the French girls viewed their vocational education as a stepping stone to exciting careers, Algerian descent girls, because of their acute awareness of the structural limitations placed on them in the labor market due to racism, were much more pessimistic about their future careers. Instead, they viewed their education and qualifications as ways to postpone marriage and negotiate better lives for themselves as education was highly regarded within their communities. In addition to pragmatic uses of their education, girls of Algerian descent also understood that their schooling provided them with knowledge (language skills, etc.) to fight their exclusion within a racist society.

In the United States, a small body of research on the schooling of young women of color also shows divergent experiences. For example, Weis's work (1985) on black women's participation in an urban community college is worth noting here. Hers is the first sustained analysis of the community college experience for such women. Though she essentially argues that achievement and outcomes are similar for both men and women in community college, there appear to be differences in what men and women expect from school. Men tend to view community college as a way to disassociate themselves from street life and its consequences. For women, however, further education usually represents a means to a better life for them and their children, to a life without dependence on welfare or on men.

In a review of literature on the impact of schooling on young black females, Scott-Jones and Clark (1986) found that a student's race appears to be the most significant attribute in accounting for future expectations regarding education and employment. In particular, the authors cite research that indicates that while white males appear to have higher educational and career aspirations than white females, no such sex difference were found for the black youth, all of whom have high aspirations. One possible explanation for this difference is that similar labor-market opportunities for black adults of both sexes may cause black adolescents and their parents to devalue "traditional" definitions of female work roles. In addition, black females seem much more motivated than white females to engage in paid labor; they tend to be concerned about contributing to the economic support of their families—a tendency also supported by Holland and Eisenhart's (1990) findings.

School experiences for girls with different racial/ethnic attributes have been found to encourage divergent expressions of femininity. This is perhaps best illustrated by Grant's work (1994) on the school experience of African American and white females in elementary schools and Goldstein's (1988) study on immigrant Hmong girls.

Grant argues that school is experienced quite differently by black girls than by white girls, though they may sit next to each other in the same classroom. These two groups of girls shape—and are shaped by—this milieu in very different ways that become manifest in markedly different forms of femininity. Grant's work illuminates how the two groups of girls occupy different "places" in the classroom, which (could) ultimately channel them into different adult social roles. She found, for example, that teachers emphasize academic achievement for white girls but for black girls they emphasize social, caring, and nurturing qualities, and encourage black girls "to pursue social contacts, rather than press toward high achievement" (p. 103). She concludes that the black girls' schooling experience seems "more likely to nudge them toward stereotypical roles of black women than alternatives . . . serving others and maintaining peaceable ties among diverse persons rather than developing one's own skills."

Goldstein (1988) studied the schooling experiences of immigrant Hmong girls, and found that the young women must carefully negotiate a path between their own cultural construction of gender and the dominant cultural ones as they are created and recreated within the school. As Goldstein states, "it is essential to consider how gender mediates the point at which ethnic and dominant cultures intersect" (p. 1). Like Raissiguier, Goldstein describes patterns where girls both challenge and subscribe to the gender order of their community. Hmong girls who drop out of school for domestic reasons, enjoy community support and a "respected identity" for moving into a "valued gender role." On the other hand, girls committed to school put a somewhat different spin on their academic experience; as one high school girl explained, "I need some education to raise my children." Goldstein concludes that the Hmong girls attempt to define their gender identities through "an inter-relationship of meanings and practices" lived at home and in school. But much as Raissiguier observed in a different context, the girls' efforts are constrained by the social marginalization and curricular limits encountered at school. Grant's and Goldstein's work furthers our understanding of the complex processes of race and other dynamics in school processes that shape and maintain gender and race identities.

Finally, Signithia Fordham's (1997) immensely important work on African American girls in a Washington, D.C. high school provides an example of divergent African American femininities and how these femininities are expressed, and importantly how they affect the young women's academic outcomes. In this compelling work, Fordham argues against the universality of gender construction by documenting the existence of diverse "womanhood" among African American female students. For example, Fordham asserts that the academically successful African American girls achieved their success by becoming or remaining silent or voiceless or alternatively by impersonating a male image. Silent girls, however, were by no means acquiescent—on the contrary, Fordham analyzes their silence as defiant and rejecting of the low expectations of school officials. In addition, their academic success comes at great cost: alienation and isolation from their community's cultural system, and seemingly little support or reward from parents, in particular mothers, for maintaining their academic and "nice girl" roles (p. 89). In contrast, underachieving African American girls are strikingly visible, and receive full support and nurturing from parents and significant others for their plans and goals. Fordham's careful attention to the various constructions of "womanhood" (and their consequences) exhibited among young African American women is one of the most important studies to date on gender diversity.

CONCLUSION

This review of literature leads to several conclusions. First, the literature suggests that when we begin to focus on gender, we find that boys and girls have qualitatively different experiences in school. Furthermore, empirical studies show that both social-class background and race/ethnicity also appear to mediate young people's schooling experience and influence their perceptions of the relevance of schooling to their future lives. Yet as Grant (1992) argues, we cannot simply extrapolate from this research on females or minority youth to conceptualize the experiences of young women of differing backgrounds. The handful of studies that attempt to push beyond such additive analyses, reveal the fruitfulness of recognizing that young women's schooling experiences and the value they attach to gaining qualifications cannot be analytically separated from an understanding of how the dynamics of race/ethnicity and class generate meaning and help to shape those experiences.

Bonnie Thornton Dill (1983) has argued that in any analysis of women's lives, we must examine both the ways in which the dynamic processes of class, race, and gender interact as well as the ways in which women perceive, describe, and conceptualize their own lives. It is precisely this dual research perspective—one that examines both the structures that shape women's lives and women's self-presentations—that is clearly lacking in the research literature.

Finally, the educational literature suggests the need for comparative research focusing on different groups of young women within an educational institution. The few studies that do suggest that young women both experience the schooling processes and "read" the ideological messages of schooling differently center their analyses on race/ethnicity and social-class configurations.

To understand young women's lives, the particular shape of their experiences and expectations, requires an understanding of context. The following chapter examines the social and economic environments of various groups of women in U.S. society—African American, white, Latina—to provide the relevant contexts in which young women today see themselves and envision their possible futures.

CHAPTER 3

The Social, Economic, and Educational Status of African American, Latina, and White Women in the United States

INTRODUCTION

Since World War II, the U.S. economy has undergone a structural shift turning from a manufacturing economy to one based on services and technology (Bluestone and Harris, 1982). The impact of this economic transformation, however, is experienced differently throughout society. It had such dramatically adverse effects as structural unemployment, unsettling changes in the distribution of jobs, and a reduced capacity for new jobs to generate adequate incomes. These upheavals, in turn, have created and exacerbated disparities in the distribution of resources, deepening already entrenched patterns of tremendous social inequality (Eitzen and Baca Zinn, 1989). In a more optimistic vein, Hartmann (1987) has claimed that this structural transformation of the economy can be credited with inducing profound changes in gender relations and furthering the erosion of patriarchical assumptions and practices. Most significantly, as women more actively and in greater numbers avail themselves of educational opportunities and participate in the labor market, they have secured a more pronounced economic independence from men.

Not all women, however, have benefited equally from these changes. Race, ethnicity, and class remain critically important to an understanding of the nature and causes of women's disparate experiences in U.S. society. In this chapter, I will illustrate how the categories of gender, race or ethnicity, and class contribute to interconnecting and interdetermining processes rather than forming separate systems; and I will explain how these processes act as central forces in determining and differentiating women's lives.

To these ends, I will situate the groups of girls in the study within a broad socioeconomic context. Because I argue that perceptions of and responses to education are, in part, influenced by the social, political, and economic status of one's group, I provide a general overview of the social and economic experiences of different groups of women in U.S. society. I also suggest that gendered—as well as racial or ethnic—identities are constructed and reconstructed relative to changing contexts, such as economic conditions, cultural and social institutions, and ideologies. By recognizing the determinant contexts for the girls' understandings of the future, we are better able to speculate about the possible relationships between the socioeconomic context in which the young women live and their expectations regarding education, paid work, and family life.

The data presented in this chapter is organized into two broad sections: socioeconomic characteristics and educational characteristics. In the first section, I cover the topics of labor force participation, occupation, earning and income, unemployment, poverty and family composition, marriage, and fertility. In the second section, I discuss educational attainment, schooling and occupation, and educational dynamics in New York City.

In the main, this chapter draws on secondary source materials to present the reader with some sense of the general social, economic, and educational trends pertinent to my study. Where possible, I have presented data based on the 1990 census. At times, I have had to rely on less recent data, which does not, however, in any way alter the nature of the trends I am delineating.

SOCIOECONOMIC CHARACTERISTICS

Labor Force Participation

Although fewer women than men participate in the labor force, their number has increased extraordinarily since the mid-1960s. By 1988, the percentage of women constituting the labor force participation rate for women (defined as the percentage of those women who are either employed or actively seeking employment) stood at 55.9 percent (U.S. Census, 1988). This host of workers is not homogeneous but comprised of many and quite diverse groups of women; one salient difference resides in race or ethnicity. As table 3.1 illustrates, white and Latina women have become a much larger force in the labor market since 1960. African American women have also become a larger presence in the workforce, but because of their historically higher degree of labor market participation, their relative increase has not been so dramatic, occurring at roughly half the rate, for example, as those of white women (Ortiz, 1994, p. 27).

TABLE 3.1
Labor Force Participation of Women by Race/Ethnicity

	Percentage of All Women			
	1960	*1970*	*1980*	*1988*
White	33.6	40.6	49.4	56.4
Black	42.2	47.5	53.3	58.0
Latina	—	39.3	49.3	52.1
Cuban	—	51.0	55.4	53.6
Mexican	28.8	36.4	49.0	52.4
Puerto Rican	36.3	32.3	40.1	40.9

Source: Ortiz, 1994, table 2.8.

As the table indicates, there are important differences between groups of Latina women. The most striking difference is the actual decline in Puerto Rican women's labor force participation between 1960 and 1970, not to mention their overall lower percentage of labor market activity when compared to that of other groups of women. It is especially unusual that their rate of participation declined at a time when those of other groups of women were increasing. Several authors (e.g., Ortiz, 1994; Rodríguez, 1989; Cooney and Colón, 1984) attribute this remarkable decline to the dramatic loss of low-skilled manufacturing jobs, particularly in New York City, in which the female Puerto Rican workforce was concentrated. Furthermore, Puerto Rican women underwent a more protracted hardship as the changes in the industrial and occupational structure of the New York region led to a significant upgrading of work-related educational requirements (Rivera-Batiz, 1994). Even though Puerto Rican females did in fact attain higher levels of education in response, these changes were unfortunately slow compared to the very rapid shift in demand for highly educated labor (Zambrana, 1994).

Women's labor force participation in New York City parallels national data trends as described above. As table 3.2 makes clear, African American women in New York have higher participation rates than other groups of women, followed by white and Latina women. Among Latina women, New York Puerto Rican women are far less likely to be employed than any other group of women.

Labor Force Participation, Marital Status, and Family Composition

Differences between groups of women also emerge with respect to the marital status of women with children. Among most women, unmarried

TABLE 3.2
Labor Force Participation of Women
in New York City by Race/Ethnicity, 1990

	Percentage
Black	58.3
White	52.3
Latina	47.9
Cuban	57.5
Dominican	48.9
Puerto Rican	40.7
South/Central American	59.9

Source: Rivera-Batiz, 1993, table 15.

women with children are more likely to be in the labor market, given the financial imperative that they work in order to support their families. (In this context, women without children tend to be younger and in school, not in the labor market.) Married women with children, on the other hand, may have employed spouses who help support the family, although many married women with children do work outside the home. However, these variables often function quite differently among African American and Puerto Rican women. As Ortiz (1994) points out, unmarried Puerto Rican women with children are less likely to be employed because they have fewer opportunities to find work with adequate compensation to support their families. Married African American women, on the other hand, have such proportionately high labor-market participation because of the economic necessity to supplement a spouse's income, given the decreasing job opportunities for minority men in a declining economy (Ortiz, p. 29).

Employed Women and Occupations

During the tremendous expansion of the female labor force in the 1980s, most of the new entrants secured traditionally female jobs in secondary sector service and administrative support occupations, since that is where most of the job growth took place. By 1990 over one-half of white (58 percent), black (57 percent), and Latina (56 percent) women were employed in secondary-sector low-wage jobs with few fringe benefits and little chance of advancement (Amott and Matthaei, 1991). Some women did make inroads into traditionally male jobs in the highly paid primary sector. Amott and Matthaei (1991) assert that white women were the major beneficiaries of new job opportunities. While white women advanced in such male-dominated fields as law and medicine, African American women followed far behind, occupying positions in social work, nursing, and teaching, newly vacated by white women. Moreover, as Higgenbotham (1994) shows, the presence of professional and managerial black women is more likely to be concentrated in the public sector. For example, in 1980, 57.9 percent of working African American women, as compared to 31.7 percent of nonblack women, were employed in public sector work. In this regard, at least, New York City presents a slightly more egalitarian prospect for black women, whose jobs are more evenly distributed between the public (49.3 percent) and private (48.8 percent) sectors. Meanwhile, only 26.6 percent of white professional and managerial women were employed in the public sector, while 66.5 percent were in the private sector (Higgenbotham, p. 121).

Among women in the labor force a conspicuous hierarchy has developed with respect to types of occupations. In 1990, 27 percent of white women held executive-level and professional jobs as compared to 14 percent of African American and 12 percent of Latina women. Further, among Latina women, a labor-force hierarchy is also quite evident. For example, women of Cuban and Puerto Rican origin (27 and 21 percent respectively) are more likely to become executives and professionals than are Mexicans (13 percent) and South and Central Americans (14 percent) (U.S. Census, 1989). While Latina women have marginally improved their prospects in recent years (with, for example, Puerto Rican women gaining ground in white-collar positions), they are still overrepresented in semiskilled jobs, typically in factories. While 6 percent of white women and 10 percent of African American women were so employed, almost 15 percent of Latina women worked in factories. In New York City, however, 32 percent of the Puerto Rican female workforce held jobs in manufacturing, as compared to 16 percent of white and 11 percent of black females (Rodríguez, 1989).

Earnings and Income

Gender and racial/ethnic hierarchies are perhaps most glaringly visible when one glances at earnings and income inequality. If we use as a standard the median weekly earnings of full-time workers, women in all racial/ethnic groups improved their occupational standing, relative to men during the 1970s and 1980s of the same racial/ethnic group; the overall wage gap between men and women narrowed, as did the wage gaps within each racial-ethnic group (Amott, 1993). But these statistics may be misleading: it has been estimated that about 40 percent of this ostensible overall increase in women's wages relative to men's was actually the result of a drop in men's earnings (Amott, p. 78). Whatever the case, if we compare all three groups of women to white men, vast differences emerge. White women fare better: in 1990, white women earned 71 percent of what white men earned, African American women 62 percent, and Latinas 54 percent. (Amott, p. 77). However, this data underestimates the full extent of gender and racial/ethnic inequality in incomes because it ignores the role of part-time work and unemployment. (More women work in part-time jobs than men because they are still usually responsible for unpaid household labor.)

These persistent gender and racial/ethnic hierarchies characterize personal earnings. Table 3.3 presents the personal earnings of year-round full-time workers in New York City in 1990, as well as the earnings ratio of white males and female workers. As can be seen in the table, women workers' earnings, when compared to white men's, ranged from 29 percent (for women of Dominican descent) to 60 percent (for white women). Among women, whites garnered higher earnings than African Americans and Latinas. Interestingly, Puerto Rican women earn more than other Latinas (with the exception of Cubans), a sharp contrast to their lower percentages in labor force participation (see table 3.1). As Ortiz (1994) argues, this is a case for Puerto Rican women where higher wages are paired with requirements for greater skills; consequently, fewer Puerto Rican women and men work (Ortiz, p. 31).

Unemployment

Just as considerable differences in earnings exist among groups of women, unemployment rates also vary across groups as table 3.4 attests. During 1990, New York City unemployment rates for African Americans and Latinos ranged from two to over two and a half times higher than those for whites. Unemployment rates in New York City were directly proportioned to a group's position in the income hierarchy, the group with lowest earnings and highest unemployment being Dominican men and women.

Family Income and Poverty

Together, lower earnings and higher unemployment rates create vast differences in family income and poverty rates between groups of people. Young families have been particularly hard hit, suffering a marked decline in family income and an increase in poverty over the last fifteen years. The real median income for families headed by a twenty- to twenty-four-year-old male in 1986 was 27 percent less than in 1973 (Halperin, 1988, p. 17). While the trend in median income is down for all groups of young families headed by persons under age twenty-five,

TABLE 3.3

Personal Earnings of Full-time, Year-round Workers in New York City, 1990

| | Personal Earnings | | Earnings Ratio |
	Male	Female	Female/White Male
White	42,731	25,484	0.60
Black	22,602	19,174	0.45
Latino/a	19,670	14,964	0.35
Central American	17,723	14,066	0.33
Cuban	30,377	20,993	0.49
Dominican	16,492	12,481	0.29
Mexican	12,330	13,811	0.32
Puerto Rican	21,049	14,661	0.34
South American	19,204	13,804	0.32

Source: Rivera-Batiz, 1993, derived from table 16.

TABLE 3.4

Unemployment Rate of New York City Males and Females
by Racial/Ethnic Group, 1990

	Male	Female
White	5.3	5.0
Black	13.8	10.5
Latinos	12.7	13.2
Cuban	7.3	5.9
Dominican	17.8	17.3
Puerto Rican	14.7	13.3
South American	8.7	12.5

Source: Rivera-Batiz, 1993, derived from table 15.

there are enormous variations among the subgroups. Married couples lost 11 percent of their real incomes from 1973 to 1986, while female-headed families with no spouse present lost three times as much—32.4 percent. Taking account of race/ethnicity, white families lost 19.4 percent; Latina families, 18.5 percent; and young black families, particularly those headed by a single parent lost 46.7 percent—almost two and one-half times the decline experienced by young white or Latina families (Halperin, p. 19).

A similar decline in household income occurred for all families, not just the younger generations, with the exception of white and Cuban families during the period from 1970 to 1987 (see table 3.5). Among all groups, female-headed families tend to have considerably less—less than half, on average—income than other families. Puerto Ricans, with the lowest family income, consequently suffer the highest poverty rates, while over one-half of African American and Latina female-headed families live in poverty.

Data trends in New York City also reflect these major income disparities between racial/ethnic groups in terms of family income, for both female-headed and other families, as illustrated in table 3.6. Overall,

TABLE 3.5
Median Family Income (in 1979 dollars)
and Poverty by Race/Ethnicity and Family Status

| | Median Family Income | | Poverty Level | Female-Headed | |
	1979	1987	1979	1979	1987
White	19,722	20,622	7.0	22.3	26.7
Afr. Amer.	12,012	11,564	26.5	46.3	51.8
Latino/a	14,550	12,975	21.3	48.2	51.8
Mexican	13,786	12,759	20.6	44.3	47.1
Puerto Rican	12,208	9,703	34.9	66.8	65.3
Cuban	16,889	17,440	11.7	27.2	—

Source: Ortiz, 1994, derived from tables 9, 10, 11.

TABLE 3.6
Family Income and Poverty of All Families
in New York City by Race/Ethnicity, 1990

	Family Income	Poverty
New York City average	47,145	17.2
White	59,582	7.5
Black	36,248	22.5
Latino/a	30,088	31.6
Central Amer.	36,323	18.3
Cuban	45,317	14.1
Dominican	27,496	36.2
Mexican	36,923	20.2
Puerto Rican	26,119	37.5
South American	36,212	20.2

Source: Rivera-Batiz, 1993, derived from table 12.

New York Latino families have lower household incomes than either African American or white families and consequently suffer higher poverty rates.[1] Comparative percentages notwithstanding, the domain of poverty contains staggering numbers of people: well over one-third of Puerto Rican and Dominican families and nearly one-fourth of African American families, live in poverty.

Family Composition

As Amott and Matthaei (1991) observe, although all women have increased their labor-market activity and income, greater economic security for women has not ensued, since their financial responsibilities have also increased. Since the early 1960s, more and more women have headed their own households and raised families without male partners. The share of households maintained by women has grown from 18 percent in 1960 to 28 percent in 1990 (Amott and Matthaei, p. 311). While the percentage of female-headed families has increased for all groups of women, the growth has been uneven across racial or ethnic groups. African American and Puerto Rican women have experienced the most dramatic changes in their marital and family status since 1960—they are less likely to be married and more likely to head families on their own. They are also more likely to have children at younger ages prior to marriage.

It is furthermore essential to recognize that throughout society, among all racial and ethnic groups, more and more people have been questioning, and in the process redefining, what exactly constitutes a family. The questions raised are not abstract speculations but recognition of societal fact, that the "traditional" family is no longer the dominant structure of domestic life. The kinds of households that people have been forming, whether by choice of through necessity, have become increasingly diverse. Amott's data (1993) suggests that perhaps the most momentous change for women was reflected by the need to create the category "nonmarriage," for single and divorced women.

The percentage of women between the ages of twenty and twenty-four who had never been married rose from 36 percent to over 60 percent from 1970 to 1988. There were, however, major differences among racial/ethnic groups. Seventy-five percent of African American women in this age group had never been married, compared to 60 percent of white women and 50 percent of Latinas. The statistics should be taken as evidence that women are delaying marriage. By 1990, the average age of first marriage had risen from twenty-one to twenty-four years of age. At the same time, the divorce rate had also risen sharply, particularly during the 1970s. In 1985, over 23 percent of ever-married women had been divorced, up from about 14 percent in 1970.

Differences in fertility rates provide another indication of differences in family composition among groups of women. In 1984, the overall U.S. fertility rate was estimated at 65.8 births per thousand women nineteen to forty-four years old, a decline from 71.7 births per thousand women in 1980. As shown in table 3.7, white women have the lowest rate and Latina women the highest. High fertility rates of Latina women stem partly from the high proportion of Latina women of childbearing age, and although declining, the fertility rate of Latina women is still higher than that of white or black women. Fertility rates for all groups are decreasing, but white women continue to have the lowest rate, and Latina women the highest.

Differences emerge, however, between different age groups of women. For example, younger African American and Puerto Rican women have a high rate of fertility, generally occurring before marriage (Darabi and Ortiz, 1987, cited in Ortiz, 1994). In 1980, the number of births per thousand for women in the age range 15–24, were 269 for white women, 537 for African Americans and 475 for Latinas (548 for Puerto Rican women) (Ortiz, 1994, p. 23).

Alongside the increase in nonmarriage was the rise in single motherhood. In 1970, only 11 percent of families with children were maintained by women alone (no husband present); by 1988, the figure was nearly 25 percent. Again, racial/ethnic groups manifest marked differences as illustrated in table 3.8. The share of African American families maintained by women virtually doubled in the course of twenty-five years, from 22 percent in 1960 to 43 percent in 1988. The proportion also rose for other racial/ethnic groups, especially Puerto Rican. Puerto Rican and African American families were over three times as likely as white families to be maintained by a women in 1988, as illustrated in table 3.8. Significantly, female-headed families have considerably lower family income than other kinds of families—less than one-half that of other families. Not surprisingly, poverty rates for female-headed households are higher than those for any other kind of family.

In New York City, the proportion of female-headed families reflects national data trends in the percentages varying across racial or ethnic groups (see table 3.9). Puerto Ricans, African Americans, and Dominicans have the proportionately highest shares of female-headed families; and suffer, as one would expect, the highest rates of poverty in New York City.

In sum, the intensified movement of women into the labor market has had both positive and negative consequences, the relevance depending largely on women's class, marital status, and race or ethnicity. While women have come to enjoy both greater financial independence from men and also, especially women of color, new job opportunities, their

TABLE 3.7
Fertility Rate of Women 18–44 Years Old,
1980 and 1984 (per thousand women)

	1980	1984
Overall	71.7	65.8
White	68.5	64.6
Black	84.0	72.2
Latina	106.5	86.1

Source: U.S. Bureau of the Census, Current Population Reports, 1984.

TABLE 3.8
Percentage of Female-Headed Families by Race/Ethnicity, 1970–1988

	1970	1980	1988
White	9.0	11.2	12.9
Black	27.4	37.8	42.8
Latina	15.3	19.9	23.4
Mexican	13.4	16.4	18.5
Puerto Rican	24.4	35.3	44.0
Cuban	12.3	14.9	16.1

Source: Ortiz, 1994, table 2.6.

TABLE 3.9
Percentage of Female-Headed Families (as a percentage of all households)
by Race/Ethnicity, New York City, 1990

	1990
New York City average	20.3
White	9.3
Black	39.2
Latina	33.9
Central American	19.7
Cuban	19.6
Dominican	38.4
Mexican	11.0
Puerto Rican	42.2
South American	17.1

Source: Rivera-Batiz, 1993, derived from table 13.

incomes vary greatly across racial and ethnic lines, with further differentiations in the poverty levels of families headed by different groups of women. Moreover, to the extent that women have achieved greater economic independence as they participate more actively in the labor market, so too have they assumed greater financial responsibilities as they increasingly establish families without male partners.

The above discussion has clearly shown how race and ethnicity mediate the economic experiences of women in U.S. society. For example, with respect to family indicators and economic well-being, African American, Puerto Rican, Dominican, and Mexican women are not doing as well as white and Cuban women. Puerto Rican women have experienced the greatest economic deterioration among all women, in part because of the drastic decline in low-skilled manufacturing jobs in the northeastern United States where most Puerto Rican women have been occupationally concentrated.

Just as women's economic activity has increased dramatically over the last thirty years, the level of women's educational attainment has also risen. But, as I will discuss, the racial and ethnic disparities in educational attainment are as great as those in income.

EDUCATIONAL CHARACTERISTICS

Educational Attainment

Since the 1970s, the trends in high school completion and dropout rates have been positive for women. Graduation rates for all women have increased. However, such aggregate data often masks important distinctions between different groups of young women. As shown in table 3.10, while the percentage of high school dropouts among women decreased between 1973 and 1993, African American and Latina women still lag far behind white women. In fact, in high school completion rates, Latina women were three times as likely as white women to drop out of school prematurely and almost twice as likely as African American women.

High-school course selection and tracking patterns also affect young women's future chances in life. Research conducted in fifty-four New York City high schools found that the overall record of female students' math and science course participation is disturbingly low (Syron, 1987).[2] The researchers found that in particular, young women of color or from low-income families demonstrated lower rates of participation and achievement in math and science than both their male counterparts and white females. Furthermore, the research suggested that young women who complete high school geometry and algebra score better on

TABLE 3.10
Female High School Dropouts by Race/Ethnicity: 1973–1996

	1973	1980	1985	1990	1993	1996
White	11.8	10.5	9.8	8.7	7.7	7.3
Black	22.8	17.7	14.3	14.4	14.4	12.5
Latina	36.4	33.2	25.2	30.3	26.9	28.3

Source: U.S. Department of Education, 1997, table 103.

TABLE 3.11
Percentage of Female High School Graduates 18–24 Years of Age
Enrolled in Institutions of Higher Education: 1976–1990

Group	1975	1980	1985	1990
White	26.7	28.6	31.8	37.1
Black	30.3	27.6	23.5	28.6
Latina	33.2	28.1	26.7	28.3

Source: U.S. Department of Education, 1992, table 9.1.

entrance exams for civil service, federal, and private-sector jobs. In addition, one study has revealed that over 70 percent of *all* majors at two universities require four years of high school math, plain proof that math skills have become a prerequisite for higher education in many other fields.

While the overall high school completion rates for women have increased there has been a worrisome decline in the numbers of African American and Latina female high school graduates who have enrolled in institutions of higher education. As seen in table 3.11, African American and Latina women have actually lost ground in enrollment rates. Between 1975 and 1985, the proportion of African American female high school graduates going on to institutions of higher learning fell 6.8 percentage points, and the proportion fell 6.5 percentage points for Latinas, although both groups regained some ground between 1985 and 1990. Meanwhile, the proportion of white high school female graduates enrolling in higher education institutions rose 5.1 percent during the same period and continued to rise, as seen in table 3.11.

The above data, however, obscures the distinction of enrollment in two-year versus four-year institutions. Some evidence suggests that African American and Latina females have been increasingly enrolling in two-year institutions or community colleges. With the reductions in financial assistance, two-year colleges are often the only viable educational route for African American, Latina, and working-class white students. As Wilkerson (1987) points out, since almost half of all college-bound African American students come from families whose yearly incomes are below $12,000 (while only 10 percent of white students' families fall in that category), it is no wonder that African American women cluster in less expensive, more accessible community colleges (Wilkerson, 1987, p. 86). Similarly, one researcher found that the majority of the Latina women who graduate from high school enroll in community colleges. Unfortunately, there is some evidence that community-college attendance has a negative impact on the academic progress of Latina women. That is, most Latina women are not completing their academic programs, nor are they transferring to four-year institutions (Asher, 1984). Table 3.12 illustrates the larger proportions of African American and Latino/a students as compared to white students enrolled in two-year colleges versus four-year colleges. Data broken down by gender was unavailable but by extending the pattern for women in general, the differences are apparent.

Although the percentage of African American and Latina female high

TABLE 3.12
Number of Students Enrolled in Institutions of Higher Education: Fall 1995

	White	Black	Latina/o
Four-Year	6,517,200 (63.2%)	852,200 (57.8%)	485,500 (44.3%)
Two-Year	3,794,000 (36.7%)	621,500 (42.2%)	608,400 (55.7%)

Source: U.S. Department of Education, 1997, table 206.

TABLE 3.13
Percentage of Female High School Graduates 25–29 Years of Age Who Have Completed Four or More Years of College, by Race/Ethnicity: 1971–1991

Group	1971	1981	1991
White	19.1	24.2	29.8
African American	12.0	14.8	13.0
Latina	6.2	11.0	18.6

Source: U.S. Department of Education, 1992, table 9.1.

school graduates who enrolled in higher education actually declined between 1970 and 1990, the percentage of African American and Latina women who completed four or more years of college actually increased, although they have not achieved parity with white women. Latina women have seen the largest percentage jump in college graduation rates, greater than any other group of women, as reflected in table 3.13.

Of those women who do enroll and graduate from institutions of higher education, most remain concentrated within a narrow band of academic majors—education, health professions, and social sciences. Women remain underrepresented in the fields of computer and information sciences, engineering, mathematics, and physical sciences. It is not known whether differences in major concentration correlates to women's racial/ethnic affiliation, though some preliminary data is rather suggestive. For example, at the master's-degree level, over half (51 percent) of all African American females received degrees in education, compared with 47 percent of Latinas and 39 percent of white females.

Important differences also emerge among groups of women with regard to the level of education demanded by various occupations. As shown in table 3.14, white women with a degree are much more likely

TABLE 3.14
Distribution of Employed Females 25–64 Years Old
with Four Years of High School by Occupation: March 1985

Major Occupation	White	Black	Latina
Executive, administrative, and managerial	9%	4%	6%
Professional specialties	4	3	2
Technicians and related support occupations	3	5	3
Sales occupations	13	7	10
Administrative support (clerical)	40	31	41
Private household	1	4	2
Other service	16	25	18
Farming	1	—	—
Precision production, craft and repair	3	3	4
Machine operators	7	14	12
Transportation	1	1	—
Handlers, helpers, and laborers	2	3	2
Total Percentage	100	100	100

Source: U.S. Bureau of the Census, *Women in the American Economy*, 1986.

to be employed in high-paying, high-status positions than African American or Latina women. In addition, as table 3.15 indicates even with four years of college, Latina women are less likely than African American or white women to gain employment in such occupations. The same holds true for middle-level occupations, where white women with high school degrees stand a better chance of access then the other two groups of women. Female African American clerical workers are more likely than white or Latina women in similar positions to have completed four years of college. This may indicate an example, not unfamiliar, where African Americans are held to a different standard, where they are required to prove their equality through superior accomplishment—or, put another way, where their comparable abilities will not bring them comparable success. It is also worth noting that exactly one-half of all African American women with a high school diploma are concentrated in the lower-level occupations, compared to 31 percent of whites and 38 percent of Latinas.

Educational Dynamics in New York City

In New York City, the uneven distribution in educational attainment among racial or ethnic groups is also glaringly apparent. Based on calculations of 1990 Census data, Rivera-Batiz (1994) found that in 1990 as much as 33.6 percent of the white population in New York City had completed college and only 20.5 percent lacked a high school diploma. On the other hand, only 8.8 percent of the Latino/a population had completed college and over one-half (51.3 percent) had not received a high school diploma. (People from the Dominican Republic had the lowest educational attainment—61.5 percent had not completed high school.) Among blacks the situation is slightly better, with 12.8 percent having finished college and 33.8 percent having no high school diploma.

There are also wide gaps in educational attainment among whites. For example, only 11.1 percent of the Russian population in New York City had not completed high school in 1990 while as much as 37 percent of the Greek population had not received a high school diploma (see table 3.16). The educational attainment of the New York City population is presented in table 3.16.

As table 3.16 illustrates, there are remarkable differences in educational attainment between groups of people in New York City. The educational lag, relative to the white population, also appears to be growing. And the consequences of low educational attainment, particularly for young women of color are substantial.

For minority females, quitting school early can have much more devastating economic consequences than for men. As Fine (1991)

TABLE 3.15
Distribution of Employed Females 25–64 Years Old
with Four Years of College by Occupation: March 1985

Major Occupation	White	Black	Latina
Executive, administrative and managerial	18%	20%	17%
Professional specialties	42	42	49
Technicians and related support occupations	5	4	9
Sales occupations	11	5	9
Administrative support (clerical)	18	25	23
Private household	—	—	1
Other service	4	2	1
Farming	1	—	—
Precision production, craft and repair	1	1	1
Machine operators	1	2	1
Transportation	—	—	—
Handlers, helpers, and laborers	—	—	—
Total Percentage	100	100	100

Source: U.S. Bureau of the Census, *Women in the American Economy*, 1986.

TABLE 3.16
The Educational Attainment of the New York City Population, 1990
(persons 25 years of age or older)

Group	Less than High School	High School	Some College	College
New York City average	29.6	26.4	19.3	24.7
White	20.5	27.2	18.7	33.6
German	17.0	27.8	20.2	35.0
Greek	37.0	23.9	14.9	24.2
Italian	31.2	34.2	17.0	17.6
Irish	16.1	31.2	21.9	30.8
Polish	21.3	25.6	18.7	34.4
Russian	11.1	21.0	18.9	48.9
African American	33.8	29.6	23.8	12.8
Latino/a	51.3	22.8	17.1	8.8
Cuban	42.7	19.3	18.8	19.2
Dominican	61.5	18.0	14.4	6.1
Puerto Rican	53.5	23.3	16.7	6.5
South American	39.8	27.7	20.5	12.0

Source: Rivera-Batiz, 1994, derived from table 11.

argues, with or without a high school diploma, African American women are two to three times more likely to live in poverty than white women and four times more likely than white men. However, having a diploma makes a substantial difference within demographic categories. Although 62 percent of African American female dropouts live in poverty, this compares with 31 percent for African American female high school graduates. Although over 60 percent of black female graduates hold white-collar positions, only 25 percent of dropouts do so (Fine, 1991, p. 23). Moreover, African American female teens who leave school before graduation are less likely to obtain paid employment than white students. African American female teens are also likelier candidates for unemployment: in 1983, they experienced a 48.3 percent unemployment rate as opposed to 18.3 percent for white female teens (Wilkerson, 1987, p. 86).

In New York City, the data on earnings and education for women is equally compelling. Rivera-Batiz (1994) argues that while the average earnings of workers in New York City increased during the 1980s, the wages of those who had not completed high school declined during the same time period. As table 3.17 indicates, the (inflation-adjusted) earnings of women with less than a high school education dropped by 3.8 percent. On the other hand, for female high school graduates, earnings increased by 2.7 percent.

Table 3.17 makes concisely clear the economic advantage a high school education portends for women in New York City. Furthermore, as Rivera-Batiz estimates, the economic benefit of a college degree relative to a high school diploma more than doubled in New York City during the 1980s. Among women, a college degree in 1979 was associated with earnings 65.8 percent higher than those a high school diploma could expect to secure. Put another way, a college degree was worth 164

TABLE 3.17
Average Earnings of New York City Workers 25–34 Years Old
by Educational Attainment: 1980-1990

		1980 (1980 $)	1990 (1980 $)	% Change
Less than high school	Men	9,038	8,945	−1.0
	Women	6,282	6,043	−3.8
High school graduate	Men	12,188	12,255	0.5
	Women	8,867	9,110	2.7

Source: Rivera-Batiz, 1994, derived from table 14.

percent more than a high school diploma (p. 57). While the data for New York City is not differentiated by race or ethnicity, it is nevertheless evident that earnings are associated with educational attainment. However, when race and ethnicity are added to the equation, it becomes clear that racial discrimination erases much of the benefits of education: in 1978, the average Puerto Rican college graduate earned what a non-Puerto Rican high school graduate earned (Rivera-Batiz, 1994).

A related aspect of educational and income inequality in New York City is the sharp residential segregation related to race and ethnicity. Residential segregation has intensified educational segregation, which, in turn, has helped to sustain economic disparities. In New York City, as in other urban areas, by clustering poor and working-class minority groups in central city neighborhoods, where public education systems are suffering from financial and other difficulties, residential segregation maintains severe educational gaps relative to the white populations.

CONCLUSION

Relying mostly on statistical evidence, this chapter has documented how African American and Latina women, especially those of Puerto Rican descent, women belonging to groups with long histories of oppression in the United States, continue to suffer a more indirect and perhaps an even more intransigently systemic oppression in the form of lower levels of income, of economic security, and of educational attainment. While all women have enjoyed greater access to income (through increased labor-market participation), their financial responsibilities have also increased, especially as family formations have become more diversified with more and more women heading families. The overall picture is certainly mixed—racial or ethnic and gender hierarchies continue to be reproduced and maintained at the same time as they break down. And it is within this context that young women create possibilities for themselves.

In the next three chapters, I will explore, through interview data, the kinds of lives that young women of white European, African American, Puerto Rican, Dominican, and South American descent envision for themselves as adult women.

CHAPTER 4

Young White Working-Class Women: Envisioning Their Adult Lives

INTRODUCTION

In this chapter, I examine the ways in which young white working-class women envision their future lives as adults. I particularly attend to the issues of employment, marriage and family as discussed by the girls[1] during in-depth interviews. I also explore two areas of the girls' current lives—romance and their participation in domestic labor—and speculate on how their experience thus far in these matters has molded their identities, shaped their expectations, and guided their imaginations when they contemplate their future selves as adult women.

Earlier accounts suggest that young white working-class females embrace specific cultural notions of femininity and romance (see chapter 1). For example, McRobbie (1978) argues that appropriate gender behavior for working-class girls throughout their adolescent years is oriented toward "winning a man" and getting married. More recent accounts, however, suggest a shift of focus from the private sphere to the world of jobs and careers. In a study of white working-class females, Weis (1990) found wage-labor identity not marginalized but, on the contrary, clearly and quite self-consciously central.

My discussions with these white working-class girls revealed a range of identities; some of them elaborated imagined lives that emphasized employment before marriage, but most envisaged lives balancing part-time work with domestic concerns. For most, the "traditional" primacy of the domestic sphere remained intact.

ANTICIPATED PATTERNS OF PAID WORK AND FAMILY

In the following discussion, I have roughly divided the girls into three groups: girls who assert a primary commitment to a job or career; girls who center their future on family concerns, with a secondary interest in a job or career; and girls who express only vague or uncertain thoughts about employment and for whom family life appears inevitable.[2]

From this first group, Chris and Terry are primarily committed to waged labor; they focus on obtaining further education while postponing marriage—Terry, in fact, does not envision marriage at all.

> JW: If you could do anything after high school, what would you like to do?
>
> CHRIS: I want to be a cop. I know you don't have to go to college for that, but I do. I want to study law. [In five years] I hope to have graduated high school and already be in college, and be working part-time, living on my own.
>
> TERRY: . . . After I graduate from high school, I'm going to play basketball at college, hopefully at North Carolina. They have the best women's basketball coach in the whole country. . . . I want to study sports medicine.
>
> JW [to Chris]: What made you think of being a cop?
>
> CHRIS: First, I wanted to be a lawyer when I went to the 104th [precinct]. And then there was this one cop, I don't remember her name, she kept telling me cops do everything . . . and she changed my mind to want to become a cop. She told me how exciting everything is and not scary or anything.

There appears to be a direct link between both girls' internship experience[3] and their future occupational aspirations. Chris was obviously favorably swayed by her encounters with law-enforcement officers.

Similarly, Terry's aspiration to work in the field of sports medicine is clearly related to her current position in a hospital physical therapy department, where she assists patients in regaining motor functions.

As for domestic concerns, only Chris spontaneously mentioned plans for a family when I asked her to imagine her life in ten years' time.

> CHRIS: I hope to be married. I want to get married like when I'm twenty-four or twenty-five. I don't want to have kids right away though.
>
> JW: What's a good age to?
>
> CHRIS: I guess around twenty-five or twenty-six. I definitely want to go to college before I have a kid.

Furthermore, she sees herself continuing to work after having children:

> JW: How do you feel about working while you have children?
>
> CHRIS: Well, I would want to work even if I had kids. I wouldn't just give up my job like that.

For Terry, the subject of marriage never arose. Even when asked directly if she thought she'd marry, she simply shrugged and said, "I don't know."

Committed to waged labor, both Chris and Terry expressed determination to go to college as preparation for a "career." Interestingly, their careers of choice are not typically female occupations. Protective service, while long an avenue to social mobility for working-class men, is an unusual choice for working-class women, although their numbers are increasing. Similarly, jobs in sports medicine, such as team trainers, are typically male-dominated, even when associated with women's sports.

The second group of girls expressed a dual commitment to future employment and to family life. These girls envision more "traditional" roles within the family as wives and mothers. In discussing their futures, they at first consider paid work and family as equally compelling goals; but in more long-term projections, their work attachments grow vaguer, while their domestic expectations become more central. In other words, although work figures in their anticipated futures, it takes second place to marriage and family.

While this group of girls appears attached to work commitments immediately after high school, future projections of work seem vague:

> JW: If you could do anything you wanted to do after high school what would you do?
>
> CYNTHIA: Oh, O.K., I don't know. I don't think about this. I don't know. I'll plan to go to college for sure. I want to do accounting a lot. [In five years] I wish in another five years, at twenty-one, I get married, probably have children. I wish I could marry Eddy, have children, have a family. I will be a career woman, I'm not gonna be a housewife. I wish for that but I don't think it will happen.

Here Cynthia, the eldest daughter of immigrant Italian parents, expresses a very real tension: she longs for the traditional female role as wife/mother at the same time that she rejects a full-time housewife position in favor of a "career."[4] Although Cynthia would like to become an accountant, a typically male-dominated profession, she also indicated to me a few months later her dream of becoming a fashion designer or "maybe being a secretary," typically feminine occupations. The shift from accountant to fashion designer may well be connected to her internship work in a hospital accounting office, work she found boring and routine. Fashion design, and perhaps even secretarial work, might have appeared to her to offer more glamour.

Laura also hopes to continue her education, although it is unclear whether she sees college as preparation for a future occupation or as a period of independence away from her parents. As with Cynthia, Laura's attachment to paid work grows vaguer after college:

> LAURA: [After high school] I'll go to college—a four-year college, somewhere away from home. [In ten years] I'd like to be a child psychologist or work in an office doing some kind of office work. If it doesn't work out, I'll work at McDonalds or something. I'll probably be married around then and thinking about having children. I want three kids, one girl and two boys. I love kids. I'm always babysitting for my mother's friends.

Laura's dramatic shift from a high-paying, high-status occupation to a low-status, low-wage service-sector job may be flip or ironic in tone, but the details surely are not accidental—indeed, they reveal an underlying, almost grim truth. Her choice of child psychology seems to convert and "elevate" her basic interest in children into an objective, respectable, remunerative occupation; while office work and McDonald's represent a more realistic assessment of the type of service jobs available to working-class women (her mother was a waitress). Or perhaps the shift indicates an awareness of the very real conflict between paid work and family responsibilities. Jobs requiring a low investment of emotion and preparation time such as secretarial work (and unlike child psychology) would allow her to make a greater domestic commitment.[5]

Indicative of their weaker attachment to paid work are their solutions to the inherent conflict between paid work and child rearing. The solutions are similar—leave the labor market to care for their young children and reenter when children are school-age. Their assumption is that they will be able to move in and out of the work force and will have husbands to provide their chief economic support:

> JW: How do you feel about working when you have children?
>
> LAURA: I wouldn't work if I had kids. I would rather stay home and take care of them until they go to school. Hopefully we'd have enough money for that.

Given Laura's desire for three children, she would be out of the labor market for at least eight years, almost certainly eliminating any realistic chance for her becoming a child psychologist.

Below, Cynthia turns to the example of her aunt's life to underscore her own anticipated dilemma:

> CYNTHIA: See, like my Aunt Laurie, she works at the stock market as a secretary. She has children. She wishes she don't have to work, but she

has to. They want to get money, right. She wishes she can stay home and be a housewife, but she has to work. My mother babysits for her kids.

JW: Working, children, what about housework?

CYNTHIA: It's a lot of work. Maybe like when I have my children, I'll probably stop working and when my children get grown up, I'll probably go back and work. If it's a girl, you know, I'll probably make her clean and pay her.

Here we see Cynthia construe domestic labor as women's (mothers' and daughters') work, but she is also aware of the tension her aunt feels between working in the labor market and being away from her home and children. As bell hooks (1984) has observed, for many working-class women, the burden of the double day makes remaining at home a more attractive alternative to paid labor ("she wishes she don't have to work"). The child care provided by Cynthia's mother (who cleans offices at night) is a typical arrangement in Italian American extended families. Close female relatives depend heavily on each other for emotional and family support (Johnson, 1988). Because Cynthia's nuclear family is part of an intact extended family structure, it is probable that she will also be able to take advantage of relatives providing child care. Interestingly, she does not offer this as a solution for herself.

Unlike Cynthia and Laura who see themselves in college before getting married, Jeannette and Beth project marriage for themselves immediately after high school, and incorporate paid work into their futures as well:

JW: If you could do anything after high school, what would you do?

JEANNETTE: I want to get married, have a family, get a great job and support my family, well, he should support my family. But I want to spoil my kids, not spoil them, spoil them like if they need something, they can have it.

BETH: Get married and go to college . . . whatever happens first it doesn't matter. I want to study some sort of law.

Both girls here evince both a commitment to marriage and family and a commitment to a "great job" and advanced education. Jeannette clearly imagines her husband providing the main economic support—her income would serve to supplement the family income ('I don't want my kids to be deprived of anything that I didn't have'). College is an afterthought, to be squeezed in somewhere between getting married and getting a job:

JW: You said you wanted to have a great job?

JEANNETTE: Yeah, a great job. I want to be a hotel manager.

JW: What do you have to do for that?

JEANNETTE: A lot, you have to go to college for like four years. So I guess I need college.

JW: How did you decide on this?

JEANNETTE: I don't know, I woke up one morning and that's what I wanted to do [laugh].

As with Cynthia and Laura, her willingness to work begins to weaken. Jeannette's solution to raising children while working in the labor force is to leave paid work for a short period of time while her children are young and to shape her work hours around her children's school schedule when they are older. Like Cynthia, Jeannette is part of an extended Italian American family, and like Cynthia, she does not suggest the possibility of female relatives providing child care:

JW: How do you feel about working while you have children?

JEANNETTE: When they're young I'm not gonna go to work right away after they're born. Once they start school, I'm gonna set up my job [so] that I could work the hours they're in school—so that I could drop them off in the morning and pick them up in the afternoon. You know, I even have their names picked out—Jeremy Adam and Alison Marie.

Beth, on the other hand, although hoping to marry, does not believe she will have to face the dilemma of working and raising children. She clearly and unequivocally rejects motherhood: "I don't want no kids, no patience. I have a sister, I tried it already." Quite possibly Beth's experience of tending her baby sister has shaped her future decision not to have children. She is also one of the few girls with an after-school job (performing clerical work in an insurance company) in addition to spending several hours a day at her internship in a police station. Beth's very hectic experience of paid work has perhaps given her a sense of the extraordinary difficulty of balancing home and work. Her mother's life as a housewife ("she just sits at home with the baby") does not represent an attractive alternative for her. Not surprisingly, she imagines having fun in the next five to ten years:

BETH: I'll be having fun, hopefully be having a wonderful life. I'll have my car. My husband and I'll move to California, cruise the strip and have fun.

Singularly, while Beth envisions a traditional marriage arrangement for herself, she has no desire to bear children, and fills in her future with images of fun and excitement; she does not mention paid work, despite having indicated earlier her fantasies of becoming a cop, an insurance agent, and a lawyer.

The third group of girls appears more uncertain about their future participation in paid work, and they are more likely to project a future life in "fantasy" terms. Not surprisingly, this group of girls is more disengaged from school, demonstrating low academic achievement and high absentee rates, which have prevented their participation in the internship program. This group of girls is also characterized by what Connell has called an "exaggerated femininity." Their appearance tends to be stereotypically feminine: high pouffed hair, heavy facial makeup, tight-fitting clothes. Each of these girls is also involved in a steady and exclusive relationship with a boyfriend. While some of these "feminine" characteristics are evidenced among some of the girls discussed above, these characteristics are exhibited by *all* girls in this third group.

For this group, material wealth and affluence figure prominently in their fantasies of the future. Below, Doreen talks about her future:

> JW: What do you like to do after high school?
>
> DOREEN: I want to be a lawyer—have a big house, with a nice big black bathroom and two kids, a boy and a girl and my son with pushed back hair, dressed in black every day and a perfect little daughter. A pool with flowers growing.

Doreen simultaneously desires a high-status profession and children, and pictures herself in an upper-class environment. It is notable that she does not mention being married here. However, given Doreen's estrangement from school (academic failure, suspensions, legal probation for assaulting another girl), symptomatic of a her not valuing an education, her aspirations to become a lawyer seem highly unrealistic.

Similarly, without mentioning marriage specifically, Debbie and Linda indulge fantasies of travel, seeing the world, having fun and acquiring material wealth (their goals, succinctly, are travel, homes, cars). These responses echo those of the young women in Sue Lees's study (1986), who confront the grim prospects of their future lives not by romanticizing heterosexual relations and marriage, but rather by trying to postpone marriage. When they fantasized their futures, it was not about marriage, but about having fun before marriage, traveling, seeing the world, and so forth (p. 104). The girls below articulate similar fantasies:

> DEBBIE: I'm gonna be so rich I don't have to work. Live in Paris, only kidding. I want to live in Florida at Daytona Beach, in a nice condo and have a maid.

LINDA: Have a Porsche, a Rolls. I want to live in Hawaii. I want to have a big house, a built-in pool, a pool in the house. I want to have a bathtub that looks like a champagne glass. I want twins—a boy and a girl. I definitely don't want to work, I want a maid!

At the heart of their dreams of affluence and travel is the desire to have enough money so they are not constrained to engage in paid or unpaid labor. It is interesting again that marriage is not *central* to their plans right after high school. It is only when I asked the girls about their lives in five or ten years' time did the subject of marriage arise spontaneously:

DOREEN: At twenty [years old] how do I picture myself? Married, going to law school, wearing my tight black pants. My hair pouffed out, I want to have my son by then. I want to spend time with him, but I'm gonna be in law school. And *maybe* have a part-time job. Go down by the pool and flirt with all the guys.

Putting to the side Doreen's seeming unawareness that one must graduate from college before entering law school, she here reveals an orientation toward both a career and a domestic life, at the same time that she senses the inherent tension involved in pursuing both successfully ("I want to spend time with my son, but I'm gonna be in law school"). What's interesting here is her projection of an assertive sexuality alongside her ambition to become a lawyer and a mother, as if to declare "I can be powerful, maternal, and sexual at the same time."

Linda, on the other hand, appears resigned to the certainty of marriage, family and paid work, seeing this future as her natural fate and best chance.

LINDA: I guess I'll be married, but I don't think, yeah, I guess I'll have kids by then. I want to be a secretary. Ah, I don't know, just bringing home the bacon.

Unlike Linda, Debbie wants to delay the eventuality of marriage and children—it's something you end up with after you've had fun:

DEBBIE: [In ten years] I'll just be getting done partying, *maybe* getting married. I really don't know about that.
JW: What about kids?
DEBBIE: I ain't gonna be having no kids yet. If I have any at all *maybe* at twenty-seven.

Furthermore, Debbie was the only girl not to mention paid work spontaneously and talked about it only after I questioned her directly:

JW: What kind of work would you like?

DEBBIE: I want to open up my own dance studio.

JW: Do you dance?

DEBBIE: Yeah, a little, I like dancing a lot.

There seems to be a certain vagueness underlying Debbie's apprehension of her future, with only a grudging acknowledgment of the possibilities of paid work and domestic life.

This vagueness imbues Jackie's discussion about her life as well. It is as if Jackie's immediate anxieties about her home responsibilities (specifically care of young siblings) prevent her from looking too far ahead. Like Beth, her responsibility for her younger brother and sister may have engendered hostility toward childrearing:

JACKIE: I want to become a model, but I'm too short and I'm not pretty enough.

JW: So do you think you'll do that?

JACKIE: I always wanted to, but my mother won't let me, so I don't understand how I'm supposed to have a future in it. I used to draw all the time, my father wanted me to become an artist, but I haven't been doing that much, either. I really don't have time for it because I'm always watching the kids. I definitely don't want to have a family because I can't stand kids.

Jackie's solution to her future is to seek economic security, if not through marriage, then at least through a relationship with a man.

JW: If you don't model, what do you think you'll do?

JACKIE: I don't know, I really have no plans for the future. I mean, I could always stick with Peter, I know I'd have enough money with him not to do anything.

In five years' time, Jackie, although presently failing her classes, imagines herself in college, "unless I get a good job, like right out of high school." Unlike the other girls for whom college is the first step toward acquiring occupational qualifications, Jackie sees college as a second resort. This may not be so unrealistic, given the high rate of teenage unemployment in New York City. Her weak orientation to paid work, however, is evident throughout this discussion:

JW: What kind of job would you imagine yourself doing?

JACKIE: I don't know, I really don't know. I doubt that I'd be able to do anything like secretary work because I can't write fast. It probably won't have anything to do with that.

Secretarial work is the only job Jackie chooses to consider. Though displaying little interest in domesticity and paid work, she is adamant in her desire to delay marriage and childbearing and to enjoy instead a period of independence from her parental home. She is also the only girl to mention an alternative to marriage, unwilling to restrict herself to a traditional marital arrangement.

> JACKIE: [In ten years] I expect at least to be out of the house by then.
>
> JW: Do you think you'll have your own place?
>
> JACKIE: I hope so. Maybe I'll find someone, I mean not get married, but at least find someone that I can be with. Just like to see how things work out.
>
> JW: You say you see yourself with someone in a relationship, but not married?
>
> JACKIE: I don't think I want to get married that early. I want to wait until I'm positive that it's the person that I want and I have no idea when or if that will happen.

What emerges from this last set of interviews is a vision of the future wrapped in fantasy. The girls' obsession with opulence and travel can only be speculated about. First, it must be remembered that of all white girls, these girls are the most in conflict with school. At the time of the interview, all were in danger of failing all their courses and ultimately would have a very difficult time amassing enough credits to graduate. In light of this, perhaps what was occurring was that as the girls became discouraged with schoolwork, they increasingly turned to more romanticized hopes, as if to escape from or deny what grim realities were more likely to await them. As we will see, it is also this particular group of girls who appeared most heavily immersed in the ideology of heterosexual romance—all involved in steady and exclusive relationships with males.

The "fantasy" responses of this last group of girls may owe something to their being interviewed, at their request, as a group. This arrangement may have fostered a dynamic in which one girl's response had to be "outdone" by the next. Nevertheless, these responses remarkably conform to findings published by McRobbie and Lees.

All the young women discussed above appear deeply hesitant about future career plans. Although some do expect to enter the formal economy, work does not claim their primary interest. Rather, these white working-class girls project futures in which attachments to men represent economic salvation. Such projections are markedly different from the expectations of African American women;[6] there has been a long history of white working-class females interpreting family and home as their "careers" and depending on their husbands' "family wage" to provide them with a decent life (Rubin, 1976). However, with the gradual demise of the "family wage" since the 1970s, white working-class women have been faced with economic and social realities that have made employment necessary for the survival of their families (Mickelson, 1992). Despite current necessities, the family-wage ideology persists, even if only vestigiously, contributing in some measure to these young women's identities.

Future Mates

Given that almost all of these white working-class girls expect to marry, I was interested in how they pictured their future husbands. The main issue for the girls is finding the right man. What follows are the girls' thoughts about the ideal husband:

> CHRIS: He has to be nice to me and to everybody. I don't want a real snotty person. Blond hair, blue eyes, muscular build—gorgeous.

> JEANNETTE: I want him to be understanding, preferably the same nationality, not for any specific reason.

> CYNTHIA: That I know he loves me, cares about me, that he's sure.

> BETH: Some looks, and as long as he treats me nice.

It is noteworthy that none of these girls, who as a group expressed strong orientations toward work or family, specify that their ideal husbands have "good" jobs or provide economic support. The affective characteristics are important—finding a man who will understand them, who's "nice" or attractive. It may be that they *assume* they will have a husband who is employed (with the exception of Laura, whose father is absent, all have employed fathers). However, given that several of these girls have boyfriends who are high school dropouts or who are unemployed, it would represent a curious assumption. There seems, that is, to be a contradiction between their direct experiences with boyfriends and their expectations for future husbands.

On the other hand, it is quite clear that for those girls most disaffected with school and uncertain about plans for future paid work, finding a man who will provide economic support is most crucial in selecting a mate.

> JW: What's the ideal husband?

> LINDA: I sit home! I want him to bring home the money. He has to bring home flowers every night, sit by my side and everything,

telling me how much he loves me. Then we go out to dinner every night. And then we just sit there romantic and cuddle up by the fire. We just sit there sipping our champagne—on a bearskin rug, next to the heart-shaped tub. Like that commercial for that hotel in the Poconos.

DEBBIE: I get to stay at home watching T.V., letting the baby walk around and everything. I go out. Then he comes home, he has dinner, we go out. He works, making some money for us.

JACKIE: I don't know, I have someone right now. He has his ways of making money.

Doreen describes her future husband by comparing him to her father in terms that challenge the sexual division of labor in the home:

DOREEN: I just think someone totally opposite of my father. My father's lazy. He's got to cook me dinner once in awhile, give me little gifts, tells me he loves me and he has to take the kids down to the park while I sit home and relax. He's got to iron once in awhile. My father does not do nothing, nothing. He lays on the bed. He doesn't do nothing. Be there for me, want to talk.

Marriage, as portrayed by most of these girls, is somewhat romanticized. None consider the possibilities of divorce and abuse. On the contrary, several describe husbands who will be loving and understanding, who will spend time with them and their children, and who will provide material and emotional support. There is a startling discrepancy between their fantasies of future marriage and their past and present experiences—of marriages breaking up (four have witnessed their parents divorce and remarry), of family violence, of unemployed and semi-employed boyfriends. They seem to hope that the "right" man (nice, loving, etc.) will rescue them from the kind of dismal life they see endured by so many married women, including many of their mothers overwhelmed with domestic responsibilities, working in jobs that are often exhausting and boring, and often trapped in abusive relationships. Ignoring such complexities and risks, they construe the issue of marriage as the more manageable individual problem of finding an understanding, sharing, considerate partner.

The possibility of abusive husbands did not arise in discussions with these girls. Domestic violence within white working-class families has a long tradition, but it "remains a well-known, shared family secret" (Weis et al., 1995). During one interview, a girl's remarks suggested that not all of these girls may be immune to male violence even though it is rarely spoken about:

JACKIE: My mother was married to two alcoholics. She was married to my dad, who's an alcoholic, and then she got married to another alcoholic who used to beat her up all the time. Now she found someone, he never talks, but he's very, very nice. He wouldn't lay a hand on her.

This passage not only documents Jackie's experience with domestic violence, but also offers insight into the definition of "nice" that many young women use to describe ideal boyfriends or mates (for example, see Wilson [1978] and Lees [1986]). "Nice," as Jackie utilizes it, is perhaps attributed to males who do not physically abuse women.

To sum up thus far, these young women revealed views about employment and marriage that are consonant with the findings of other researchers exploring the construction and expression of female gender roles. For example, young women who adopt traditional stereotypical traits of femininity—women who are dependent, self-sacrificing, relatively passive, and submissive—are disproportionately at risk for dropping out of school and for unwanted pregnancy.[7] In other words, for girls who adhere strongly to traditional feminine behaviors, the consequences can be severe. Girls, such as those above, who expect to be marginal economic contributors to their households, or who subscribe to traditional gender distinctions in work/domestic roles, may end up leaving school prematurely, or may find themselves as adult women thrown into the least secure sector of the economy, unable to provide for themselves in the event of divorce or loss of a mate's income. Economic dependency on males may also lock them into exploitive and abusive relationships with their mates. However, as we also saw above, some girls fluctuate in the extent to which they embrace traditional notions of femininity—some not wanting children, others desiring some independence before marriage, and so forth.

A feminine gender ideology, with its attendant conceptions of wage work and domestic life, is significantly shaped by the young women's own personal experiences as daughters and sisters within families, and by their experiences as "girlfriends" in romantic heterosexual relationships.

DAILY LIVES

Household Labor

To explore the girls' participation in domestic labor, I asked them to describe a typical day in their lives. Much of the emphasis in research on women's/girls' labor has been on their *paid* labor. As Griffen (1985) points out, previous studies have minimized the importance of young women's involvement in domestic work. This is not only a serious deficiency in scholarship but also a recapitulation of the dominant culture's tendency to discount girls' nonpaid work in the home. We know, therefore, very little about class (and racial/ethnic) differences in girls' contributions to domestic labor. There is, however, evidence that white middle-class girls are likely to have fewer domestic responsibilities than working-class girls. In one of the rare studies to examine class difference, Griffen (1985) determined in her study that only 20.6 percent of the white middle-class girls—compared to 51 percent of the white working-class girls—performed household chores. This difference was partly (and hardly convincingly) attributed to the presence in some middle-class families of employed female daily help (a small minority, really); more often, this difference is attributed to the middle-class girls' families exempting them from domestic work because of their heavy load of academic schoolwork.

What emerges from the following data provides evidence to show that all girls are already participating in their future roles in domestic labor by helping their mothers in the home. Without exception, every girl comes from a home with a traditional sexual division of labor vis-à-vis childrearing and housework.

The girls in my study spent, on average, about fifteen hours a week engaged in domestic labor—the same as McRobbie (1978) found in her study of 14–16-year-old girls. With one exception,[8] the girls had no help from their brothers or fathers, as the following exchange illustrates:

JW: Does your brother do anything around the house?

LINDA: Well, he's supposed to do his bedroom.

JW: Does he?

LINDA: No, not really. I end up making his bed everyday.

JW: Does your father or brother help?

CHRIS: No (laughs).

JW: Who makes dinner?

JEANNETTE: My mother, or I do when she works overtime.

JW: Does your father ever do anything?

JEANNETTE: No!

DOREEN: . . . My father's lazy! . . . My father does not do nothing, nothing. He lays on the bed. He doesn't do nothing.

DEBBIE: The only thing my father does is change the thing [duck pen] that the ducks are in—his babies.

Because so little is known about such girls' daily lives and the work they do at home, it is useful to quote some of the girls' descriptions of their household duties.

> LINDA: I get home from school around 3:30, clean the house, babysit my brother.
>
> JW: What kind of things do you do when you clean?
>
> LINDA: I have to vacuum, dust, do the living room, do the dishes in the kitchen, clean the kitchen, the dining room, my bedroom, my parents' bedroom, the bathroom.

Linda's household labor and child care for her younger brother make it possible for her mother to work outside the home in a physically demanding job as a meat cutter in a supermarket six days a week. In Linda's words, "all she does is come home, cook and go to bed. . . . On her day off she sits around and cleans the house."

Cynthia, as the oldest of four daughters, carries the major burden in her family, since her mother works at night as an office cleaner, entrusting Cynthia with the care of three younger sisters after school.

> JW: Who does the housework?
>
> CYNTHIA: I do, I do most of it, I do the laundry, I wash dishes, I clean the house. My mother'll do it too and sometimes my sister.[9] They all [sisters] go out, play games. I don't mind, I always clean. My mother's like, "do this, do that." I clean the hallway. It's a six-family house, I have to clean the hallway every week. When my mother works, I have to cook, too. I always have to watch my sisters.
>
> JW: Does your father do anything?
>
> CYNTHIA: Yeah, he comes home and then he goes to the club [Italian American Club]. I don't mind, once in a while I go out. I make my father watch my sisters.

What's interesting here is Cynthia's comment about "making" her father watch her sisters as if her father is assuming *Cynthia's* child-care responsibility.

Even when mothers are not active in the labor force, daughters are not exempt from a major share of housework and child care. Jackie, whose mother has temporarily left a real estate position, spends most of her intended leisure time after school and on weekends babysitting her seven-month-old brother and two-year-old niece.

> JACKIE: I used to draw all the time. That was in New Jersey. I haven't been doing that anymore. I really don't have time for it because I'm always watching the kids. I think it's unfair.

Chris's mother was recently laid off as a telephone operator and provides most of the unpaid household labor. At first, Chris indicated her mother did all the housework; however, it later emerged that while Chris performed few chores at home, she was in fact providing a substantial amount of help to her aunt with three young children:

> JW: Do you have any chores at home you're responsible for?
> CHRIS: Just my room (*giggles*).
> JW: Who does all the housework?
> CHRIS: My mother (*giggles*).
> JW: How about at your aunt's house, do you help her?
> CHRIS: Yeah, all the time. I babysit for her kids, well I babysit for my mother too and I help my aunt cook almost every night. I help her a lot more than I help my mother.

The above quotations illustrate the type and frequency of household tasks that the girls perform throughout the week. No girl was completely exempt from the responsibility of household work, unlike brothers and fathers who were. The two girls who had commitments to wage work (after-school jobs) performed less household work than the others simply because they spent so little time at home. In fact, neither ate dinner at home most nights.[10] Debbie works as a waitress and is exempt from *daily* tasks; her seventeen-year-old sister and her mother perform most of the domestic labor. As she explains:

> DEBBIE: I just do wash, my sister does the ironing, my mother cleans. I got to clean my room, but that's it. I'm usually gone at night. I eat dinner at work.

Beth, who works as an office assistant in an insurance company and arrives home around 8:00 every evening, is also exempt from household work. While she is expected to participate, she states simply:

> BETH: I'm *supposed* to [do housework], but I don't do anything.

Lees and Griffen have argued that early domestic commitments can shape girls' expectations of their future position within the family. However, these practices, especially as they reflect the traditional division of labor, are not necessarily automatically internalized or accepted (Valli, 1983). In the girls' descriptions of their domestic work, many instances emerged in which girls expressed, in various ways, their opposition to such responsibilities. The clearest example is Beth, who is able to avoid household chores probably because of her holding an independent position as a wage earner as well as having a mother at home full-time with a two-year-old child. In Beth's case, her opposition to domestic work and care of her young sister has turned her off to having her own children. When I asked whether she intended to have children someday, she responded:

> BETH: No way. I have a sister. I tried it already, no patience.

Similarly, Jackie states emphatically:

> JACKIE: I'm always watching the kids. I definitely don't want to have a family because I can't stand kids. I'm dead serious, I cannot stand them.

Other girls also do not accept unproblematically their household responsibilities:

> LAURA: I do most of it [housework], like I cook dinner and clean up the house when my mother goes to school. My sister's supposed to make her bed. But when I was her age [eleven years old], I used to watch her and do much more. I think she's spoiled.

For Jeannette, the negotiation of domestic work usually leads to conflict with her mother:

> JEANNETTE: I help my mother do the laundry, clean, stuff like that. Then we always fight about it and I get punished and sit in my room for the rest of the day.
> JW: What do you fight about?
> JEANNETTE: She won't let me go out until I finish and it's too much work.

Cynthia, who carries a large share of the care of her younger sisters, as well as housework, avoids weekend trips with her family. While weekend trips may be restorative for other members of the family, for Cynthia and her mother the division of household labor does not change and is simply transplanted to another location.

Another strategy employed to avoid domestic work is to perform the household task so ineptly that one is exempt from doing it routinely. During a discussion about housework, Linda and Doreen brag about their ineptness at cooking:

> LINDA: I help my mother cook, but I just can't cook (*lots of laughter*).
> DOREEN: My mother won't let me come near her 'cause I wash the chicken (*whoops of laughter*).

JW: You mean with soap?

DOREEN: She told me to wash the chicken and I washed the chicken. Well, what would your interpretation of wash the chicken be?

DEBBIE: Rinse it out.

DOREEN: And pull all those things out? Oooh (*laughter*).

It is evident from the preceding discussion that the division of labor in these working-class families assigns child care and housework to the wife/mother and daughters. A girl's femininity is constructed in part by the unpaid labor she provides for other family members which is considered women's work. Unlike middle-class adolescent girls, who are less likely to have domestic responsibilities (because of female daily help employed in the home or a heavy academic load), working-class girls spend a significant amount of time participating in household labor. Through these activities, young women learn about conventional definitions of femininity. However, as we saw, many do not accept these definitions unproblematically. Domestic work is only one of the ways through which young women learn about their present and future positions in the family and labor market. I now turn to another aspect of girls' lives in which they learn about cultural conventions of "womanhood."

Boyfriends and Romance

As Christian-Smith (1990) states in her pioneering work on adolescent romance novels, romance is one of the "organizing principles" of the home and school lives of teenage girls (p. 16). Indeed, love relationships with males and dating seem to be so central in my discussions with girls that it is imperative to explore how it works in relation to female subjectivity (Taylor, 1989). Myra Connell (cited in Taylor, 1986) and others in their work on romance and sexuality state:

> The way in which they accept it [romance], use it, and experience it is part of a complex social process. . . . [R]omance "keys" into various aspects of women's lives and connects up with their subordination in a far from simple way.

Holland and Eisenhart's (1990) recent work on college women also underscores the centrality of romance in young women's lives.

Heterosexual pairing among these adolescent girls is very common, and is generally viewed as proof of "normal" femininity. Most girls interviewed spent a significant amount of time discussing their relationships (often spontaneously introducing the topic) and sometimes producing photographs of their boyfriends. Not quite appreciating the centrality of romance in girls' lives before my data collection, I was surprised to discover how prominent a role boyfriends played.

The duration of an exclusive relationship with a boy was a much-discussed topic and revealed the importance girls gave to their relationships. Girls often kept track of exactly how long they have been with a particular boy. In this exchange, three girls compare their situations:

> LINDA: We been together a year and seven months.
>
> DOREEN: It's too long, believe me. You've got me beat by a week and four days.
>
> DEBBIE: My longest was a year and four months.
>
> DOREEN: Me, a year, six months, two weeks and three days.

Such accuracy is not unusual. When I asked other girls how long they have been going out with their boyfriends, they responded:

> BETH: A little over two months, like two months and one week.
>
> CYNTHIA: It's almost seven months now. We met September 9th.

What constitutes a steady, exclusive relationship as opposed to a casual relationship seems, in the girls' terms, to be fairly well-defined:

> CLARICE (to Connie): How long you been with him?
>
> CONNIE: You mean physically or mentally?
>
> CLARICE: All of the above.
>
> CONNIE: Mentally, I been with him for one year; physically, two months.

Jackie explains the rules thusly:

> JACKIE: You have one boyfriend, that's it, unless you're just seeing the person. If you mess around[11] with anyone else, your boyfriend wouldn't speak to you the rest of your life for that.

Steady relationships seem to comprise an exclusive sexual relationship as well.

Relationships with boys are not always a source of fun as the following girls attest:

> CYNTHIA: He's the kind of guy that minds his business. He's always telling me what to do, but he won't tell other people what to do. But I guess it doesn't matter anyway, now he's going out with my friend. It hurts a lot.

LINDA: He can be a real tart when he wants to be. He can be all laughing and happy and everything and then he could just change his mood like that and not say anything.

JEANNETTE: He was a real sweetheart, but now I can't see him no more. He's a big liar, he started seeing someone else behind my back.

Through casual dating and through more serious exclusive relationships with boys, girls learn about the gendered relations of power between men and women (Christian-Smith, 1990). Boys can control the terms of a relationship by making girls their exclusive "property." (This exclusivity in girlfriend-boyfriend relationships mirrors monogamous marital relations.) Being the exclusive "property" of a boy means that he can "legitimately" control his girlfriend's contact with other boys, effectively setting the terms of the relationship (Christian-Smith, 1990). Girls, however, can be quite ambivalent in their response to this attempt at domination:

DOREEN: I can't go dancing, my boyfriend won't let me.

JW: Why not?

DOREEN: 'Cause he's jealous. I used to go all the time [without him] and now he won't let me.

JW: What about with him?

DOREEN: I can go with him, but I don't consider that dancing. Like what am I gonna do, there's my boyfriend standing over there. I'm not gonna dance with them [other guys].

JW: So he gets jealous?

DOREEN: Yeah, he's like really jealous, overprotective.

DEBBIE: Every boyfriend is jealous and overprotective. I'm sorry, but they are.

DOREEN: Yeah.

Although Debbie relates this complaint with some sense of injustice, boyfriends' jealousy and overprotection (possessiveness) appear to constitute normal and expected male behaviors.

In some cases, "protection" provided by a boyfriend can benefit a girl. As Anyon (1984) has noted, girls are increasingly encouraged to accept femininity in the form of male protection as the source of their power. In the following passage recounted by Jackie, it is evident that "protection" is providing her with a sense of "empowerment."

JACKIE: He has David and Eric his bodyguards, so everywhere I go like, when I go dancing, if any guy even tries to get next to me when Peter's not around, they're there right away. 'Cause the night we went to the hotel, we got a flat tire . . . then all of a sudden, a truckful of guys came up. And like, they drove up and were sitting there whistling and everything at me. Peter wasn't there, all of the sudden David and Eric come back to the car, right, and like they get out of the car, and they're sitting there like this and they're big too. Sitting there on both sides of me. And I was just sitting there smiling *like come next to me, I dare you.* They both carry guns. (Emphasis mine)

In this situation, Jackie clearly experiences a temporary sense of power over the guys who harassed her. Sandwiched between two big, gun-toting bodyguards, she is able to challenge her harassers. But, more important, as this passage highlights, Jackie is learning about gendered power relations. Standing alone on a dark street, she is vulnerable to harassment and possibly to violence—"protected" by her boyfriend's bodyguards (an extension of her boyfriend's protection), she is able to challenge them. Her status as Peter's girlfriend confers recognition and imbues her with a sense of empowerment; however, there is a limitation to that power. It does not affect the balance of power between Jackie and her boyfriend. Moreover, the display of power by the bodyguards could as easily turn into violence against her. For Jackie, this possibility is not missed—she has witnessed male violence against her mother by a former husband.

There seems to be an important public and even utilitarian dimension to romance for girls. Christian-Smith makes the point that romance "ultimately involves the construction of feminine identity in terms of others, with boys in the powerful position of giving girls' lives meaning" (p. 92). This is most clearly expressed in the ritual of inscribing a boyfriend's name over books, papers, desktops, and even on classroom chalkboards. It is not unusual for a girl[12] to announce her exclusive relationship with a boy by writing his name on the board or even writing other couples' names all over the board. I think this practice highlights the importance many girls place on being "paired off" and is a means of calling attention to themselves through their involvement with boys.

Relationships also provide girls with companionship. Girls' intense involvement with steady boyfriends organizes much of their time. This frequent and close contact between girls and boys is illustrated below:

DOREEN: [Every day] I go to the pool hall, and everybody hangs out. I wait for my boyfriend to pick me up. We drive around, eat, whatever.

DEBBIE: I'm like forever shopping, get my nails done, go home, hang out with my boyfriend, then he takes me to work . . . he sees me at work. He sits there for three or four hours, gets in the way. When it's not busy, I tell him to come in and we eat, talk, watch T.V.

BETH: Usually after work every day I go to my boyfriend's . . . on the weekends, I go by his job, hang out with him, he drives me home.

LAURA: We talk on the phone every single night, sometimes for hours. On the weekends we go to the movies, hang out.

JACKIE: I don't want to go on an internship in the spring. I'll be going to the beach all day. I go to Jones Beach to see Peter since he doesn't work during the day.

Over half of the girls (six out of ten) are involved with steady boyfriends who are at least four or five years older than they are. Most of these boyfriends either dropped out of school or rarely attend, and are unemployed or not steadily employed. The fact that boyfriends have so much "free" time, often puts pressure on girlfriends to spend time during the school day with them. As one guidance counselor put it:

> Some of them are involved with boyfriends who simply don't want them going to school. They go to a different school, some don't even go to school, and they don't want them to walk in the halls with other boys. And there's this dependency thing, the girls want to spend all their time with their boyfriends.

Again, boys control girls' movements and contact with other boys. The guidance counselor articulates the central problem here, that for some girls, their lives are given greater meaning through their contact with boyfriends, but such contact almost always is predicated upon an unequal exchange of power (Christian-Smith, 1990).

In nearly all instances where one of these girls has a steady boyfriend, the boyfriend has visited the girl's home and met her parents. Such a visit is here taken to sanctify the relationship, not necessarily as an "unofficial engagement" (Whyte, 1973), but as a serious and exclusive commitment. Public acceptance and acknowledgment of a girl's steady relationship makes romance a seemingly "normal" part of being a teenage girl (Christian-Smith, 1990). Steady and exclusive relationships with boys can also function to render sex a legitimate activity. As Lees (1993) comments, "the only really safe place for the expression of female sexuality is in a long-term relationship, usually leading to marriage" (p. 112). "Love" plays a crucial role here—it is the existence of affection in the form of romantic love that legitimates sex. Love either precedes sex to render sex legitimate, as Wilson (1978, p. 70) states, or love is used as a rationalization after sleeping with someone (Lees, 1993, p. 109). In any event, "love" directs girls' sexuality into the only "safe" place for its expression—steady and monogamous relationships.

As I have tried to show, boys can control the terms of the relationship by making girls their "exclusive" property, regulating their girlfriends' contact with other males through their "protection" and jealousy. The benefits and disadvantages of romance form a circuit (or vicious circle) of exchange—the girls put up with the boys' domineering behavior in exchange for public recognition and approbation, as well as for the feeling of personal security, of belonging to someone. As Christian-Smith (1990) suggests, these are "the kinds of bargains adult women strike as wives and mothers. Romance is as a training camp for marriage—as such, romance is an important social dynamic for the learning of gendered relations of subordination and domination" (p. 29).

It could be argued perhaps that these girls are learning not only how to negotiate unequal gendered relations within their relationships, but at the same time learning how to balance the demands of a steady and exclusive relationship, the demands of schoolwork, and the demands of work (both paid and unpaid).

CONCLUSIONS

This chapter has attempted to shed light on the formation of identities and expectations among a group of young white working-class women. Although these girls generally envisaged being employed, many tended to think they could move in and out of the labor market with relative ease. While many indicated a desire to have jobs or "careers," this desire was swiftly suppressed in favor of domestic commitments. The wish for domestic fulfillment was perceived as incompatible with a permanent commitment to the labor market. Feelings about being wives or mothers were not, however, without ambivalence. Most assumed housework and childrearing would be their responsibilities and most seemed committed to traditional marriages.

Many of the young women also mentioned obtaining some sort of higher education, although, in many cases, such a goal came as an afterthought ("you have to go to college for like four years [to become a hotel manager] so I guess I need college"). There seemed an awareness at some level for the need to prepare for a "good" job through higher education, without which they could face a typically more constrained and limited job market.

Several of the girls, however, expressed a great deal of uncertainty, vagueness, and "imagination" about their futures in terms of both paid work and family life. While they desired children and material wealth, their commitments to waged labor were marginal at best. For this group of girls, who were disaffected from school and who possessed few skills to enter the labor market, the best chance for economic security will be through forging advantageous attachments to men. It is precisely this group of girls who were, in fact, heavily involved in steady and exclusive relationships. Indeed, for most girls presented in this chapter, romance played a central role in their lives. In this sense, my findings parallel other studies in which the ideology of romance plays a prominent role in young white working-class girls' lives.

The experiences of these young women validate McRobbie's (1978) argument that specific (working-class) cultural notions of femininity and romance appear to direct working-class girls into marriage, childrearing, and part-time work, and that these notions do not appear to be greatly changing; we will see in later chapters, however, that the gender code of the school, while at times contradictory, does in fact create some pressure for change.

My findings depart, then, from more recent studies (Weis, 1990; Raissiguier, 1994) that suggest that changes are developing in the "culture of femininity." Such departure may be linked, in part, with the specific economic and cultural contexts in which the studies have been conducted. For example, Weis argues that the stress among the girls in her study on a wage labor identity is elaborated *in relation to males* who were experiencing joblessness, underemployment, job displacement, and so forth, within a deindustrializing economy. Although the prospects for employment among white working-class men continue to decline, the young women in this study can still count on employed fathers to bring home a paycheck (and mothers, if they do work at all, are not the primary economic support).[13] In this context, in which fathers are still providing for their families, the young women may not be fully cognizant of the overall contraction of economic opportunities for white working-class men. While they do know that their boyfriends are unemployed or not working steadily, it may appear to the young women that these are individual instances, rather than a more structural problem of working-class male unemployment.

Weis's study exemplifies how working-class female gender ideology gets redefined in the wake of deindustrialization and that women take on economic roles only when their men are prevented from doing so. Perhaps for these young women, the redefinition is only just beginning.

CHAPTER 5

Young Women of African American and Puerto Rican Descent: Anticipating Lives as Adult Women

INTRODUCTION

In the previous chapter, we saw how a particular group of young working-class white women largely adhere to a "traditional" working-class femininity emphasizing dependency on male wage earners and discouraging women's participation in the economy. In this chapter, I will recount how a group of seven U.S. Puerto Rican[1] and three African American girls intend to structure their adult lives. In contrast to the girls in the previous chapters, these young women ascribe importance to educational credentials that will qualify them for the good jobs or careers they intend to secure.

My rationale for grouping together these young women of African American and Puerto Rican backgrounds is based on their common history of "nonvoluntary" migration to the United States. According to Ogbu (1989), "involuntary minorities" are people who were initially incorporated into United States society through "slavery, conquest, or colonialization" (p. 186). As such, they are to be distinguished from "immigrants," people who more or less voluntarily moved to the U.S. in search of greater economic opportunity or greater political freedom. While U.S. Puerto Ricans admittedly share cultural bonds with other Latino groups (bonds derived in part from a common history of Spanish domination), they arguably have more immediately in common with other U.S. "involuntary minorities" such as African Americans, Native Americans, and Mexican Americans, particularly insofar as experience and perceptions are forcefully determined by their "castelike" status within U.S. society (see chapter 1).

While both groups experience racism and discrimination in all spheres of life, Ogbu points out that these two groups (voluntary and involuntary minorities) interpret their plights quite differently. Unlike immigrants who tend to regard social, economic, and political inequity

as a temporary predicament susceptible to melioration through education, nonvoluntary migrants construct their experience according to a
different model whereby they understand racism and discrimination as
permanent constituent elements of social reality. Minority youths may
underachieve in school as a result of an accurate, even if subliminal,
assessment that education does not, ultimately, pay off, given the recal-
citrant constraints of class and race; the plain evidence for their parents
and others in their communities testifies daily that economic returns
have rarely been commensurate with educational qualifications (Mickelson, 1990). Although my intention here is not to apply Ogbu's thesis
to African American and U.S. Puerto Rican female students, this chapter does provide some evidence that not only do these young women
abstractly value schooling as a way to improve their social and economic opportunities, but most actually behave in ways that are consistent with successfully completing high school.

The history and abiding legacy of racial oppression and U.S. colonial domination have powerfully shaped African American and U.S.
Puerto Rican women's lives, importantly distinguishing this group from
white women and, as we will see in the next chapter, from immigrant
Latinas. Unlike white working-class gender ideologies in which women
have been almost axiomatically identified with the domestic sphere,
African American and U.S. Puerto Rican women have long inhabited
more flexible gender roles, to a large extent dictated by the historical
necessity that they participate in the labor market to compensate for
persistent discrimination against their men.[2] And while immigrant
Latina women do have much in common with the others in this study,
it should be recognized that their experiences have been shaped and
defined by immigration in unique ways; therefore, I will discuss the
immigrant Latina girls separately in the next chapter.

In this chapter, I will first focus on the African American and U.S.
Puerto Rican girls' plans for education, paid work, and family, as
elicited through open-ended interview questions. I then turn to a consideration of the girls' engagement in domestic labor (in their own
homes) and their relationships with males.

HIGHER EDUCATION AND LABOR MARKET PLANS

Significantly, most of the girls in both groups identify their primary aim
immediately after high school to be the pursuit of further education and
paid employment. The goal to obtain paid work did not, for most of
these girls, preclude the possibility of marriage and children. However,
almost without exception, the girls gave temporal priority to continued

higher education as the first logical step toward establishing themselves in "good" jobs or careers, an implicit prerequisite to seriously entertaining thoughts of marriage and childbearing. This emphasis on higher education and employment holds both for those girls doing well academically and those performing poorly.

The following quotations illustrate the girls' commitment to higher education. Here they respond to questions about their plans after graduation from high school, and speculate about their lives five years hence.

> SAUNDRIA: I'm going straight to college. I want to go to Syracuse, that's it. [In five years] I know I'll still be in college, I'll be living in a dorm. Everything will be alright. I'll have my car. I'll be preparing for my career. I want to be a broadcaster. I know you have to do English and communication classes like that. I won't have no kids (*laughs*). That's about it. I'll be doing good in my schoolwork.

> BARBARA: I think I'll go to college. I want to go to a good college, but I don't know where I want to go now. [In five years] I'll be a career woman. I was thinking about being a social worker and then I was thinking about being a doctor, you know, one of them that work with babies. I think I want to be a social worker or a doctor. I'll probably be living in my own apartment or house. I don't really know, but I could see myself doing that.

These two African American girls forthrightly assert their independence, envisioning life outside the parental home, and both voice the desire to attend "good" colleges. Moreover, they both expressly use the word "career," recognizing a strong connection between acquiring solid education and acquiring solid future employment. Neither, significantly, mentions marriage. Both find compelling the image of themselves as independent career women, though Barbara miscalculates the time it will take to complete her education and Saundria sees as added incentive the avoidance of having children. Only one African American girl did not evince such a commitment to further education and wage labor:

> CHERYL: I want to marry my boyfriend [after high school]. That's it and move far away from my mother as I could. I want two kids.

Although Cheryl here in the "formal" interview seems primarily bent on an early marriage, she had earlier confided in me her hope to become a writer. She had also been giving thought to transferring to a vocational/technical high school in order to "get some job skills." Perhaps in the above response, she is tacitly assuming a future of paid work; nevertheless, she is the only girl in the whole group not to indicate a desire to attend college.

Similarly, higher education represents a primary goal for girls of Puerto Rican descent, whether or not their academic achievement warrants the possibility.

DELORES: I'll be going to college, of course; I want to study law.

ANGELA: [In five years] I'll be in college then, studying business management, mostly doing math and reading, trying to get to know people. I'll probably be going to college somewhere in Manhattan.

EMILY: [In five years] my life will be hectic because I'll be in school. I'll be in college, studying, working, you have to study. If you have an exam the next day, you gonna be like breaking night studying real hard. I see myself in college doing well. That's how I see myself.

GLORIA: I want to become a teacher, actually I want to be an English teacher. I'm planning on moving, living in Puerto Rico. So I want to be an English teacher over there. First I'll have to go to college, though. I'm graduating high school when I'm nineteen since I got left back. I'll go to at least a two-year college and I'll become what I want to become.

CLARICE: I want to own a dance studio and I'll probably go to college to study choreographing. I already have experience doing it. . . . [In five years] I'll be in college, hopefully.

AUREA: I'll either get a job or go to college. Well, this is what I really want to do after I get out of high school. I'm gonna go into the army and I'll get the G.I. bill for college and I'll get on scholarship, part-time in the army for college. Then either become a teacher or a lawyer. I like criminal law. Something else I would like to do is the doctor that does the babies. Oh forget it, I would like that.

MARTA: I want to go to a college with a nice campus. I'll be walking down the hall going to class with all my books. And I'll have a room in the dorm with a roommate and it'll be decorated so nice. I'll be far away. [In five years] I'll be in college. Hopefully, I'll fall in love and get engaged. I don't want to get married in college, but I want to get engaged.

The fact that, without exception, these girls of Puerto Rican descent envision attending college is important. According to Amott and Matthaei, only 39 percent of U.S. Puerto Rican women over twenty-five are high-school graduates and only 5 percent have completed four years or more of college.[3] These figures stand in sharp contrast to the educational attainment of African American and white women in the United States. In 1988, 63 percent of African American women and 79 percent of white women over the age of twenty-five had graduated from high school (Amott & Matthaei, 1991, p. 190).[4] In addition, white and African American women were also more likely to have held a college degree than U.S. Puerto Rican women (17 percent and 10 percent, respectively).

Attending college for these girls is usually associated with training for future employment. Marta is the only one to somewhat romanticize college, conjuring images of decorated dorm rooms and alluding to marriage ("Hopefully, I'll fall in love and get engaged"), but she discounts getting married while attending college.

In general, these girls of African American and Puerto Rican backgrounds reveal a strong attachment to the ideals of higher education and the pursuit of a career. They possess a vivid sense of themselves as potential career women, and they seem to be firm believers in the value of education, especially as it confers the qualifications necessary to procure "good jobs."

A topic that arose spontaneously during the interviews with these girls was the imperative to avoid early pregnancy, an issue that was not addressed by the white working-class girls. This contrast may reflect differences in the meaning and consequences attached to early childbearing among African Americans and whites (Geronimus, 1991, cited in Irvine, 1994). As Geronimus notes, among low-income families, black females are much more likely to become teen mothers than white females. While one in twelve white girls becomes pregnant, one in four black girls does (Geronimus, 1991).

The girls seem acutely aware that early pregnancy can interfere with college plans and a career:

> ANGELA: I don't want to get married at a young age. Like if I was twenty-five maybe. But that's too early. I'll still be in college, and I don't want to be married and then I get pregnant and then I can't go to college, that's why. So now, I have to put everything off to have a kid.

> GLORIA: . . . If you do it young [have a child], it messes up your career. I want to get into my career first before I could start thinking about babies. I'm not saying I got anything against babies, I love them, I was born around them. What I'm saying is I don't want to get married and then divorced. I want to find the right man first.

While an early pregnancy would clearly impede college and career plans, Gloria also seems aware that an early marriage precipitated by pregnancy is also a likely path to an early divorce. It is worth remarking the two girls' perception that they lack control over their own fertility. Clarice, on the other hand, appears to have an unusually firm sense of control over her fertility, as she here elaborates on her wish to postpone pregnancy:

> CLARICE: I'm on the pill now. My cousin she's twenty and she's having a baby. I think she's too young to have it. And I have a friend who's nineteen and she never been to a gynecologist and don't use any birth control. She's stupid. She been having sex since she was thirteen. I keep telling her she's gonna get pregnant and she'll be sorry, 'cause having a baby is not funny. If I got pregnant, I don't know, I'm against abortion. That's why when I have sex I use everything, foam, condom, everything. . . . My mother's strict with me. That's why she would *kill me* if she knew I wasn't a virgin no more. She was lenient with my brothers and they dropped out of school in tenth grade. With me I'm the baby of the family so they all want me to do good in school so my mother is strict with me.

Here we can see the correlation between "doing good in school" and delaying sexual activity that can lead to pregnancy. Clarice's mother apparently believes that her daughter's continuation in school depends upon sexual abstinence. For Saundria and Emily, the prospect of adolescent pregnancy is not in the least "funny": not only would it interfere with school, but it would destroy any chance of the fun adolescents and young women should experience:

> SAUNDRIA: When I'm twenty-five I won't be having no kids cause I'll be in college. . . . I know a couple of my friends, fourteen years old, pregnant. All of them on welfare. They going with their mother, trying to let their mother take care of their baby and in the summer we all having fun, going swimming. They have to say, "No, I have to watch my little son; no, I have to watch my little daughter." That's when they look cute, to be fourteen and pushing a little baby around. That's why I ain't having sex until I'm twenty. And I ain't having no kids until I'm twenty-six.

> EMILY: I love kids, but I can't have them too soon because, as I said, I was only fourteen and having kids at that age is not joke because you have kids and you want to go dancing, you have a hard responsibility. I mean the responsibility, like when you drive a car, you make sure you don't get in a accident. That's responsible. But with a kid, it's harder, you have to stay home. You can't go out. How you gonna go to school?

Barbara and Gloria further understand from the example of their mothers' experiences how early pregnancy can disrupt educational plans.

BARBARA: My mother had me at a young age [sixteen], so she didn't work and she couldn't finish high school. She's always telling me how I should finish my education.

GLORIA: My mother had to get married. She got pregnant. Well, they had problems with my family, my mother had to get out of school and work for her mother in the factory and get married. So she had a divorce, she went on welfare, then she met my father. He helped a lot and things started changing, but there were always problems. So my mother didn't finish high school at that time. She wanted to go back to school, but she can't because right now she has a daughter she has to bring up.

In sum, these girls' views about early pregnancy seem to strongly reinforce their commitment to education.

Young Women's Thoughts on Marriage, Children, and Employment

What then do these girls think of marriage and domesticity? The interviews revealed interesting patterns of association—only when asked to reflect on their lives ten, not five, years ahead (when most would be twenty-five years old) did the subjects of marriage and family emerge; and even then several girls did not spontaneously address marriage, but had to directly be asked. Generally, the girls seemed to want to delay marriage in order to have time to become qualified for satisfying employment. For the most part, this group of girls also expected to enter into a traditional marriage arrangement.

Among the three African American girls, marriage and family figure quite prominently in their projected futures and in Saundria's and Barbara's cases, alongside careers:

SAUNDRIA: [In ten years] I'll have my career by then. I'll probably have a husband. I'll have my house. My house will be in Cambridge Heights in Queens. I'll have my car, a little dog. I won't have no finance problems. That's it.

BARBARA: I'll probably have a husband and kids, probably be a mother and a career woman. But I don't want to get married too young, you know. You want to have time to explore life and everything, have fun.

CHERYL: [In ten years] I want to live in Queens, I want to have two kids, a boy named Jabral and a girl named Kristen, and I want to marry my boyfriend, that's it. I said I want to, I'm not saying I am.

The fact that these three girls stress marriage is noteworthy. All three of their mothers are divorced (although they all have contact with their fathers). This discrepancy between desiring marriage and knowing first hand that marriages often end in divorce will be discussed later. The important point here is that Saundria and Barbara envision themselves as both having a "career" and being a wife/mother. Importantly, the three girls share the experience of mothers who work outside the home. This dual role of wife/mother and worker has historically characterized African American women. As Collins (1990) describes:

> Black daughters learn to expect to work, to strive for an education so they can support themselves, and to anticipate carrying heavy responsibilities in their families and communities because these skills are essential to their own survival and those for whom they will eventually be responsible. (p. 123)

Indeed, the majority of African American female adolescents grow up expecting eventually to assume the dual role of mother and worker (Smith, 1981). According to Ladner (1971), young African American girls learn directly from their mothers and female relatives and indirectly from their observations of their mothers' relationships with men that they must one day strive for economic independence. Although African American women rely on African American men for emotional support and understanding, they consider persistent economic discrimination against African American men to be a poor basis for relying upon them for their economic well-being (Holland and Eisenhart, 1990).

Among the girls of Puerto Rican descent, while all express the desire for further education and for a "good" job or career, there are some discrepancies in their professed feelings about marriage. Some anticipate marriage and work in ten years; others believe they will be engaged in waged labor but are uncertain about marriage.

Marta, Delores, Angela, and Gloria all imagine they can integrate marriage and employment:

> ANGELA: [In ten years] married and have a baby, a babysitter and have a good job. I'll be a manager in some business. I'll be managing, helping people. I like being with people.

> DELORES: I'll be in law school studying for law. Yeah, I'll still be doing that. And I'll probably be married and I want to have four kids. Well, maybe not all then. I want four kids because I was the only child.

> MARTA: Hopefully I'll be finished college. I probably be getting married and starting my career. I want to go into some kind of business, like be a businesswoman.

> GLORIA: I'll be married and have a career, a nice house to live in and a good husband. I'll have at least one kid—one or two kids, that's it.

It is worth noting that although these four girls mention marriage first, their future employment also remains key. In other words, they seem to possess a very strong commitment to paid work and, at the same time, combine marriage and motherhood. The wish for marriage, children, and family does not necessarily preclude the desire for labor-market experience.

In thinking about their futures, these girls seem intent on combining work and parenting throughout their lives. Several of the girls, however, are less certain about the prospect of marriage:

> AUREA: I want to be successful. I do want to get married, but like I want to be successful. First I want a college degree, then a good job. I ain't gonna think about getting married. I could have a boyfriend here and there.
>
> CLARICE: [In ten years] I have no idea, I guess I'll be doing something with dancing.
>
> JW: Do you think you'll get married?
>
> CLARICE: No, I want to live my life first. Maybe I'll have children then. I don't know.
>
> EMILY: I'll be a lawyer, well, going into law school something like that.
>
> JW: Do you think you might get married?
>
> EMILY: Maybe I think well if I do, I do. Look, I think if I find the right man, I'll settle down and get married. But until then, Lucy goosey.

The above quotations reflect the girls' commitment to the idea of waged labor and, for many, to a possibility of a family.

I would like to digress briefly to analyze more closely the types of jobs these girls are aspiring to. All of the occupations are professional, promising high wages and enhanced status (see appendix B) and they will require a college degree. According to Amott and Matthaei (1991), only 16 percent of U.S. Puerto Rican women and 15 percent of African American women (compared to almost 30 percent of white women) are in managerial and professional jobs. A high proportion of African American and U.S. Puerto Rican women in professional positions continue to be employed in the public sector. For women of color, public sector jobs are tenuous because of their dependency on the size of government and their level of commitment to affirmative action.

Although women's representation in professional work has been increasing in all groups, much of this growth has been confined to jobs historically dominated by women. Several of the girls' occupational choices reflect this restrictive tradition—social worker, nurse, teacher,[5] dancer. Sex-typing also occurs in so-called nontraditional jobs such as medicine and law. For example, both Aurea and Cheryl express the desire to become "baby" doctors.

It is particularly striking that six out of ten girls want to be lawyers. It may be that, as Ruth Sidel (1990) points out, television shows that depict glamorous women lawyers (such as "L.A. Law") have crystallized this occupation as a popular locus on which to project fantasies of high pay and status. But there is also a more altruistic, less economically motivated explanation for this preoccupation; as Emily puts it:

> I always wanted [to become a lawyer] cause when I was small I used to see a lot of law films and everything and I would always be like if they can make a difference, so can I. I don't know, it's just, I have the attitude and the mouth for it. I mean I could stand there and argue with you if I feel I'm right. And I feel that if I can do that for myself, I can do that for another person and prove that person's innocence. That's why I thought about it.

The question remains as to how this group of girls envisions negotiating the inherent tension between domestic responsibilities and employment. In other words, how do these girls intend to organize their lives around employment while assuming domestic responsibilities? Unlike the group of white girls, most of whom posit typically middle-class solutions to the problem by restricting themselves to part-time work or by foregoing employment altogether once children are born, African American and U.S. Puerto Rican girls expect to rely on extended family or paid babysitters to provide child care while they continue to work in the labor force. They all agreed that they would work regardless of childrearing responsibilities. It is important to note that *none* of the girls consider support from an employer while parenting young children. Below, the two African American girls, Barbara and Saundria, discuss their options:

> SAUNDRIA: One's the limit. It will be easy for me cause I have parents. They'll help me out. And hopefully my grandparents they'll be living. And I know where I live now, I don't know if they'll be living there by the time I get the house, but they good people. I'll make sure my neighbors are good. And there's some nice daycare centers around the house, and I'll have my children in there. It's all right having children there while you're working.

> BARBARA: That's what I was thinking cause on this, I think it was a week ago [on T.V. news] you know, that babysitter hitting, beating that child, so like I was thinking, when I'm working and I have kids, should I like stay home, or should I get a babysitter. But how this

world is going now, I'd like to stay home with my kids. But maybe if my mother would say that she'll watch them, yeah, then I would definitely work.

Similarly, girls of Puerto Rican descent expect to engage in paid labor while maintaining domestic and family responsibilities:

AUREA: That's OK, but you have to find the right babysitter. My mother had us with the babysitter and she was like my aunt. My mother used to pay her, right. She used to pick us up at school. That lady used to be our neighbor downstairs. We did that for about a few years, then we got old enough that we could stay home by ourselves and that's what happened.

CLARICE: I would probably stay home for like four months and keep on my career, get a babysitter and take her to the babysitter.

ANGELA: I'll have a babysitter for the kids. It'll be kind of difficult, I'll be coming home, you know, cooking dinner for them, packing their lunches in the morning then leaving. It's hard to say goodbye to kids when you have to get to work at 8:00 in the morning. I hope it doesn't get too out of hand and I can't see my kids.

GLORIA: I think it's all right to work when you got the responsibility with children cause my mother works and she got kids. She done things her way and she always had the time to listen to us. If I got a good career, like if I was a teacher, I know I couldn't quit that, maybe do what Edie did—she went on vacation from school and gave birth. But I want to keep on with my career. I don't want to stay home and just watch the baby. . . . I'll have to get used to the schedule, getting up in the morning and going to work and coming home, cook dinner, clean the house, it'll be hard. I don't want to do everything at the same time because it would cause me stress and I'll probably feel guilty for what I did and probably won't even have enough time to spend with my kids. I don't want that to happen.

Both Angela and Gloria clearly recognize the likely tension between pursuing a career and providing unpaid domestic labor (viewed as their work). Interestingly, they both fear that they may not have sufficient time to spend with their children.

The girls count on help from their mothers or from babysitters in caring for their young children so that they can maintain their position in the labor market; this is further evidence of their strong work orientation. A significant source of this proclivity resides in the examples set by the girls' grandmothers and mothers, who also worked. Aurea and Gloria see their mothers as successful exemplars of women who work(ed) and simultaneously raise(d) a family. It is furthermore note-worthy that these mothers did so while experiencing marital disruption and desertion.

Here the girls describe the paid work their mothers did and continue to do:

> SAUNDRIA: She was working when I was little but I don't know how did she start. My father felt it was all right because they both got good parents that cared for me. Now, she's a secretary.

> BARBARA: My mother works at the post office. She works on a machine or something like that. Before that she worked at P.S. 10 doing secretary work in the school. And then that's when she came to the post office. But before she went to work at the post office, she had my little brother.

> JW: Did she work when you were small?

> BARBARA: Yeah, but not really, she didn't work 'cause she had me at a young age, so she didn't really work. I lived with her and my grandmother. . . . Right now my grandmother got like two jobs. She works at B. Altman and then she works at this lady's house cleaning and stuff. It's like two jobs.

> AUREA: My mother *had* to work when we were small. Well, we're not rich, we're middle class, like. We're not on welfare and all of that. So we don't get no type of help. We don't even have Medicare, none of that. We have like an insurance plan, but you have to pay everything, dental, all of that. . . . My stepfather never really helped out. But I get everything I want, anything I want, I get from her [mother].

> EMILY: . . . When she [mother] was younger she worked. My mother's crippled now. She has MS so when she was younger she did. . . . She used to sing.

> CLARICE: She's still working at the same place. She's a boss! Yeah! She works in a pencil factory and they make crayons there. My mother is the boss of all the secretaries on the whole first floor.

These quotations illustrate various strategies and the resources available to the girls' mothers while raising small children without, for the most part, the economic support of husbands or partners. African American women and, more recently, U.S. Puerto Rican women, have long integrated economic self-reliance with mothering, often with no support from men. As Collins says, African American communities recognize that "vesting one person with full responsibility for mothering a child may not be wise or possible" (1990, p. 119). As a consequence, "other mothers" (grandmothers, sisters, aunts, cousins) take on child care or mothering responsibilities, thus allowing "bloodmothers" to engage in waged work while raising children. The place of grandparents in these girls' lives is apparent:

> SAUNDRIA: I have three grandmothers. My grandmother in Jamaica [Queens], I love her for the world. That is my heart. If anything happen to her I wouldn't know what to do. She took care of me for a long time. And the grandmother I live with, I live with everybody, the other grandmother that I stay with, my grandma and my grandpa, I like staying with them, too. I live with my mother, too, but I have my own room at both houses. Sometimes I stay with grandma and grandpa and sometimes I stay with my mother.

> BARBARA: I lived with my mother and my grandfather in a house in Jamaica [Queens] and then I lived with my other grandmother, my father's mother. . . . Her husband left her, so my grandmother, she was working real hard to keep the mortgage and stuff and had all that stress. . . . She moved into an apartment and I be going over there the weekends.

> AUREA: . . . During the week I usually go to my grandmother's. She's too strict, but she's not so strict, she just worries about me a lot because she's seen a lot, shooting and everything. I stay over there because she's lonely, her son isn't coming back til September.[6]

The point here is that extended family members frequently play major roles in the care and raising of younger children. The young women's experiences within their communities have conditioned their understanding of how they might be able to construct their lives around employment while also raising a family.

In a study of child care patterns of U.S. Puerto Rican women, Hurst and Zambrana (1982) found that all women felt it was most desirable to have a grandmother take care of their children, preferably in their own home. In general, relatives were the preferred source of care. The authors conclude that, as a result of this preference, it is not marriage or childbearing per se that makes Puerto Rican women drop out of the labor force, but the question of the availability of *acceptable* child care. The authors feel that family continuity is the most important facilitator of U.S. Puerto Rican women's employment. Again, the anticipated dependence on an extended family member or a babysitter (who sometimes becomes an "aunt") for child care becomes an important part in the construction of a girl's future plan regarding work and family. This is very different from the construction of white girls' future plans, which entail withdrawing from the labor force or engaging in part-time employment while their children are young.

One question that needs to be addressed is why so many of these girls desire marriage when they recognize that marriages break up and husbands/fathers can leave. At the macro level, African American and U.S. Puerto Rican women are more likely than white women to be the single support of their households (in 1988, 56 percent of African American children, 35 percent of U.S. Puerto Rican children, and 20 percent of all white children lived with their mothers only). While the same factors—divorce and separation—are affecting African American, white, and U.S. Puerto Rican families, they affect African American and U.S. Puerto Rican families disproportionately and increasingly so. The following remarks typify the girls' experience with family disruption:

> SAUNDRIA: My parents, they don't talk that much. They don't talk. I try to get them back together so much, but they both got girlfriends and boyfriends, so I gave it up. . . . They separated when I was ten. I had to go to family court. Who got custody. It was sad 'cause I couldn't say well I'm going to stay with my mother, and I couldn't say I'm going to stay with my father, and then I was like, when they first told me that I said, forget it, I don't want to stay with neither one of them. I want to stay with my grandmother, you know. They just told me I should stay with my mother 'cause it's best that a girl stay with her mother and everything and I could see my father on weekends. So that's the way it is.

> BARBARA: . . . My mother never finished high school and then my father was living with us, and there was problems so him and my mother separated. . . . Then when I lived in the house with my grandmother, her husband had left her, so my grandmother, she was working real hard to keep the mortgage and stuff and had all that stress. So she gave the house up, everything, she couldn't pay the bills.

> GLORIA: . . . Actually my father[7] left over Thanksgiving. He used to be a cop and then he retired. . . . I have no idea where he is. I don't know whether he's all right or not, he hasn't called. His wife wanted to move, so they probably went to Kentucky.

> AUREA: . . . My mother she was having problems, you know marital problems, so we don't live with my stepfather no more. My mother threw him out. So then we just left town, we went to Chicago for three weeks.

> CLARICE: My father left before I was born. But then when my mother was in the hospital having me, my father came. But then he left again. He's the one who named me Clarice. He's married now in Brooklyn. They have three daughters and a little boy who's four.

DELORES: . . . My mother went through so much before. See, my father went back to Puerto Rico. He's married now and has two boys.

Despite their experience of estranged or single parents, all the girls expressed some degree of commitment to marriage. Perhaps, as Michelle Fine[8] points out, watching their mothers leave bad marriages paradoxically reinforces their faith in the possibility of successful marriage, given the right circumstances and more reliable men. This fantasy of an ideal marriage was also described by Ladner (1971) in her study on low-income black female adolescents. Ladner found that marriage persisted as an ideal goal to which all the girls aspired, though it was marked by some ambivalence. Ladner explains that

> [t]hey [girls in her study] viewed future marriage in a positive manner if it took place under the ideal circumstances [professional husband, etc.], but at the same time, marriage was viewed as very tenuous because they knew that the odds were stacked up heavily against this kind of ideal arrangement working out. (p. 236)

Joseph and Lewis (1986) are also helpful in understanding the apparent contradiction. Data from their study on African American mothers and daughters showed that the majority (67.1 percent) of mothers either explicitly or implicitly communicated to their daughters favorable messages about marriage, while 77.1 percent conveyed negative attitudes about men. Joseph and Lewis explain:

> There is acute awareness and sensitivity on the part of black women to the problems associated with and encountered in the traditional monogamous marriage or in other marital living arrangements. . . . The seemingly incompatible messages about men and marriage are in actuality honest assessments and realistic responses to an oppressive and restrictive society. (p. 121)

As a means of assuring a secure economic future, marriage may in fact represent a pragmatic desire. While most of these girls have mothers who work outside the home, it is also true that the median income of U.S. Puerto Rican families headed by women (including individuals) has fallen sharply relative to U.S. Puerto Rican husband/wife families (from 67 percent of their median income in 1960 to only 32 percent in 1980) (Amott and Matthaei, 1991, p. 282). Similarly, the median income of African American single-mother families is only 35 percent that of an African American married-couple family (Amott and Matthaei, 1991, p. 186). In other words, the relative position of U.S. Puerto Rican and African American female-headed families compared to husband/wife families has been deteriorating, while the relative position of white female-headed families has improved. It is no wonder, then, that African American and U.S. Puerto Rican girls may cling tenaciously to the hope that they will find themselves in the economically more favorable position that marriage today represents.

Future Husbands

Since many of the girls interviewed anticipated marriage, I asked them what they would look for in a future husband. Some of the girls specifically responded that they hoped for husbands who could provide financial stability. For Saundria, perhaps intuitively aware of the insecure status that blue-collar workers occupy in today's economy, a white-collar job is key:

> SAUNDRIA: He will be either doing the same field of work I'm doing or higher, better. I know he be a white-collar worker in an office or something. He don't have to be, if I love somebody, I love him, but that's what I feel. We won't have that many problems.

Aurea and Angela fantasize about attractive husbands; they interestingly emphasize intelligence; and they cite a "good job" as an important criterion as well:

> AUREA: Tall, dark, and handsome. Has a good job. He knows everything. He's successful, or he could be.

> ANGELA: Probably tall, smart, fine. He'll be smart in things, have a nice job. He'll help me when I'm under pressure, come up to me and talk to me.

Noteworthy about Angela's comments is the emotional support she expects from a husband—perhaps anticipating the inherent difficulty in simultaneously parenting and working.

For several of the girls in this group, finding a husband who shares in domestic labor is a priority, reflecting a more egalitarian view of marital relations:

> MARTA: The perfect husband, um, loyal, looks nice and helps with housework. That's it.

> BARBARA: He should know how to cook and clean everything and watch the kids, and not just come home and lay on the couch and drink and everything. I think he should help, too. You know, a husband, equal, equal, fifty/fifty. He should be smart, intelligent respectful and good looking, muscular like, nice height.

CHERYL: He cooks sometimes, I cook for him. Um, he gonna work, I'm gonna work.

If we piece together the girls' various comments, a picture emerges of a group oriented both toward future employment and toward future marriage and childrearing. They express a certain pragmatism with regard to future mates—"good job," potential for "success," participating in domestic labor, and so forth. Such a profile differs considerably from the more "romantic" image of an ideal husband described by the group of white girls in the last chapter.

GIRLS' DAILY LIVES

Domestic Labor

There has been very little research done on African American and Latina women's unpaid labor in the home. Collins (1990) suggests that research on African American women's unpaid labor within extended families remains less fully developed than that on African American women's paid work (p. 44). Similarly, Amott and Matthaei (1991) found they were unable to locate any studies that compare the distribution of household work across racial-ethnic groups. However, scholarly work done by African American feminists has emphasized the contributions African American women make to African American family well-being by keeping families together and teaching survival skills. This work suggests that African American women see their unpaid domestic work more as a form of resistance to oppression than as a form of exploitation by men. However, as Collins states:

> less attention is given to ways that African American women's domestic labor is exploited within African American families, an omission that obscures investigations of families as contradictory locations that simultaneously confine yet allow African American women to develop cultures of resistance. (p. 44)

Simply put, the unpaid work that mothers/housewives perform may not have the same meaning for women who experience racism as it does for women who are not subject to racial or ethnic oppression.

In a reworking of traditional Marxist-feminist theories about women's oppression, Evelyn Nakano Glenn (1985) argues that many key concepts—such as the public-private dichotomy, gender conflict within the family, and the division of reproductive labor—need to be reformulated to explain the experiences of women in oppressed groups.

As for the division of household labor, Marxist-feminist analysis sees it as benefiting men, who receive a greater share of services while contributing less labor. Glenn suggests that "in the racial ethnic family, conflict over the division of labor is muted by the fact that institutions outside the family are hostile to it . . .this is not to suggest there are no conflicts over the division of labor but struggles against outside forces take precedence over struggles within the family" (p. 104).

In other words, while most high school girls participate to some degree in domestic labor, it may mean different things for African American and U.S. Puerto Rican girls as opposed to white working-class girls, given these groups' different historical experiences with regard to productive and reproductive labor. It is reasonable to assume that such differences—in history, in culture, and in personal experience—will make productive and reproductive labor exert a variable determinant force in the construction and definition of feminine identity.

In one of the few cases where girls' participation in household labor has been studied, Griffen found differences in the distribution of household labor between white (middle- and working-class) families and Afro-Caribbean families. According to Griffen (1985), overall domestic work was most unequally distributed in white middle-class families and most evenly divided among the members of Afro-Caribbean households. Among white families, working-class female family members shared household work more evenly than did white middle-class female family members.

In analyzing this group of girls' responses to questions about their participation in unpaid household labor, I found that, where the father or stepfather is present, there exists a strong sexual division of labor, similar to that found in the white girls' households. Also similar is the finding that older brothers do not significantly participate in household labor.

> BARBARA: I take care of my little baby brother, he's six. I pick him up after school, or when I can't another lady picks him up. I watch him and help him with his homework and everything.
>
> JW: So who cooks dinner?
>
> BARBARA: Sometimes my mother cooks, and sometimes I cook dinner when I feel like it or sometimes she cooks dinner and I cook for my own self. Or sometimes I buy my own food around where I live.
>
> JW: Who does most of the housework?
>
> BARBARA: My mother, but I have my chores that I have to do, clean my room, vacuuming and I do the bathroom, wash the dishes every night. My brother helps me 'cause he likes to clean.
>
> SAUNDRIA: I come home from school at 2:30 and I do my chores.
>
> JW: What kind of chores do you do?

SAUNDRIA: I have to wash the dishes, my grandmother makes the dinner. I have to clean the bathroom and wash the dishes.

JW: Who does most of the housework?

SAUNDRIA: My grandmother. She do the work.

The following comments are by girls whose mothers are not in the labor market, but who babysit at home for the children of relatives or friends.

JW: Who does the housework in your home?

ANGELA: My mother does it mostly. She stays home and babysits my niece.

MARTA: My mother. I have to wash the dishes usually and clean my room.

JW (to Emily): Do you have to do any chores?

EMILY: I'm supposed to but I never do anything. My mother does everything, the dishes, the clothes, the floors, everything. It's not that easy for her 'cause she's crippled now. She has MS. My cousin [female] helps her sometimes.

In families where the mother is employed full-time, mothers receive more help from their daughters. In contrast to the white girls, these girls do not appear to resent their household responsibilities nor do they try to escape them.

JW: Who does most of the housework in your home?

CLARICE: I do. I have to vacuum, clean the furniture, do my brothers' rooms, my room, my mother's room. Then I do the wash. My mother cooks dinner, sometimes I do, though. I wash the dishes.

AUREA: Well, I do and my mother. I have to do the dishes and pick up the house everyday. I'm a very neat person. My mother and I clean the house every Saturday unless we go somewhere.

GLORIA: My mother. But I have to clean my room and the kitchen. My mother do the upstairs, the bedrooms and the living room and she does the wash. It depends, sometimes I'm in a bad mood and so is my mother so we just leave the house in a mess.

These data suggest that, similar to white working-class girls, this group of girls does participate in a substantial amount of unpaid domestic labor. Although the data are somewhat sketchy, what appears to make a difference in the amount of housework girls do, is whether their mothers are employed full-time. When they are, daughters assume more of the responsibility. What is key here is that as in white working-class families, unpaid domestic labor is associated with being female.

Romance and Girls' Relationships with Boys

Studies on working-class girls highlight the importance that girls give to heterosexual relations and romance (McRobbie, 1980; Valli, 1986; Lees, 1993; Griffen, 1985) and the role romance plays in the social construction of femininity (Christian-Smith, 1990), although there are important differences between working- and middle-class girls. As Holland and Eisenhart (1990) discovered, romance and attractiveness had a great deal of significance in the lives of the young white and African American women they studied. As Taylor (1989) points out, "romantic ideology" or meanings associated with romance (romantic love) "operate as a regulatory mechanism and, as such, it is pulled about by social and economic forces and as an ideal it can act as a force in the regulation of behavior between the sexes" (p. 443).

Research on black and Asian girls in England suggests that minority girls may have a different attitude toward romance than white girls. For example, Griffen (1985) found that Asian and Caribbean girls in her study were more critical of the ideal of romantic love than their white peers. Similarly, Miles (1987) found that working-class Asian girls in her U.K. study did not place the same emphasis on the romance of marriage or on the "cult of femininity" as white working-class girls. Riley (1985), moreover, argues that in terms of sexuality and relationships with the opposite sex, the black girls in her study totally negated the stereotypical vision of women as potential dependents of men.

As we saw in the last chapter, many of the white girls seemed to be pulled fairly strongly into an ideology of romance by engaging in steady and exclusive relationships with older boys. In this section, I will suggest that while this group of African American and U.S. Puerto Rican girls also participate in sexual relationships with boys, they do not seem to be as immersed in the ideology of romance to the same extent as the white girls. By exploring how groups of girls of different racial/ethnic backgrounds participate in and understand romance, we may understand more fully the differences in how girls learn about conventional definitions of femininity and how these differences shape or reflect their expectations.

Many of these U.S. Puerto Rican and African American girls do not have "boyfriends" as such, but are involved in friendships with boys, although the girls express some romantic interest. For the most part, the form of their relationships with boys is not typified by the same intense involvement as the white girls. In the following, some of the girls discuss their relationship with boys in response to the specific question, "Do you have a boyfriend?"

> GLORIA: Well, actually I don't have a boyfriend, but I'm seeing somebody, you know. We're not really girlfriend and boyfriend. He's in this school, nobody knows about it. Just his friends and my friends. His name is Tray, he's a Puerto Rican guy. He's tall, spacey, hangs out with a black guy named Tyrone. We're like working things out between us. . . . If he has a problem, he comes to me, we work things out. We listen to each other, we play with each other, we make fun of each other.

> BARBARA: Well, there's this boy, I just talk to him. He live in my project. He's fifteen, he's athletic, he likes to play basketball. But we just talk.

> SAUNDRIA: Yeah, he's so nice. I been going with him like off and on a month and a year. What's the date? The twentieth, the tenth? He's fourteen, too. He's in an all boys school, got nice parents.

> ANGELA: No I don't [have a boyfriend].

> JW: Anybody who likes you?

> ANGELA: Yeah, but he doesn't go to this school. We talk lot because his mother knows my mother. We're the same age, we grew up together. I like him, he's funny, but sometimes he's a pain.

> AUREA: . . . It's not my boyfriend. I know him from the bus. The way it started I asked his name, and I said where's he from, 'cause, you know he looked Puerto Rican right, he goes, Honduras. I thought he was Hindu [East Indian], but he's not so I started to like him. . . . We don't hardly know each other, that's why I want to get to know him, first. 'Cause I know nothing about him. If I notice I'm starting to like him more, you know, he only been with his girlfriend one month, he could start to like me too. It's working out alright. He's Honduran, he talks Spanish. He's gonna be fifteen.

> Marta: Um, you know Leo, right? He's in Core, we talk a lot.

It seems fairly clear that these girls, unlike the white girls, are not involved in steady and exclusive heterosexual relationships. At times they allow for the potential of particular friendships turning into romantic relationships, but by the end of the school year, with the exception of one girl, none of the girls quoted above were involved in such steady or exclusive relationships with boys.

What is also interesting here is that unlike the white girls involved with older boys, several girls mention being interested in boys of their own age group.[9] Age seems to be an important factor, as Saundria below explains:

> JW: You said that girls go out with guys that are so much older, how do you feel about that?
>
> SAUNDRIA: I feel that's wrong, guys should not go out with girls too much younger. The oldest guy I've ever went with, you know, at fourteen was seventeen. I don't care if his birthday tomorrow, he turn eighteen, he too old. I feel age do make a difference. Everybody say age don't mean nothing. That's when you get grown. As long as you young, age mean a lot. And it's wrong for a guy to pick up a twelve-year-old and he's about twenty 'cause it's like your daughter, and all they got do is maybe buy the girl a outfit or something and then they try to have sex with you. And that's wrong too. 'Cause if it was their daughter that went out with an older guy, they wouldn't even do that. I know a lot, a couple of my friends, fourteen years old, pregnant, and how old is their boyfriend? Thirty. And I feel all girls that go out with guys that age is a fool. They dumb and they stupid, they going out with them 'cause they got a car or something, they gotta take a cab with their little fifteen-year-old boyfriend.

One motivation for the girls restricting relationships with boys to their own age group, as Saundria suggests, may be to reduce the pressure to engage in sexual activity, and thus also reduce the risk of early pregnancy and an interrupted education. Again, Saundria explains:

> You can't do nothing without a high school diploma. Most of the girls I know older than me finished. And some of them didn't *'cause they found a little older boyfriend.*

Furthermore, involvement with a peer may make a girl feel less subordinate to a boy who himself may be restricted by parental limitations on his activities.

Another distinguishing feature of these U.S. Puerto Rican girls' relationships with boys is that several have more than one boyfriend, referring to their multiple attachments as not being settled. This is quite a departure from the monogamous relationships characteristic of the white girls. The significance of the U.S. Puerto Rican girls' behavior is that they are not constrained to depend on one boy for filling leisure time, and so forth. In other words, having several boyfriends ensures some degree of independence.

JW: Do you have a boyfriend?

EMILY: Probably too many. It's not good to have one when you're young. It's good to have associates, not settle down. There's two that I really care for.

DELORES: I'm not really settled down. I'm just you know, I have three right now.

JW: Now, do they all know about each other?

DELORES: Oh no. You can't let that happen. You get in trouble.

Another difference between the white girls and the African American/Puerto Rican girls lies in the degree of acceptance their families accord to their boyfriends. We saw how the parents of the white girls, for the most part, were both aware of and tolerant of their daughters' romantic involvement with boyfriends, in fact, often encouraging the young couples to spend leisure time at the girls' homes. Some of the girls betrayed ambivalence about their family's role here—interest seems to easily become interference or domination (for example, some girls have older brothers who take on a disciplinarian role and control over the girls' sexuality).

AUREA: He called me on Sunday. I told my cousin, I told my brother. It was really hard to tell my brother. I got to work on that more. My brother thinks he's my father. 'Cause he's seventeen, he thinks he's my father. When I told my brother, he was like, "if he does anything to you, you tell me, I'll beat him up." . . . My brother likes it when I tell him. Like, when I messed with this guy named Marty, and he found out, he was mad 'cause I didn't tell him. So then he got angry with me. He said, he kept threatening me that he was gonna tell my mother, until I got tired of it and I told my mother. And she didn't like it, but she has to handle it so what was she gonna do, nothing. I had already passed ten.

CLARICE: My mother thinks I'm still a virgin. If she or my brothers ever found out that we [ex-boyfriend] had sex, they would sew me up and chop off his part! . . .

BARBARA: I have the feeling that my mother don't really want me to have boyfriends, but I do anyway. . . . She doesn't say nothing, but when she talk to me, she could tell me about trying not to get pregnant and stuff, finish your education because she never did. She like telling me everything, she be talking to me like girl talk and everything.

SAUNDRIA: I don't like telling my father I have a boyfriend. 'Cause he's like, oh my God. He like, you're not supposed to have a boyfriend until you're seventeen, not supposed to do that. Like Daddy, shut up.

Nevertheless, like the white girls in the last chapter, some of these girls are learning about unequal gender relations. Here, Emily describes two of her "associates" whom she "really cares for":

> EMILY: Carlos is sweet, but overprotective, and Joey's outgoing. He lets me be free. I can't be too free, I have to be *with him* when I'm free. But you know, I could deal with that 'cause it shows that they care. So I like feeling that sort of protection if they really care.

And consider Saundria's description of how some boys treat their girl-friends:

> SAUNDRIA: He knows how to treat you right. Some guys, they like "yeah, this is my girlfriend" but then tell you to get out of here. You know how they just neglect you or something, but when we're together, he'll like hold your hand, when you're walking in the street and everything. He always buying you things. He real nice. He's into basketball. All he do. . . . It's hard to keep up with him because he don't keep girls a long time. It's like if you have a week with him, that's all you gettin'. He goes with girls like a drink. If you don't want it, throw it away.

Clearly, both girls are learning how to "get along" with their boyfriends, which means ultimately accepting the idea that boys will be in charge, and that girls must adapt themselves to boys' demands, desires, likes and dislikes, and activities.

Girls also learn about unequal gender relations by observing their mothers' relationships with men.[10] Despite Saundria's own increasing accommodation to her boyfriend, she offers the following critique of her mother's relationship:

> SAUNDRIA: . . . Now my mother has a boyfriend. I kicked him out so many times. He don't stay there. He'll come over and visit if I say so. I do not like that man. Oh my God, I don't like him. He has a nasty atti-tude, it's just the look on his face. He's younger than my mother, and I don't like that. I said, "Ma, if you want to get a boyfriend, get a man. Don't get no little boy. He's too young for you." He feel, you know, he want her to run. You know, he say something like Angel, come here, and she's supposed to come. It's like he's her father, he like where're you going? Like what are you talking about, where you going, like what you talking about, where she going. She going where she want. When she going to work, she call him on the job. I'm like what you call him for? You know, when she come home, if she ain't home, where was you? You know, you don't ask my mother all these questions, she do what she want. That's the way I feel. That's why I ain't gonna have no man younger than me. I have to kick him in the butt.

JW: So your boyfriend doesn't act like that to you, does he?

SAUNDRIA: No, he know me 'cause I'm bodacious. I'll do what I want. That's the only way a relationship work with me, 'cause I'll do what I want and you do what you want. That's it.

To sum up, when compared to the white girls discussed in the previous chapter, these girls appear less intensely preoccupied with boyfriends and romance. In other words, they do not seem to be so immersed in an ideology of heterosexual romance. This is not to suggest that the African American or Puerto Rican girls were not "interested" in boys or that boys were not a topic of conversation between friends. However, romance does not seem to be an organizing principle in the girls' lives to the same extent that it is in many of the white girls' lives.

DISCUSSION AND CONCLUSION

This group of young women of African American and Puerto Rican descent expressed a positive orientation toward gaining educational credentials and a strong commitment to future paid employment. Their hope for marriage, children, and a family life did not preclude a desire for labor-market participation.

For these girls, employment was not defined in opposition to and as incompatible with motherhood. Paid work appeared to be an important dimension of their definitions of motherhood. They planned to depend on mothers, babysitters, or relatives to help with the care of their children. And while most saw the domestic sphere as their responsibility, they clearly wished to negotiate more equitable terms in the division of labor with their mates.

The above findings appeared to hold for girls of all academic abilities. Unlike the case of the white girls, where there seemed to be a correlation between poor school achievement and a weak labor-market identity, all of the African American and U.S. Puerto Rican girls, regardless of their academic performance, expressed a primary orientation toward a "good" job or career.

Whereas romance formed a central concern for many of the white girls, the African American girls and the girls of Puerto Rican descent seemed less preoccupied by romantic longings. While many expressed interest in boys and dating, they were not apt to enter into the same type of intense and exclusive involvements that the white girls favored. This is not to say that boys were marginal to their lives, nor that they did not expect to have relationships with men in the future. My conjecture is that for these young women who express strong labor-market identities, having a boyfriend does not assume the same significance as it does for girls more primarily invested in a domestic identity, where finding a future mate is essential. Furthermore, several girls spontaneously addressed the limitations early pregnancy would have on their aspirations. It may be that they were choosing to postpone sexual activity to prevent possible pregnancies that would interfere with their future plans. It may also be that these girls were less focused on finding a man because they understood, through personal experiences and community examples, that men should not be counted on to provide financially (especially in a society with a history of economically discriminating against African American and Puerto Rican men).

Unlike the white working-class girls, these girls largely came from families in which men were not consistently present or were not steady contributors to household income. Most had mothers who were employed and provided the sole support for their families; several of the girls came from families headed by mothers relying on public assistance. The girls' recognition of the economic and emotional hardships faced by their mothers cannot help but influence both their self-understanding and their expectations.

These girls of African American and Puerto Rican descent who articulate a primary labor-market identity are not only responding to the *immediate* economic inability or unwillingness of men to provide for their families, but rather come from communities in which women historically have contributed to the economic well-being of their families.[11]

It is, of course, important to acknowledge differences in the situations of African American girls and girls of Puerto Rican descent. Puerto Rican women's roles have traditionally been more circumscribed by a "traditional" Spanish-influenced gender code. However, through the process of assimilation since their migration from Puerto Rico, gender roles have changed and been renegotiated. Early accounts of immigration to New York City (during the 1920s) document that the survival of Puerto Rican families depended on women's economic contribution. While Puerto Rican women basically thought of themselves as "women of the home," many engaged in economic activities that supplemented family income, and various home-centered economic ventures emerged in response to their economic needs (Korrol, 1983, p. 48).

Finally, the data presented in this chapter appear to corroborate Mickelson's (1990) postulate of an "achievement paradox" for young women of color. Mickelson sets out to test Ogbu's theory that because minority youth accurately perceive that schooling is unlikely to pay off for them as it does for members of the dominant group, they (minority youth) consequently put less effort into scholastic performance. Mickelson found, however, that in spite of this awareness of limited future opportunities, minority girls still valued and strove for academic achievement. Clearly, Ogbu's theory must be expanded to take into account gender differences in educational motivation.

CHAPTER 6

Young Women of Dominican and South American Descent: Constructing Possibilities for the Future

INTRODUCTION

In this chapter, I will recount how several immigrant Latina girls[1] hope to organize their lives as adult women. I focus first on their plans for education, paid work, and family. I then elicit some of the experiences that have shaped their hopes and survey some of the foundations they have established to support these hopes for the future: specifically, the girls discuss their participation in domestic labor in their households and their relationships with boys.

LIFE AFTER HIGH SCHOOL: WORK AND FAMILY

For most of the girls (seven out of ten), the most important and immediate goal after completing high school is to attend college. As with the other groups of girls, this desire is not limited to those whose academic history would ordinarily support such a prospect. However, though the desire may be equally shared, significant differences do emerge between the girls faring well academically and those appearing academically disengaged.

In the following, academically motivated girls talk about their immediate post–high school plans and how they envision their lives five years hence. As Antonia, Toni, Carolina, Magda, and Paula imagine their individual futures, they are as one in their express desire to attend college to prepare for a career.

> CAROLINA: I'll go to college. Maybe someplace like FIT (Fashion Institute), but you know, if I only study fashion, that could be boring after four years. What if I don't like it anymore? So I'd really like to go to N.Y.U., but it's so expensive. I'm saving for college now. . . . I'd like to go to a four-year college. I'll study something like accounting. My par-

ents say I could do that and work with one of my uncles. They're in accounting. I don't know, maybe something like stocks, Wall Street. [In five years:] In college, maybe go away somewhere and live on campus.

ANTONIA: Go to college. Why I want to do that? First I'd like to make commercials, but my brother,[2] he says I should work on computers because that's what the future's gonna be about—computers. So, he says I'll make a lot of money on that. Probably there will be a lot of computers in the future, so if I know about them, that's why I'm gonna do computers in college. [In five years:] The same, I'll still be living with my brother. I hope not 'cause I want to leave. If I do leave, I'll be living, I'll be twenty, my sister will be eighteen, I'll take her and rent somewhere. I'll be going to college.

TONI: I want to go to college. I want to go to college somewhere else, like Europe. I'll study science or architecture. [In five years:] I imagine myself in college and yeah, studying. Then when I get out of college, I'd travel around the world, become an architect and be professional. . . . First I want to go to college and I want to be prepared. I want to be a professional in case I get a divorce or something. I don't want to get like my mother. My mother got married right away [after high school].

MAGDA: Well, college and graduate, go to my country [Ecuador], be a secretary and know computers. They say to be a secretary you have to learn a lot, typing, know a computer. I want to find out now, so I could get in a good college and everything. If you're bilingual, right, then you get a lot of money. [In five years:] I think by then, around seventeen, I graduate from school. Then I'll be still studying around eighteen. My mother's planning us to be in California. I think I'll be working by then, studying, living in California in a house. That's how I see myself working and everything.

PAULA: I have no idea. None. Right now I'm not really sure. Maybe next year or later this year, I'll think of something.

JW: What do you think you'll be doing [after high school]?

PAULA: That's something really hard because I'm not into school. I'm more into just bugging out with my friends and not worried about school. I might go to another school or just stay here for four years and *maybe* go to college, but not to this college, I'm going away. If I decide to go to college, I'm not sure yet. I'll maybe be a secretary. *Maybe.* Like a management secretary. Something that pays good. Something that pays well enough and that I could support myself. I don't care what it is. Well, I do care, but right now, I'm not into it. [In five years:] Twenty-one? I'll have my independence. I won't live with my mother. That's one thing, my mother wants me to. She wants me to live with her until I get married. She says I have to leave the house married. Engaged, married, then I could do what I want. I don't know, she's too overprotective. And I don't like that. And I laugh in her face when she tells me that 'cause I ain't gonna wait until I get somebody and stay with my mother.

The girls' intentions all disclose the assumption that attending college will prepare them and be conducive to high-paying, high-status jobs. Interestingly, in considering careers in accounting, computer technology, and architecture, Carolina, Antonia, and Toni expect to venture beyond the sphere of traditional "women's work"; nevertheless, they also fancifully allude to more "glamorous" or exciting pursuits after high school involving fashion, commercials, travel. Antonia is quite candidly driven by the desire to make a lot of money: Toni also seeks financial security but with the rather hopeful gloss that "professional" credentials would provide a back-up resource in the event of divorce.

This theme of fuller economic independence is reiterated by Magda and Paula, who both see themselves as engaged in secretarial work. But they both pointedly qualify the position they would occupy (management secretary or bilingual secretary) suggesting that this type of secretarial work is both more remunerative and more prestigious. Magda's response, like the others', clearly represents a college education as a direct conduit to a satisfying career. Paula, on the other hand, is much vaguer about the prospect of attending college, despite her superior academic performance and attendance. While college may be an iffy proposition, there is no doubt about the necessity to obtain a job, for the clear purpose of achieving economic self-sufficiency ("something that pays well enough that I could support myself"). Paula rejects her mother's suggestion that she remain home until she marries; indeed, Paula implicitly rejects reliance on marriage to promote her goals—for her, it is work, rather than wedlock, that will secure her independence.

Indeed, none of these young Latina women expressed interest in marrying—let alone plans to marry—immediately after high school. Most of them voiced an eagerness to establish independence from their parental home, but not by merely exchanging one family for another that marriage would signify. For them, independence requires some achieved sense of separate identity and self-reliance. Hence, attending college to prepare for jobs or careers was their primary goal for the five forthcoming years. These girls appear to be delaying marriage in order to focus on what they need to accomplish for themselves before they become emotionally involved in relationships with others.

Future Projections of Family Life

Given their recognition of the imminent need to enhance their capacity or credentials as wage-earners, what expectations do they entertain for future family life? Naturally, an emphasis on education and career does not preclude their desire to enter into romantic attachments and the hope one day to have children. In the following comments they describe how they imagine, or hope, life will be in ten years:

> ANTONIA: In ten years I'll be married and I'll be going to my job for computers.
>
> JW: What about kids?
>
> ANTONIA: Let's see. I want to marry when I'm twenty-three. So I'm probably gonna have kids then. Well, I want to wait two or four years before I have kids after I marry.

> CAROLINA: Married, living in a house. I don't know, have my career.
>
> JW: Will you have children?
>
> CAROLINA: Of course. I'll have children when I'm twenty-five. That's a good age. That's like half-way. You can still be young for your kids, but not too young when you have them.

> TONI: I'd get married, have a couple of kids. I wish at that age I'd be a mother and working. Around twenty-four or twenty-five is a good age to get married at. First I want to go to college and I want to be pre-pared. I want to be professional in case I get a divorce or something.
>
> JW: Do you want kids?
>
> TONI: Oh yes, I want to have kids. I'd want to have one or two. I don't want to be an old mother. But I don't think when you get married you should have kids right away.

> MAGDA: I think I'll have an education already. Be in nice office, dress nice, have a house already and get married, have my family, live with my mother taking care of her. . . . I think twenty-five is a good age to have kids. I have to first get my education, cause when you get mar-ried, get kids, you don't got time to do this. You have to take care of your husband, clean the house. I prefer to get first my education and then have children.

> PAULA: At twenty-six? Have a big house, not a big house, but a house, and maybe kids and I know I'll have maybe one or two, but no exag-geration and have, you know, a career. Something too so I could know that nobody has to take care of me. That I could take care of myself. Just have at least a job. . . . I think I might be an executive secretary, the secretary that works for the boss. Something that pays. I ain't say-ing that I want to be greedy or anything, but at least something that I could support myself with my kids.

The most striking aspect to these girls' forecasts is the dual emphasis on employment and family life. The two are not particularly dichotomized; work and family are parts to be accommodated simultaneously ("I'll be married and I'll be going to my job for computers"; "married, living in a house . . . have my career"; "I wish at that age I'd be a mother and working"; " I think I'll have an education already . . . be in a nice office . . . have a house already and get married"; ". . . have kids and have a career"). There is a further shared emphasis on the desirability of postponing childbearing after marriage, but not for too long. In their projections, the girls convey little sense of complication in "having it all" and handling it easily; even the possibility of divorce, which Toni mentions, assumes the character of an inconvenience rather than a crisis. Only Magda alludes to an inherent tension in trying to maintain a family and work at the same time, suggesting that once she is married her domestic responsibilities (defined as primarily her own) will not allow her time to attend school.

Paula and Toni make specific reference to being able to provide economically for themselves. They clearly eschew financial dependence on a man's income. Although Paula does not outright reject the possibility of a relationship with a man, marriage does not loom large on her horizon:

JW: Do you think you might get married?

PAULA: Yeah, maybe, if the right guy came along I would be married. If not, I would just live with my kids. Maybe, I don't know, if the guy came along or just have a relationship.

The corollary of financial independence seems, not surprisingly, to be a greater sense of freedom of choice, a willingness to keep open one's options, to wait for the "right guy" rather than, so to speak, an all-right guy.

The priorities and aspirations conveyed by these girls markedly differ from those of their Latina peers who are academically weak students, characterized by high absenteeism and low or failing grades. As the following interviews testify, those girls, though they similarly acknowledge their prospective status as wage earners, tend to focus on their future family life, more emphatically ascribing to a role in the domestic sphere rather than in the labor market.

MARLISSA: Go to college and get my career. That's it.

JW: What career is that?

MARLISSA: First I wanted to be a cop, but I don't want to become a cop, I want to become a C.O. (Corrections Officer) or a guidance counselor.

[In five years:] I think I'll probably have a baby. I think I'll have a kid. As long as you're gonna be responsible for it and not just leave it there so you could go hang out, having a kid is ok.

LUCY: I want to go to college. I don't really know where yet. [In five years:] I'll be in college. Um, I'll have my job. I would like to have my apartment. And, I would like to be married at that age [twenty years old] cause I would like my kids to see his mother young and everything. I guess 'cause I want to be a pediatrician, so I really want to work hard for that. I like to handle the babies. I guess my life is gonna be studying nursing, my own apartment. I want to be independent. That's what I want.

TINA: I hope I even graduate high school (laughs).

MARISOL: I want to be a teacher, mathematics. That's it.

[In five years:]

TINA: By that time Marisol'll be married three times.

MARISOL: By that time I'm twenty-one or twenty, I have my career. I'll be having my career. I'll be probably married, 'cause I want to get engaged early with this guy that I really like and he likes me. And I'll *probably* be married and have my career but I know my father wants, he goes, you know what age he says I can get married? At twenty-seven! I said twenty-seven? I don't want my kids to have an old mother. I want my kids to have a cool mother. I'll be telling my mother that.

TINA: I'll be married for sure, maybe be having a kid.

BERTA: Get married in a white dress and a honeymoon, I don't know where. A white dress. I don't want no kids. [In five years:] I hope I am in college.

JW: Do you know what you want to study?

BERTA: I don't know. I really can't make up my mind. I really wouldn't want to get married at twenty. I'd like to get married when I'm twenty-four.

JW: Kids?

BERTA: I don't want no kids. Yo, man you get stuck with a baby, you won't be able to go dancing.

As illustrated by a rather remarkable specificity, Marlissa, Lucy, and Marisol plan to have "careers" or jobs (protective service/guidance counselor; pediatrician; math teacher). As with the girls in the first group, they assume without question their participation in the workforce. All three also spontaneously mention attending college or "getting a career" after high school. In contrast to these three, Tina worries about graduating from high school while Berta quips that she intends to "get married in a white dress and go on a honeymoon," although later she discounts early marriage in favor of college.

What is particularly striking about this group of low-achieving girls is their anticipation of domestic responsibilities (marriage or children) soon after they graduate from high school. Marlissa imagines she will "probably have a baby"; Lucy hopes "to be married at that age" so that her children will have a young mother; Marisol surmises, "I'll probably be married, 'cause I want to get engaged with this guy"; Tina asserts that she will "be married for sure, maybe having a kid"; and Berta, facetiously perhaps but nevertheless tellingly leaps to the thought of marriage after high school.

Unlike the more academically successful peers, these girls do not foresee enjoying a period of independence or undergoing some preparation for a career immediately after high school. Rather, they appear to have an equal or primary commitment to enter into domestic life. Lucy expresses some ambivalence, she wrestles with conflicting feelings; she desires marriage but she also yearns for independence.[3] Particularly striking is the emphasis both Lucy and Marisol place on becoming mothers while they are still young, an attempt perhaps to preserve a youthful image of themselves: "I want my kids to have a cool mother." In any case, they do not reject the possibility of getting married or having children at an early age, in contrast to the other group of girls for whom a college education is the immediate next step in life, to prepare them for "good" jobs and for whom postponing marriage and childbearing presents little problem. The domestically oriented girls remain consistent in their projection of life ten years ahead; although several mention the possibility of careers or jobs, it is not asserted first. Instead, domestic concerns take priority:

MARISOL: Twenty-six, twenty-seven. Well my life I'll probably have a home already, a condominium. I'll have a kid, I want to have a boy and girl and my husband, I'll still have my career. I'll be taking my kids out to the park. . . . I imagine me with a big condo, a husband, two kids, a boy and a girl.

LUCY: For sure I'll be married. Then I'll have my career, and then I'll have my kids. I want to get married at twenty, but that's if I find the right guy and everything. I want my kids to see me young. I won't really want to get married. I want to be with someone, you know, to share my life.

Marisol's future at twenty-six years old will center around domestic life and although she imagines "I'll still have my career" it is not at all elaborated on. Lucy as well appears to focus on domestic concerns in her response, but interestingly becomes less sure about marriage, although mentions some kind of emotional attachment to a man. Again, Lucy's conflicting feelings are given voice.

Marlissa, however, does not spontaneously address marriage, using the example of her mother's life as sufficient reason to reject marriage. There is little doubt that she imagines herself independent of any husband:

> MARLISSA: With a kid it'll be hard, without a kid it'll be easy. I'll probably be working as a C.O. (corrections officer).
>
> JW: Do you think you might get married?
>
> MARLISSA: I don't want to get married. I don't want a husband. I never had my father by my side.
>
> JW: So you think if you had a husband, he'd be the same way?
>
> MARLISSA: I don't know, I never had a father, so I think I could make it on my own like my mother did.

Tina and Berta, on the other hand, concentrate primarily on marriage. Berta had previously given "lip service" to attending college, but makes no mention of it again, instead emphasizing marriage and economic dependency:

> BERTA: In ten years I want to be rich, have a rich husband and a maid. And I don't want no kids.
>
> TINA: Yeah, I'll probably have a house, three kids, a husband. That's all I want. No more, and probably be having a husband. If my parents are still there, probably with them.
>
> JW: Do you think you'll have a job?
>
> TINA: Probably, I don't know.

Berta here is reminiscent of several of the white girls with their romanticized futures of travel, wealth, and so forth. And like several of the other girls, her experience with young children (her niece and nephew are part of her household) has produced a negative disposition to childbearing. Also, paid work does not stand in as a priority for these two girls.

In thinking about their futures, most of these young women, both "academic" and "nonacademic," aspired to securing "good" jobs, entering into traditional marriage arrangements, and bearing children. The salient differential between these groups is timing: while those girls most engaged in school anticipate obtaining educational credentials and "settling themselves" before marriage, the girls most disengaged plan on soon entering into emotional attachments with men or early childbearing, rather than a period of independence or further schooling.

An interesting question arises as to how the "nonacademic" girls envision negotiating the inherent tension between domestic responsibilities and employment. In other words, how do these girls intend to organize their lives around employment while caring for children? Unlike the group of white girls, most of whom foresee solving the problem by limiting themselves to part-time work or forgoing employment once children are born, these Latina girls are adamant about maintaining their labor-market status by relying on paid babysitters. Only Magda indicates that she will avail herself of her mother and pay her to provide child care:

> MAGDA: If my mom, right, if she's still alive, she could take care of my children 'cause when she used to go work my grandma used to take care of me. And I never used to be in a babysitter. If she's still alive I will leave them with my mother and pay for my mother. It's now me and my mother, my mother, my grandmother takes care, she cleans, works in the house.

The other girls as well make it clear that they will continue to engage in paid labor:

> ANTONIA: I won't work when I'm pregnant, ready to give birth, not. I'll leave them with a babysitter and then work.

> TONI: If the father works and I work, I would take them to a nursery, have somebody care for them while I work. Like then on my lunch hour, I could go home. I would like to work near my house. When I get home late, when it's time for dinner, my husband and I will have to cook the food.

> PAULA: That's hard, but I would do it. I wouldn't, I just don't like to be home stuck in the house. I would stay home maybe for a couple of months, because the baby will be newborn, but after I would go back to work and pay someone to watch the baby.

> CAROLINA: I'd work, but when they're babies, I guess I'd have a live-in maid. I would want to work.

> MARLISSA: I would have to work and my boyfriend would give me money to take care of the kid.

> LUCY: Yeah, I'll be working because I think I'm showing my kids, you're not unable to be a mother and work when you got kids. I think you have to be an example to them. . . . I'd have a family member [take

care of the kids]. I don't trust somebody else. I've seen those babysitters that abuse the kids, so you know I don't trust them. Or maybe I'll send them to daycare. If they're really young when I get a job, I'll send them to daycare. You know, I'll try to be the best mother I could.

These quotations suggest that the girls do not see family responsibilities as distinct from or competing with their paid work responsibilities. What's interesting here is that the prospect of domestic responsibilities (child care) does not diminish the attraction of paid work just as with the white girls. Most assume that having children will not interfere with their employment status in the labor market.

Schooling, Social Mobility, and a Changing Division of Labor

It remains to explain both the importance the girls ascribe to education and their motivation in seeking careers or jobs. In other words, why does paid work in the future seem to be such a salient determinant of identity? Two complementary explanations are useful here. First, as daughters of immigrant parents seeking a better life for themselves and their children in the United States, these girls see education as a vehicle for individual mobility. That many of the girls place emphasis on obtaining a college education can be seen partly as a product of the high value immigrant parents place on educational qualifications to make something of their children's lives. Secondly, education represents a means for many of the girls to achieve independence and enable them to enter into relationships with males on more equal terms.

As part of an "immigrant ideology," there is a strong desire by parents to see their daughters use the schools to maximum advantage (Pessar, 1990):

> MAGDA: When we came to this country, right, my father worked in a factory. And every time when I call him, he goes "I want to see you with education and I don't want to see you working in a factory."

> PAULA: . . . She always wants me to be like my brother, he's a 90 student, 95 or 98. And that's how, I know, she tells me she don't care if I'm not like my brother, but I know deep inside, she wants me to be like him. Never be in fights, always be a goody, goody, always getting 90s and stuff—honor role.

> [From field note: This summer Antonia is going to summer school to get more credits. She would like to work, but she hasn't asked her brother yet, afraid he'll say no, "because he says I don't need to work and it will get in the way of school. He wants me to graduate in three years."]

In the following, Lucy and Paula describe their mothers' abbreviated education in Colombia and the Dominican Republic and their desire for their daughters to lead a different kind of life:

> LUCY: My mother got married when she was fourteen. She had my older brother when she was thirteen, then the other when she was seventeen and I was an accident. You know, I guess she didn't finish all her school. And in Colombia, it's tough cause back then you had to pay for the schools and everything. And you know, we were middle class, we weren't rich, we didn't have that much money. And there were eleven kids they had to send to school. My grandmother she had to have that much money for eleven kids to send to school. So I guess they stayed home. They went to elementary school and I guess to junior high school, but they didn't finish high school so you know, my mother stayed home and helping my grandmother and everything until she met my father. Then my father brought her over here. . . . My mother wants me to be someone. She wants me to have all my diplomas.

> PAULA: Like my brother, he's gonna be a lawyer, a politician, one of these people. That ain't gonna be for me, that's what my mother wants me to do. Do something like that, do something that's better than a secretary or something. Because that's something she never did. She never finished high school because they couldn't afford it. I don't know, back in those old days, I don't really know. She's just trying to make us, she's that way because she don't want us to be the way she is. I understand where she's coming from, but she can't worry too much.

The desire on the part of these mothers for their daughters to pursue education parallels findings from several studies on immigrant Dominican and Colombian women in New York City. Pessar (1990, 1991) and Castro (1982) found that their women informants attributed extreme importance to education and viewed their children's education as a primary vehicle for the family's social mobility. Castro found that Colombian female household heads and married women frequently cited the lure of economic opportunity and the "desire for a better education for their children" as reasons for migration. Pessar's Dominican informants reported asserting a more equal voice with men concerning their children's education after migration. The Dominican informants frequently observed that this change (having a more equal voice in their children's education) greatly benefited daughters, "because it is the wife far more than the husband who realizes that both sons and daughters will likely have to work after marriage" (1990, p. 100).

Educational qualifications are also valued by the girls because they will lead to good jobs or "careers." At the very least, a high school diploma will be necessary for even the most low-paying service-sector job. This understanding is expressed by Marisol in describing a friend's situation:

> I prefer for her to stay in school and if she wants to work, get herself an apartment. But for her to drop out of school and not get out with a diploma, and then whenever she goes to look for a job, they'll be like, do you have a diploma? I don't want her to go through that.

Many of these girls hope to maintain both some independence from husbands and control over their domestic life. The girls seem to give voice to the realization that they will also have to provide financially for themselves and their children; they do not expect that they will ever be fully supported by a man (nor do most seem to want that). In explaining these attitudes, the girls constantly refer to their mothers. They understand from their mothers' experiences that men cannot be counted on to provide economic security (whether because of low wages, sporadic work, or abandonment through divorce):

> MARISOL: My mother works, she's the only one in my house that works. She works at this place where they sell clothes. She's supposed to put the tickets on and the price. They sell them in Alexanders, Macy's, send them out to Pennsylvania. My mother doesn't make that much. She makes $5.75 an hour. And once she gets that she has to pay the rent, gas, everything. . . . I would like to help my mother with the money. My stepfather once in a blue moon when he feels like it he brings money for the house. I told him if you're gonna bring money, bring money every day. It's not right, he comes back on Monday he says that he works, comes back on Saturday he don't have money. . . . Once my mother goes to me, "I want you to have your career, be independent, depend on yourself."

> TINA: She [mother] works in a factory, sewing clothes. She doesn't make that much but she gives it to my father so my father could pay the rent. Like, my father works in a taxi and it's not that much, and my mother doesn't work that much. Sometimes he doesn't work that much. They never have money.

> TONI: . . . I want to be professional in case I get a divorce or something. I don't want to get like my mother. My mother got married right away. I think she got married at twenty and she was very alone and she didn't finish her career. And when my mother got pregnant, I was born with a problem[4] so she left her career, she left her studies and she started working. My father's irresponsible. So my parents are divorced. That's how we are now. My mother tells me to prepare myself and know what to do with something like that.

MARLISSA: I don't want to get married. I don't want a husband. I never had my father by my side. I think I can make it like my mother did.

MAGDA: He [father] thinks it's my mother's fault [their divorce] and everything. I don't believe him because he wasn't there. He was supposed to be taking care of us. He wasn't there for us, not even the day I was born.

These girls seem to strongly identify with their mothers' situations—so much so, in fact, that Marisol and Magda hope to support their mothers in the future as compensation for their fathers' failure to have done so:

MAGDA: Then [I'll] buy a house for my mother 'cause my mother never had a house, or my father never gave her. And I would give her everything she wants, a house, everything. I wish I could make her happy, 'cause she was my mother and my father.

MARISOL: I'll tell my mother [in ten years] "I have a condo and you can have the basement as soon as you hit fifty." I said to her, "Mommy, you're gonna live with us, I'll give you the money you never had" 'cause if me and my husband are going to be working, we could give her money and I'll buy all her clothes and all that.

In the following, Lucy and Paula suggest that their future role as wage earner will enable them to maintain a sense of independence from husbands and will, particularly, provide them with authority to control the household economy. Both girls directly challenge the traditional division of labor within the home:

LUCY: I think you have to be an example to them. When they [children] grow up you're not gonna be sitting around the house waiting for the husband to bring some money. And if he don't make money then you're not gonna eat or something. You know, I'll have a steady job and I could bring home the money and everything and my kids could learn that. You know that you can't always be sitting around waiting for your husband to bring whatever you want. YOU have to go out and get it.

PAULA: Me, I ain't gonna be a housewife. If I stay home to take care of the kids, OK, but he has to help. But I will go work. And not that I have to give him all my money either. I'll pay for half for whatever and I'll keep the other half to buy clothes and go out, but it's not like I'm gonna give him all my money. Because he don't have to give me money. He just has to put in for the rent. I know that things are expensive, but I know that it ain't right for guys to think that you're slaves cause this ain't no 1940s.

It seems clear that these girls plan to parlay their status in the workplace into greater equality with their domestic partners. For Marlissa, who expressed no desire to enter into a traditional marriage arrangement, paid work will lay the foundation for her dream of marriageless motherhood. These girls have learned directly from their mothers' experience the necessity to establish themselves as wage earners to ensure the economic stability of the family. I do not mean to imply that these girls are embracing a "go it alone" strategy (Mirza, 1992). Rather, the point is that these girls are articulating a belief that both partners are expected to participate in establishing the financial security of their household. With two exceptions, they seem to neither want nor expect the full support of a man.

These girls echo the findings of Pessar (1987) in her research on immigrant Dominican women in New York City. She proffers the following statement by a Dominican women as a typical attitude about household management:

> We are both heads. If both husband and wife are earning salaries, they should equally rule in the household. In the Dominican Republic, it is always the husband who gives the orders in the household. But here when the two are working, the woman feels herself equal to the man ruling the home. (Pessar, 1987 p. 121)

Future Husbands

Most of these girls anticipate marriage; in the following responses, they imagine what their prospective husband will be like. As they discuss what needs they expect their partner to fulfill and what responsibilities they expect a partner to assume, two themes emerge as most significant: finding a mate who is emotionally supportive, and avoiding abusive relationships with men.

MARISOL: OK, a straight man, a sincere man.

TINA: My ideal husband is gonna be an understanding person. He will always be with me. We'll be able to understand each other. . . .

PAULA: . . . At least he would treat me right with the respect and the love that he should give me. I would give it to him back. And not to hit me, or, he could scream at me if I deserve it, OK, and he could be upset with me, but to hit me, or to treat me bad, or treat me like they own me, that would be bad. At least treat me with respect. I ain't asking for a rich man, either.

TONI: . . . He has to be, you know, not those type of men who feel like they're the head of everything and they have to prove it, think the woman doesn't know how to do nothing. I don't like that. I like the man who feels alright with you. . . .

MAGDA: To respect me, to be honest with me, not to be that kind of man that they're alcoholic, don't be a playboy. You know, a decent one, right. And like what happened to my mother, 'cause my father had education and my mother didn't and that's, they had to separate for that reason. And I think, I don't want that to happen. He work, I work, so we can get along.

These girls are looking for supportive and nonabusive relationships based on understanding and respect, relationships through which they hope to challenge unequal gender relations within marriage. It is particularly interesting that Magda should cite her mother's lack of education as the grounds for divorce, implying that more education might have better equipped her to negotiate a more equal position in the marital relationship. Paula and Toni directly challenge a husband's presumptive dominance and control; Marisol, Tina, and Magda express concern about faithfulness and honesty.

That these girls should so expressly voice concern about finding a nonabusive mate perhaps stems from their own lived experiences of male domination and violence in the home. Below are several examples. In Tina's painful account, we see how the traditional role of male dominance and privilege was carried out to a pathological extreme:

TINA: When I was at the age of thirteen, I got raped by my own brother, and that's what my mother doesn't understand. Me and my mother never got along, and when she found out she cursed me. She just told me straight out, she said that now that you're not a virgin it's easy for you to go to bed with anybody. That got me more depressed you know 'cause I couldn't take it no more. Every time I came home I used to sleep 'cause I was really depressed. . . . I told my counselor about it and she said she's gonna do something about it and she put me in the hospital and I stayed a month there. When my father wanted to take me out, he lied to the doctors saying that my brother was out of the house. When I went back home, he was still there. I said though that I ain't going back to the hospital staying all locked up all alone like if I did the crime. My brother was out there having fun and me stuck there like that as if I had done the crime.

Sexually violated by her brother, Tina was "cursed" by her mother as if she were responsible. With her brother not only unpunished but even held not accountable, her parents tacitly condoned incestuous rape and insidiously conveyed to her both their and society's estimation of the relative worth of the sexes. Violence against female members of the household was also described by Marisol:

MARISOL: Once my stepfather smacked my mother in front of me. I came out of the room and I said, "What the hell are you doing." He

came to hit me and my mother took an umbrella. . . . My brother
and my sister were just standing here looking at my father beating
my mother. I could hate my mother, but nobody messes with my
mother. I told my mother, he lays a hand on you don't worry. My
mother wants to go to work with a black and blue eye? She had to
wear dark glasses for nobody to notice. I felt like calling the cops
and telling the cops this man is abusing my mother. He don't got no
right. You know how in New York state the law is no man is
allowed to hit no wife. He got no right to hit my mother. He don't
belong in this house. He don't bring no money. He don't bring no
food.

Paula, in the following account also passionately criticizes the presump-
tion and operation of male privilege.

He never gets hit, I mean the last time she ever hit him, oh my Lord,
she never hit him, only a smack. But she hits me that you might call it
abuse. I never had a good relationship with my mother like she has for
her son, my brother. It ain't right.

I include these quotations in order to suggest that perhaps the girls'
experiences with male dominance and violence have given them a critical awareness and wariness: for them, the search for an equitable relationship is not idle romantic daydreaming but a sensible imperative—
they have acutely witnessed how the lack of equity can so quickly issue
in violence and abuse.

Several of the girls also hope to find husbands who will reliably provide a regular income. This criterion, however, seemed almost inciden-
tal to the girls; they mentioned but did not dwell on it:

ANTONIA: He'll work something big, I guess, like something you make
a lot of money in.

MAGDA: Have an education and nice job. Have a nice paycheck with a
lot of money. . . .

TONI: He has to be professional.

LUCY: He'll be working.

What strikingly takes center stage in these girls' specifications for an
ideal mate is a partner who will participate in household labor.

PAULA: I wouldn't want for him to take advantage of me saying you
better have food on the table by the time I come. I'll be like you crazy?
Not me. If they really love you they should do 50/50. I don't believe

that a female should just be home and cleaning and cleaning and cooking and cooking, making sure her husband gets everything. Unless you want to, then it's your business.

TONI: . . . I like a man, you know, if you have to do the dishes, we share the work. He helps me clean, 'cause I'll have to work too. I wouldn't want to be a live-in maid. I want to be his companion. A great father, take the kids out now and then.

MARISOL: . . . Not depending on me to take care of him and the children. Not to be irresponsible. To be responsible for the house, like if I get late to the house, to cook for him to already cook. To help me out with the laundry. To be a man, a real man. Not one of these men that they get home late and they're like "Give me my food." I would like the man to when he gets home first, to serve himself the food.

LUCY: Well, he'll work and at home do things like cooking. I come home late, he comes home early, I would like to have everything done, the kids picked up wherever they are. I would like him to help me. But if he can't 'cause he's working late, I wouldn't mind doing it 'cause I already got a brother and I know how they are. They lazy, so I guess I'll probably be doing mostly everything. He'll be working.

ANTONIA: Well, I'm planning to get a maid. I hate housework, so you know, I want to become rich, so I'm gonna, if I can, I'm gonna have a maid.

Except for Antonia, who resorts to an upper-class solution to the dilemma of who does the housework by hiring a maid, the other girls exhibit an important shift in female expectations regarding the traditional sexual division of labor, a shift toward true domestic partnership where men will assume a greater share of the household responsibilities. Interestingly, this ideal is not held only by those girls who plan to be wage earners. The battle against the unequal division of labor within the home is also trumpeted by the two girls who anchor their future identity in marriage:

TINA: It's not gonna be like, you get married, he's gonna be expecting everything. We're gonna share things, half, half. We will work together. If something comes up, he'll help out in the house. We could help each other. We do everything together.

BERTA: I don't want to be no housewife.

HOPE: You don't have to be no housewife. You could get a babysitter.

BERTA: If I do everything in my house right now, I ain't gonna cook for my boyfriend, it ain't no restaurant.

HOPE: You'll get tired of that. You're gonna have a babysitter. He gonna work, and you're gonna work.

BERTA: I do not want to work. I'm gonna have me a maid.

HOPE: She's lazy. You want to marry a rich man, what about your poor boyfriends?

BERTA: I'm gonna marry Adam [boyfriend]. He gotta give me everything. Hell no, I ain't gonna cook for no asshole. You think I'm gonna cook for my entire life? I been cooking for all of them [family] and I'm gonna cook for somebody else? Guys are so lazy. They're gonna get up and get tired for their women? What's up?

While there is a somewhat romanticized quality about Tina's response, she makes it clear that her future husband will participate equally in domestic labor. Berta, on the other hand, really evades the issue by implicitly casting it as a false dilemma, namely either they will have a maid or no one will do the housework (as a reality check, her friend states with appropriately symmetrical and plainly accurate conciseness: "he gonna work, you gonna work"). Nevertheless, that Berta's spontaneous remarks should issue forth as contempt for household labor and for the very word and idea of "housewife" is rather telling, evidence of further erosion of traditional expectations and roles.

What seems to come through in the above quotations is, at one level, a desire for greater equality within the domestic sphere but, at another level, a disbelief that greater equality can actually be achieved.

What is noteworthy about these Latina girls is their attempt to insert ideals of greater equality into the framework of a traditional marital arrangement. They seek partners who will respect them, who will not dominate them, and will participate equally, or at least peripherally, in household labor.

That these girls lay so much stress on a more equitable division of household labor, particularly compared to the white, African American, and U.S. Puerto Rican girls, may reflect the changing power relations between men and women within patriarchal Latino immigrant families. As Pessar (1987) noted in her study of Dominican women, patterns in the division of labor and authority in the household shifted after the family emigrated as a consequence of women's entry into the labor market. Their economic activity as wage earners provided them with leverage to make their husbands view them more equally. Many immigrant Dominican women reported their husbands' willingness to participate in housework (typically cooking and shopping) and viewed this as a "moral victory." (It is interesting to note that Pessar (1987) found the man's contribution increased when children were young and decreased once daughters were old enough to help their mothers.) In addition to establishing cooperation in household labor, Dominican immigrant women also were able to increase both their authority over budgeting and their freedom to engage in a quasi-independent social life. After migration, which forced many women into the labor market (necessitated by economic need), women were allowed to negotiate more equitable relationships with men. This alteration in traditional gender relations may play into daughters' expectations about future husbands participating equally in domestic work.

In the following sections, I will explore several areas of girls' daily lives—their participation in household labor and their relationships with boys and with family members—which may shed light on how this group of Latina girls negotiates and constructs different definitions of themselves from their families and peers and shapes their vision of themselves in the future.

DAILY LIFE: HOUSEHOLD LABOR AND ROMANCE

Domestic Labor

All the girls had participated in domestic labor, which included performing a series of household and child-care tasks throughout the week. While they all reported having household responsibilities, the amount of work seemed to vary depending on the girls' particular family composition.[5] For example, in families where no male head was present, girls carried fewer responsibilities for household labor or it was more equally divided between mother and daughter. On the other hand, in families where a male head was present, girls engage more heavily in domestic labor, carrying out household tasks for the whole family.

Marlissa and Toni live alone with their mothers and household labor seems fairly equally divided between mother and daughter:

JW: So who cooks at home?

MARLISSA: Me and my mother. Usually most of the time her. I do it once in a blue moon.

JW: How about housework?

MARLISSA: We both do it.

JW: Who does the housework?

TONI: Well, I do really. Everyday I go from school and I eat something and then I prepare dinner. My mother comes and we cook together. And I clean the house every Saturday. My mother keeps the kitchen clean and does the laundry.

Magda, in contrast, is completely exempt from housework as her family includes a domestically active grandmother: there is a conspicuously uneven distribution of domestic work between female family members, most chores being assigned to her grandmother:

> MAGDA: My grandmother cooks 'cause my mother comes home late. My grandmother mostly cleans the house, you know, my mother's working.

Similarly, housework does not feature prominently in Paula's daily life. However, she is assigned primary responsibility for housework when her mother travels to the Dominican Republic:

> JW: Do you do the housework?
> PAULA: Only when my mother ain't there.
> JW: What kinds of things do you do then?
> PAULA: Clean the house, everything.

In families where a male heads the household (father, stepfather, older brother), the girls assume sometimes massive amounts of domestic duties. It is not clear whether there was, say, simply more work because the families were larger, or whether perhaps the presence of a man as authority invoked the traditional patriarchal expectations regarding housework. Pessar (1990) has observed that men who experience a drop in their economic and social status after immigration due to discrimination may attempt to counteract this by trying to maintain their patriarchal privilege within the household to include demands like clean clothes, tidy house, cooked food, and so on (see Tancer, 1973), thus creating a greater burden for women in the household.

What is certainly clear is that in families where there are younger siblings (or young cousins, or nephews/nieces), these girls assume a large share of the reproductive labor:

> CAROLINA: I get home about 3:15. My brother gets home at 3:00, but my mother's home all day. I have a little baby sister who's one year old. So I play with her when I get home. Sometimes I'll do the laundry and help my mother cook. Like last night I made dinner. Then we eat and then I talk on the phone. I do the dishes every night. I don't mind because it helps my mother out. My brother can't do it, he just doesn't know how, he's not responsible that way. I'm always pulling out his dirty socks from under the couch. I just do it all to help out my mother. We split the housework, I mean we don't have an agreement, but it works out.

ANTONIA: . . . I get home around at 3:00. I go to pick up my little cousin. I babysit and when I come back, I give him the food. Then I help him with his homework. But like around 4:30, I'm finished and I start cooking. I finish around 5:30 or 6:00 and at 6:30 we're eating. By 7:00 we're finishing eating and I start seeing my soap opera.

TINA: . . . In my house I take care of my three nephews.[6] . . . I used to buy them everything when I was working. I say to myself, it's not hard raising a kid, it's not. I mean people say it is hard, but it's not, you just got to get patient, have money for the baby, buy clothes and they grow up to go to school and that's it. I went through it, I know how to raise a kid. I mean it's hard when they're little babies. But enjoy yourself, see how he grows and everything. My nephew, he's now six years old, he's starting to call me mommy. People think he's my son.

That these girls come from families with a strong sexual division of labor does not mean that they accept unproblematically their household roles. In the following, the girls' sense of injustice about how their compulsory participation in housework is used as a lever of control over their freedom of movement:

MARISOL: I get home, I pick up the living room, I do what I have to do. When I come home, my grandmother tells my mother, "your daughter came home at this time and you better tell her and my mother was raised in the days the girls would only go to school and come back home right away and do their [house]work." I'm not that. My grandmother's home and she does everything, it's done. I can't do that while she does everything. The days I do cleaning is Fridays, Saturdays, and Sundays.

TINA: . . . You know, it gets me mad cause as soon as I get home from school, you know, I have to go to my house and I clean the whole house and then I go outside when everybody's home. And I go to my cousin and I come back at 9:00 or 9:30 and they [parents] complain about it. I say so who does the house when you come, the house is already clean. I mean, I been doing it since so long. I mean I'm responsible for it, but they giving me too much responsibility and I can't take it. A teenager this day want to hang out. I have my chores but I need to be out and have fun, too. I just can't be locked up and just do what they tell me 'cause I take good care of my nephews [their mother is living in a homeless shelter]. I clean the house and they expect me to stay home.

PAULA: . . . The last time my mother went back to Santo Domingo, he [brother] thought he was in charge and he wasn't. He was like he's in charge of me. But it wasn't that way, I was in charge of myself. If he don't let me go out, I'll say, I have to leave, the house is clean and everything. So he has to let me go out.

Though the three girls feel unfairly treated at home, their sense of injustice derives not from resistance to household labor per se, but from displeasure at the curtailment of their social freedom. Lucy is the only girl to openly express her hostility at the domestic role to which she has been consigned—she must take care of all household chores, which she perceives as unfair particularly because she is employed:

> LUCY: My brother is lazy. Sometimes before [when] my mother was here,[7] he didn't cook, he didn't do nothing. Now that she left he has an obligation, so he leaves. Now when I come after school, I don't go to my house, I go to my aunt's house 'cause I like staying there and it's near my job, so then I go, and my brother has to clean the house. Sometimes he don't want to. So I says what do you think I'm always been working and going to school. Then we'll be having an argument. So we both end up half half. Yesterday I was telling him to wash his clothes. He didn't want to. My father had to go wash them. . . . I've been doing a lot. 'Cause I work, too. So on my days off, I clean the house and then on Sundays, I be doing, I be washing clothes.

Interestingly, Lucy is able to use her paid work as leverage to render a fairer division of domestic labor with her brother and father during her mother's absence.

It is evident from the preceding discussion that the division of labor in these girls' families assigns domestic tasks and child care to the wife/mother, grandmother, and daughters. It does not, however, appear that these girls uncomplicatedly accept this traditional division of labor.

Romance

In a previous chapter, I introduced the idea that boys and "romance" appeared as an organizing principle in the lives of white girls. For the most part, the girls were involved in steady and exclusive relationships with older boys, which mirrored the traditional pattern of monogamous marital relations. On the other hand, an analysis of the role of boys and romance in the lives of African American and U.S. Puerto Rican girls suggested that they were not as immersed in the "ideology of romance" to the same degree as the white girls. Many did not have boyfriends as such, but had instead friendships with boys; and they expressed romantic interest but not intense involvement, though this is not to imply that boys were marginal in their lives. Furthermore, while families of white girls condoned the girls having a boyfriend, such acceptance was not so readily bestowed by African American and U.S. Puerto Rican girls' families.

In general, this group of Latina girls does not appear to focus on romantic relationships as the core of their lives, although there are important exceptions. These girls are dissuaded from pursuing romantic relationships by the imposition of strict rules concerning boys and by the constraints on the girls' social freedom consequently enforced. These prohibitions perhaps derive from the purportedly "Latin" tradition that the honor of families is strongly tied to the sexual purity of its women (Medrano, 1994). Daughters are still charged with maintaining their virginity until marriage (Espin, 1992, p. 143). Below Vicky articulates the code:

> I'm proud to be a virgin. . . . My mother was a virgin until, you know how old? Until she was twenty-two, that's when she got married. Spanish feel you should be a virgin when you get married, and then you can get married in white. Only one person brought dishonor to my family—my cousin who's living with this guy in California and got pregnant.

The tradition of maintaining virginity until marriage does not mean, however, that girls cannot and do not have boyfriends, but only that the relationships can be more circumscribed than, for example, those in which we have seen the white girls involved.

JW: Do you have a boyfriend?

ANTONIA: No.

JW: Ever?

ANTONIA: Yes, three of them. I went to Mexico with my sister and I got a boyfriend there, only for a month though. When we came back I didn't want him no more. He was ugly. I couldn't have one anyway.

JW: So who doesn't want you to have one?

ANTONIA: My brother, I don't think he wants me to have one.

JW: Do you have a boyfriend?

CAROLINA: Yeah, I have a boyfriend. He goes to Art and Design [high school]. He's nice, but I have like mixed feelings about him and I try to explain to him but he says I should just tell my mother. I say fine, but you're not the one who gets hit.

JW: What would your mother do if she found out?

CAROLINA: She would kill me. Really kill me.

JW: Do you have a boyfriend now?

PAULA: No

JW: Did you before?

PAULA: Yeah, I did before. I don't know. My mother freaked out. It was like in '85. I had a crush, oh my Lord, it was crush. He was a player so

I said forget it. And then I had this other guy recently, who my mother never knew about it. We went out and stuff, but it was not in the sense, you know, we didn't do nothing [sexual]. It only lasted three weeks, and then he went his way, he went back south, and I stayed around. . . . I got in big trouble 'cause somebody [on the block] saw me with this guy. Just we were talking, and my brother freaked. I got punished by HIM. I could not believe it. I got punished by him for a week, I could not go out. By HIM!! I could understand if it was my mother, but him. I understand that he could do whatever, my mother didn't say anything. I got punished by him.

JW: Do you have a boyfriend now?

MAGDA: Kind of boyfriend. He lives far away, he lives in Long Island. Sometimes I see him, but I don't feel nothing for him no more. It's like, I want to be alone right now.

JW: Does your mother know about him?

MAGDA: She doesn't let me go out. If she found out, she would hit me. She would call me this, she thinks, she always says she's gonna send me to my father. I say OK, she starts crying if I say I want to go to my father. I know she would hit me, and she wouldn't let me go out. . . . She gives me a lot of freedom but I have little ways. I know I have to be careful. She lets guys call my house, we're just friends, sure. . . . I have to listen for the telephone, when it rings, I have to go running. My mother doesn't like guys calling me a lot.

JW: What about your brother?

MAGDA: Ohh, he'd tell me, "If I see you with a guy I'm gonna hit him. I'm gonna kick your butt, and I'm gonna hit, oohh, watch it, I don't ever want to catch the guy." I'm like yeah, yeah. But we're good friends now. I love my brother. We fight and everything, but he still there.

LUCY: Yeah, but he doesn't go to this school. He has dark skin, he's Dominican. He's not here right now, he's in his country. He'll be back at the end of the month. We been seeing each other for the past four years and my parents know about it and everything. He goes to my house.

JW: Do they approve or object?

LUCY: At first they didn't. They used to hate him. But then on Mother's Day three years ago, he sent my mother these roses, and then one thing led to another. They were friends. My father didn't like him at first. My brothers hated him. I got two older brothers, twenty-four and twenty-three, and they were talking about like "Take care of my sister real good."

Lucy is the only girl involved in a long-term relationship, which was ultimately endorsed by her family. But, as with the other girls, Lucy's romance initially encountered family resistance. In trying to ban boyfriends, these girls' parents (or brothers) adopt preventive measures to deny the girls opportunities for social or physical contact with boys. Particularly striking in the girls' responses are their resentful accounts of older brothers assuming the role of "protectors" of their younger sisters' sexuality. But, as revealed above, these girls find ways to subvert the efforts of their parental/fraternal control. For example, Antonia limits her involvement with boys to vacations, when she is far away from her brother's watchful eye. Even though Carolina's mother "would kill" her if she discovered her boyfriend, she still manages to maintain this involvement, even spending time at the boyfriend's house. Paula, similarly, "had a guy" whom her mother never knew about; and Magda remarks, "I have little ways, I know I have to be careful."

Not all the parents were reported to ban boyfriends so completely. Marisol's mother and Marlissa's mother give qualified consent:

> MARISOL: My mother also asks me if I have a boyfriend now. I don't want to have a boyfriend. It's like I want to have my fun now, go out to the movies, have a job, party. . . . My mother goes to me, "I don't care if you have a boyfriend as long as you go to school and have your career, you don't have to depend on your husband, on nobody."

> MARLISSA: My mother said I could have a boyfriend only if they know how to treat me, not get a mistreatment.
> JW: Does your mother know Thomas?
> MARLISSA: She liked him before, and then things happened between us. A lot of shit started between us. And then we got back together and she still doesn't like him.

For Marisol's mother, a boyfriend could thwart her hopes for her daughter's further schooling and career, especially should she get pregnant. Marisol's description of a friend's situation captures succinctly and distinctly the environment some of these girls inhabit:

> Her father wants her out of the house. Her father says, if you have a boyfriend and you're gonna get married, get married and get out of my house already. And that's all they say.

Tina adds another variable to this complicated equation. Given the fact that she was failing at school, there is a likelihood that pressure will be exerted on her to get married, despite being only sixteen years old, since her prospects were not promising, perhaps at best a low-paying job. Almost by default, Tina seems to be falling into a reliance on men and marriage for economic support and security.

Some of the girls are quite clear that they value their prospective independence and that they give priority to pursuing education rather than relationships:

> MAGDA: I want to be alone. First I want my grades to get better 'cause finals are coming right? And I have to make up, I hope they're gonna give me a good grade. Now when he comes I'm gonna go, "No, look, I'm sorry, my grades, my school come first and everything." I don't want to be with him.

> JW: Do you have a boyfriend?

> TONI: No

> JW: Ever?

> TONI: No, I don't know, I'm too quiet. I don't have a boyfriend but I consider everybody my friend. I like these two guys, they're twins. They live around where I live. But that's it. I'm a kind of independent woman. I don't like to be attached to anybody.

What the above quotations illustrate is a "tempering" of girls' involvement with boyfriends where going out with boys is either controlled or completely banned, or simply not desired. Girls are similarly reared in Latin American societies where their involvement with a boy is carefully monitored. As Lucy explains:

> You know over here you could go with a guy. But over there [Colombia] you have to let the family meet him and then you go out with him and the next day you have to get married with him. Even if you don't want to. Some families are like that. A girlfriend I got, she was going out with this guy. She only like him and they made her get married.

Although Lucy's example is exaggerated, it conveys her mother's culture's heavy investment in traditional and stabilizing sexual conduct and familial structure, values and regulations in turn transmitted by parents who, if not forbidding, at least strictly controlling their daughters' behavior. These mores receive even greater emphasis here in the United States since education and job opportunities are at stake.

Although these girls generally experience a more circumscribed involvement with boyfriends compared to the white girls (who are engaged in steady and exclusive relationships and who spend vast amounts of leisure time with their boyfriends), I do not mean to imply that these girls are not learning about unequal gender relations in romantic heterosexual relationships. Circumscribed though they may be, it is clear that romance involves not only emotion and caring, but also control:

MARISOL: The guy that I found right now, he's nice, he's sweet. He's the kind of man, he would do anything for his girlfriend, wife, whatever. I think he's the perfect one. The thing that I was looking for was a strict man with me. 'Cause if you go out with a man that you could control, what's the use of going out with him?

MARLISSA: . . . I could talk to him as a friend. Every time I have a problem I know he'll listen to me. I know he'll stand by my side no matter. . . . I usually stay with him in the park after school. He plays ball and everything. And then we go to his house and we take something to eat. But I don't get high when I'm with him. He don't let me get high around him.

TINA: I need someone that could control me you know. I'm still seeing this guy. He's twenty-one, he is a real man. He's nice and everything. We just get into arguments 'cause he found out something with his cousin so he got mad at me. I was just talking to his cousin. His cousin is after me, he likes me. So José got mad at me. He's real mad, he's making me suffer for this.

MARISOL: Why don't he hug her once in awhile in front of everybody so everyone knows that that's your girl. So nobody will go after her.

LUCY: He's sweet, he's caring. When I have a problem, I talk to him and everything. Like I stopped coming to school, I guess you noticed right? And then I called him. He yelled at me and he told me to go, go do it for me, do it for yourself, become someone. He gets mad when I used to be absent one day. He used to scream at me, and I'm like don't scream at me. He goes I don't want you to be like those girls on the corner. Hey man, he made me think a lot about that—going to school. And he's real sweet, he's real kind and he helps me when I need it. We been together for a long time, four years. . . . He be telling me that we're gonna get married, we're gonna have three kids, we're gonna move somewhere out of here. I hope we get married.

JW: When do you think?

LUCY: I'm too young now. I don't know how I could handle myself married. I mean I do a lot of things that a married person when they're married. I clean the house and everything, I wash clothes, I cook, it's like being married. So I said to myself, this is a test. I wonder if I could pass it. If I could pass it, it means I'm ready for my next step when that day comes. But I'm too young. 'Cause like my mother's not here right now, so I'm taking care of my father and my brothers. So I have to wash and cook and clean and everything for them. So I make believe my brother's my husband and when he comes home, you know, I have to have everything ready. That's like a test, I'm testing myself. I don't know if I could pass it.

"Sweet," "caring," "nice" are words that girls use to describe what they like about their boyfriends. Also evident in their responses is a description of male domination and possessiveness that seems hardly contested at all: "I was looking for a strict man with me"; "I don't get high when I'm with him, he don't let me"; "I need someone that could control me." In the situation that Tina describes, her boyfriend is making her "suffer" because his cousin is "after her." Marisol's perspective that it is the boyfriend's fault for not signaling clearly that Tina "belongs" to him (why doesn't he hug her in front of everyone) reflects the persistently patriarchal view of women as men's property.

Caught up in these descriptions of relationships is a sense of ambivalence. On the one hand, these boys/men are sweet and caring and provide emotional intimacy; but at the same time involvement with them costs a girl her autonomy and personal agency. Perhaps the reason girls may rely on boys who are controlling or domineering derives from a partial acceptance of the traditional power differentials between Latino men and women. Medrano (1994) explains that from a very young age, Latina girls are groomed for their primary duty of caring for men (brothers, fathers and later, husbands) even to the exclusion of their own needs (p. 108). Later when a woman marries, the relationship becomes a mutually dependent one in which the husband provides for his wife and defends her from others, while she is expected to cater to his needs, sometimes putting up with abuse (Medrano, 1994, p. 107). This power differential between men and women often becomes mirrored in relations between Latina and Latino teens (p. 108).

Earlier the girls had expressed an apparent desire for equality in future relationships; but on the basis of the preceding remarks, their actual relationships bespeak great male-female disparities, with men expected to control women, even be strict with them. Men are the ones who are responsible for making the relationships official and women perceive their involvement as a test, the rules of which are defined by males. I would like to speculate here and suggest that perhaps the apparent contradiction between the girls' desire for greater gender equality and their actual relationships in which males appear controlling or domineering reflects ruptures in traditional patriarchal gender codes and the changes in gender consciousness that take place after immigration. As discussed in the case of Dominican women, the economic necessity for women to work, which takes them out of the domestic sphere, results in renegotiated gender roles that were traditionally sharply enforced and restrictive. But in spite of women's employment and consequent victories within the home (in which men assumed some responsibility for household labor), this has not provided women with a new status that challenges or subordinates their primary identities as wives and mothers

(Pessar, 1984, p. 1192). Espín (1992) points out, people often pay lip-service to traditional values without actually enacting them. Nevertheless lip-service can affect behavior, subconsciously reinforcing a sense of the naturalness and inevitability of those values and traditions—such as the subordination of women to men, the expectation of and consent to men's assertions of authority over women. Even if such values are not enacted, believing in them is sufficient guarantee that tradition will continue, perhaps subtly, to define and support appropriate gender roles.

In Lucy's reference to marriage, it is clear that marriage entails shouldering a domestic burden that she would do well to practice and prepare for in her present household—"it's like a test." But a test she clearly does not wish to pass. In Lucy's conflicted discussion, she seems like others, to wrestle with opposing definitions of femininity derived from family and community, the dominant society in which she is assimilating, and her own sense of personal agency.

There appears to be an important correlation between failure at school and investment in boyfriends. Those girls most estranged from school (Lucy, Marlissa, Tina, and Berta) all have boyfriends and all harbor the desire to marry or have a child in the near future, before going to college or getting a "career" underway, if at all. For these girls steady and exclusive relationships play a more central role in their lives and seem to be closer to their core of interest and, in this sense, parallel the findings of white girls.

CONCLUSION

For this group of young immigrant Latinas, gaining an education appears to be partly the product of the high value placed on educational qualifications to make something of their lives. For the most part, these girls' families placed a great deal of importance on their education, viewing it as the primary vehicle of social mobility. Many of this group of immigrant Latina girls plan to enter the labor market, hoping to achieve and maintain some degree of economic independence and control over their domestic life. Their mothers' experience and example have taught them the necessity of women's access to wages if their families are to remain economically stable and secure. While most hazily envision their doing some sort of work outside the home, their desire to marry and start a family prevailed.

However, there seemed to be differences between those who were performing well academically and those whose academic performance was weak. While all the girls saw themselves working at "good" jobs, getting married, and having children, the girls most engaged in school (i.e., those who attend regularly, received passing grades, etc.) anticipated obtaining educational credentials and "settling themselves" before marriage, and those less engaged (those who were failing classes, frequently cutting school, etc.) foresaw themselves soon entering emotional attachments with men or bearing children without first obtaining further schooling or at least a period of independence in which to explore job opportunities and consolidate their identities. This is somewhat similar to many of the white working-class girls' future projections of themselves. Perhaps, as I argued, these girls understand that, without qualifications or sufficient skills to enter the labor market, their best chance at economic security lies in marriage (or some near equivalent).

What they hope to establish in an ideal future relationship is a domestic partnership with a man who is emotionally supportive and nonabusive, a partnership not defined by the inequities that characterize conventional gender relations. In some cases, such criteria for a successful relationship may reflect their own domestic experience of male domination and violence: they are powerfully aware of what they do *not* want their futures to hold.

The problems presented by their desire to have boyfriends and to possess more social freedom underscore the difficulty these girls face when trying to redefine the boundaries of traditional gender roles. On the one hand, the girls express acute resentment over the control that parents or brothers exercise in restricting their social life. But, on the other hand, they sometimes accept the legitimacy of male prerogative in their own relationships with boyfriends.

The range in responses to future work and family also appears to reflect the tension that these girls experience, finding themselves sometimes caught in the middle when the traditional values of family and community cultures contravene the liberating, new possibilities presented by education. The fact of their family's recent immigration appears to create conditions for a change in gender consciousness within families, but this process is far from smooth. Many of the girls struggle to redefine gender boundaries, as some of their mothers have done since arriving in the United States. But the struggle is not without contradiction—girls can both offer critical insights on women's oppression and at the same time behave in ways that perpetuate male domination.

The next chapter, the first of three in which I examine the school processes that have the power to significantly influence the emergent identities outlined in the last three chapters, focuses on several innovative ways by which the school identifies and redefines "at-risk" girls, and then I will consider some of the strategies the school has developed to keep them in school until graduation.

CHAPTER 7

Redefining Relationships to Schooling

INTRODUCTION

The purpose of this chapter is to analyze several features of this school's school-based factors that appear to impact on the formation of the girls' identities as outlined in chapters 4, 5, and 6. I examine three aspects of school culture and suggest possible effects on incipient female student identities.

First, I show that the success A.H.S. has engendered in graduating its students acts as a powerful incentive for many young women, with previous histories of school failure, to view school as instrumental in attaining their goals of future economic independence. I will also examine important differences between groups of girls in their reasons for attending. Next, I argue that the disciplinary structure in place at A.H.S. allows young women to redefine their previous negative relationships to schooling. Finally, I suggest that the administrative practices at A.H.S. positively influence the shaping of teacher-student social relations. Teachers not only encourage students to aspire to higher education, but students believe teachers care about them.

The alternative school portrayed here differs profoundly from traditional public schools that serve working-class youth and youth of color. In general, as previous research on schooling and class has documented, schools with such students are often characterized by demoralized staff, school overcrowding, pedagogical practices such as tracking, and fiscal constraints, all of which contribute to a high rate of student dropout (Fine, 1991; Wexler, 1992). Ultimately, as Fine writes, "the school perpetuates the social inequities that constrain the material opportunities and psychological visions of their teen students" (p. 43).

As an alternative high school that serves working-class and poor students from all backgrounds who have experienced previous school failure, A.H.S. differs from "traditional" working-class schooling in many important ways. A.H.S. has implemented school practices that have made it possible for many of their working-class youth and students of color to graduate, continue in higher education, and find employment. While the school enables its students to envision for themselves higher education and careers, A.H.S. students' ambitions are expressed and created amid adverse circumstances. It is within communities characterized by high dropout rates and persistent labor market inequality (see chapter 2) that A.H.S. attempts to reshape and shape their students' expectations and aspirations. While a school in isolation such as A.H.S. apparently can affect educational achievement and student aspirations, it cannot, on the other hand, compensate for social inequality. Schools are subject to the wider social and economic forces that ultimately affect a school's independence as a social institution. Thus, the social, political, and economic environment in which the young women live also greatly influences and shapes their destinies.

I turn now to a discussion on the young women's reasons for attending this alternative high school, which help to shed light on the value the girls place on acquiring a high school degree.

THE INCENTIVE TO STAY IN SCHOOL: A CHANCE TO GRADUATE

What is striking about this group of girls is their strong desire to attend A.H.S. despite their previous negative experiences with schooling. As will be shown, their reasons for attending A.H.S. are quite pragmatic— many understood that coming to A.H.S. was their best and only chance at completing high school, and for others, work experience through the internship program might help them secure decent jobs in the future. For many of these young women, schooling and the acquisition of a high school degree are instrumental in attaining future goals. However, does this hold for all groups of girls? In other words, are there divergences between young women in their reasons for attending A.H.S.? If so, how can we account for these differences? Below I will present excerpts from the girls regarding their reasons for attending A.H.S.

Perhaps the most common reason for attending A.H.S. shared by all groups of girls, is the likelihood that they will eventually graduate from the school. (Indeed, the school graduates 85 percent of its students.) This is important because it is within a context of very high dropout rates within their own communities that the girls believe they are getting a second chance. Many understand that, given their previous educational failure, coming to A.H.S. is a unique second chance:

MARLISSA (LA):[1] I came to Alternative [High School] because I wasn't gonna make it in another school. I was a regular truant. They wanted to send me to court to take me away from my mother 'cause I wasn't going to school and they thought that she knew I wasn't going. I had a lot of absences and then they put me in AIDP [attendance improvement dropout prevention], and then I passed and my guidance counselor told me to come here cause *if I was to go to a regular high school, I would've dropped out.* [Emphasis mine]

CHERYL (AA):[2] . . . When I got suspended [in junior high school], my guidance counselor said, "we think A.H.S. is a break for you, you should go there." . . . *I would've failed in that school.* They said I cause a lot of problems. [Emphasis mine]

BERTA (LA): . . . My guidance counselor told me it was a good school and they have a lot of reading and *I thought I wasn't gonna graduate ever.* I failed everything, reading, math, Spanish. They didn't want me in the school no more. [Emphasis mine]

It is apparent that the girls believe they were on a trajectory toward certain failure. Accepting the recommendations of their guidance counselor, they recognized that admission to A.H.S. provided them with a second chance at completing high school.

In addition to opening up the possibility of earning a high school diploma, the school is attractive to several of the girls of Puerto Rican and African American descent because of the career education/internship program.[3] The girls believe that the program will enable them to secure better jobs in the future:

AUREA (PR):[4] I came because of the internships, you get to work 'cause in the other schools, they didn't give you the opportunity. This is better, for like a resume, you got experience when you look for a job.

SAUNDRIA (AA): It was the closest school and I saw they had an internship and I wanted to do that 'cause I want a good career.

BARBARA (AA): . . . My aunt's friend went here and was telling me how they go on an internship here and all that and how she got a good job.

ANTONIA (PR): Well, I came because my language arts teacher . . . he told me that it was a good school, to come here. Some of his students that were in the class came to this school, and when they came back to say hello, they were decent, and they were well dressed and they got a good job.

Other girls describe the attraction of A.H.S. because of its affiliation with a community college:

LUCY (LA): I was hearing from my guidance counselor about all the good classes they got here and everything, like how you can take college classes. And it's close to my house. I like it here. I used to hear a lot of things about it, that it was good and everything.

TINA (LA): My guidance counselor was telling me that it's a good school . . . and the college is here.

PAULA (LA): 'Cause this is like near the house and it's a good school because the college is right next to it.

And still, for others, A.H.S. offers an alternative to overcrowded and often dangerous comprehensive high schools:

MARISOL (LA): Well, I heard it from my counselor, and she told me about it. She told me that the school is good and then I said I want to try it out to see how it is because my mother didn't want me to go to my zoned [neighborhood] school, it's one of the worst schools.

MAGDA (LA): My guidance counselor told me that it was a good school. . . . I was gonna go to Livingston [zoned high school], but I been there and it's a bad place. My friend just transferred here because she had a lot of fights. I think this school's a good place 'cause it's easy to get credits and graduate.

The girls below, of white European backgrounds, similarly articulate troubled relationships to schooling. What is striking is not so much their own personal motivation to graduate and complete high school but rather the pressure their mothers exert on their behavior. It also appears significant that the attendance of these young women seems influenced by the prior attendance (and completion of high school) by a sister or female family member.

DOREEN (WH):[5] I wasn't going to school and my mother told me I have to go here so she could force me to go [to school]. My sister graduated from here two years ago.

DEBBIE (WH): Same story [as Doreen]. When I went to Calvin [High School] for ninth grade I messed up really bad. I never went to school. Then I got left back and my sister used to go here, she graduated in May so my mother made me come.

LAURA (WH): I came here because I wanted something new. My mother thought I could have a better chance [of staying in school] if I didn't hang out with the people I was at my old school. They [were] the troublemakers.

CHRIS (WH): Well, my aunt, she graduated [from] here and she told me about it so that's why I came.

JACKIE (WH): . . . It's a law that once you hit fourteen [years old], you can pick which parent you want to live with, so the minute I hit fourteen I came here [to NYC] to my mother's. . . . I came to A.H.S. because my sister went here and my mother told me if I wanted to graduate [from high school] I better go here.

Several other white girls cite those features of A.H.S. that distinguish it from traditional schools such as size, proximity to college, or discipline structures as their motivation for attending A.H.S. Notable is Beth's comment about attending A.H.S. "to see the [college] guys" as if attaching oneself to an older male could be equally as important as obtaining a high school diploma.

> JEANNETTE (WH): Because I felt it was a small school and they'd pay more attention to us, so I felt that in high school you need more attention, so I came.

> CHRISTINA (LA): I came because I was always hearing about how good the school was, like when old students came back, they were always talking about how free it is and everything.

> BETH (WH): It was on a college campus, [to] see the guys.

The students here seem aware that attending A.H.S. is equated with their perceived unwillingness to perform at their previous school. At the same time the interviews also suggest that the girls understand, on some level, the importance of obtaining a high school diploma.

Furthermore, many of these Latina and African American girls perceive A.H.S. as a school where they might become better prepared to secure a good job. As Antonia suggests when she says "when they [former A.H.S. students] came back to say hello, they were decent, and they were well dressed and they got a good job," A.H.S. is perceived as a place that can facilitate individual social mobility. For the white girls, while they too express a desire to complete high school, their motivation to do so appears to stem from female family members' (mother's or aunt's) pressure rather than their own pragmatic concerns about obtaining educational qualifications and securing a job. Since I did not interview the mothers of the young women in the study, I can only speculate that white working-class mothers are perhaps pressuring their daughters to complete schooling because of the inevitability that their daughters must find future employment that will provide for the family in the event of male unemployment.

The reputation that A.H.S. enjoys for graduating its students has enabled many of these girls of all backgrounds to construct optimistic possibilities for the future. In the previous chapters that outlined the young women's visions for their futures, there was a certain sense of "makin' it" in spite of the previous educational failures. It should begin to be clear that A.H.S. represents a novel opportunity for them to reimagine themselves and their futures.

DISCIPLINARY PRACTICES

A school's disciplinary measures structure its general operations to help create a particular school "ethos." The discipline structure at A.H.S. differs profoundly from other working-class public schools: while many schools are looking for answers to student failure in stricter discipline and the maintenance of law and order, A.H.S. has been much more concerned with changing students' "oppositional" behavior through more subtle means of control—peer pressure, extensive counseling, modeling of college student behavior, and so on. The discipline code at A.H.S. attempts to promote self-regulation and self-control rather than distribute punishment and flex authority. Previously defined by their relationship to a punitive disciplinary structure (discipline deans, detention, suspensions, etc.), the students are now in a more hospitable environment without such threatening structures. Thus, students have an opportunity to recreate alternative self-images vis-à-vis school (Wexler, 1992).

In his book *Becoming Somebody* about students' identity formation within a working-class school, Wexler describes the "social feel" of the school as one of containment. The young people themselves liken their school to a prison or a penitentiary. Similarly, in his account of an urban school, Wexler describes hallways monitored by "professional sentries" who apprehend students in the halls after the bell that announces the beginning of class (called a "blitz" or "attack") and the closing of corridors and swinging shut of heavy doors, all of which communicate to students "a blockage to 'makin' it' to class and beyond."

These accounts stand in direct contrast to the "social feel" of A.H.S., which does not restrict the physical mobility of its students either in the hallways or outside of the school, contributing to a sense of "freedom." Even within the A.H.S. administrative offices, the absence of official boundaries is noteworthy. The principal, several guidance counselors, and vice principals have small offices located in the interior of the office to which students have easy access. (My first field note describes in detail seeing students walking throughout the large office, very unlike typical public schools where students are prohibited from entering a variety of spaces by large barrierlike counters that separate staff from students and outsiders.)

The relaxation of regulatory control over students' mobility throughout the school day is the most common distinction the girls of all backgrounds make between their previous schools and A.H.S.:

MAGDA (LA): Here you could walk out. In the old school you couldn't chew gum, you couldn't hear a walkman, hardly talk, very strict. It's much better here.

CHERYL (AA): . . . It's freedom in this school. My friends are talking about their school like, "well we had to sneak out the back door in order to go to, in order to get this." Oh, we just have to walk out the front door and nobody says nothing. . . . I think all schools should be like this so kids could have more freedom.

BERTA (LA): Over there, they're not really guards, but as soon as they see you, somebody is gonna see you and report you. You go straight to the dean's office. This school has a lot of freedom. Before you gotta raise your hand to go to the bathroom. Here you just walk out.

MARLISSA (LA): I have a lot of freedom here. When I cut out [leave school], they don't call my mother, whatever I do. I could smoke, come in and out any time I want and they got no say in it.

ANTONIA (LA): . . . The freedom is good here, . . . ten or twenty minutes free before class starts, and being able to walk outside. And smoking, which I don't do.

DEBBIE (WH): It's better here because like over there they treat you like you're in jail. There's like five guards sitting there in the morning. Then in the afternoon, they're all walking around the school and everything. You can't even go in the yard.

Moreover, for many girls, freedom is akin to feeling more "grown-up" or being treated like an adult:

JEANNETTE (WH): In junior high school, they didn't give you any freedom. You were like a baby locked behind bars. They wouldn't let you out for lunch or anything.

EMILY (PR): The rules were real different. Like in my junior high school, you weren't allowed to smoke. In A.H.S., you can smoke. In A.H.S., they give you more freedom. They treat you more like an adult.

BARBARA (AA): They don't treat you like kids here. And, you don't have to get on lines, everything and wait for the teacher to take you to lunch or sit in the auditorium or something like that. You don't have to write a pass to go to the bathroom.

DOREEN (WH): . . . Like here you can walk out whenever you want to. There you had to sneak out to go someplace. They treat you more grown up here.

The issue of freedom appears to be uppermost in the girls minds. That they choose this focus indicates the prominence of the school's disciplinary structure in defining their more general school experience. As Wexler (1992) has described, a school's disciplinary apparatus creates a kind of public grid that selects students, labels them negatively or positively, shapes their relationship to schooling, and ultimately contributes to the "production of self" (p. 21). For many of these young women, their relationship to school has largely been felt as one of punishment—feeling enclosed ("they treat[ed] you like you're in jail), spied upon ("someone [was] gonna see you and report you to the dean") or being treated as children ("you were like a baby locked behind bars"). At A.H.S., they experience "freedom," they feel like "adults." Removing symbols and practices perceived by students as repressive has the benefit of diffusing student oppositional behaviors, behaviors that in the past have labeled them "at-risk." At the same time, eliminating such symbols and practices enables students to redefine themselves in relation to school. The interview data above suggest that freedom and adult status are important issues for many of the young women who appear to be in the process of recreating self-images that are positively connected to school. This becomes possible in the absence of a disciplinary structure that brands certain behaviors antischool or oppositional.

While the disciplinary structure of A.H.S. does not appear to differentiate between boys and girls, there is certainly a difference in its relevance and meaning. For boys who have generally enjoyed fewer family restrictions on their mobility and freedom than girls, their freedom of movement during the school day is quite consistent with their out-of-school lives. Girls, on the other hand, have a long history of restricted mobility and constrained freedom. Sharpe (1987) explains that for white working-class girls, their restriction was accompanied by a concern for "respectability"—"respectable" families did not let their daughters wander the streets (p. 213). In a related way, as we saw in chapter 6, Latina daughters are closely monitored in their movements because of the notion that a girls' sexuality is in a sense "owned" by males and tied to the honor of the family. Girls are also constrained by parents' fears for their safety at night and their fears about male violence. Sharpe also highlights other ways in which freedom has been constrained for young girls. For example, there is little encouragement for women's desires for exploration and adventure, and girls' upbringing does not allow them to develop much confidence in fulfilling these desires (p. 213).

The ability to adapt to the various kinds of freedoms in place at A.H.S. is fundamental to the young women's academic survival. Indeed, the school attempts to foster an ideological link between the ability to discipline oneself and academic achievement. As we will see in the next chapter, a student's behavior and academic performance are criteria for being placed in an (unpaid) work internship. According to the rationale of the internship program, unacceptable school behavior (the inability to regulate oneself) and poor academic performance can therefore jeopardize a student's future chances in the labor market by preventing her from obtaining valuable work experience. Below several of the young women express their belief that too much freedom can have deleterious effects on their academic achievement:

> AUREA (PR): I liked the last school better because it was stricter and it made me learn more. This school, you don't want to go to class? It's like telling me, you don't want to go, don't go. The last school was like, you have to go.
>
> JW: Why did you come to A.H.S.?
>
> AUREA: I was getting in trouble at my old school and I didn't want so many strict rules 'cause I don't like discipline that much. But I think I would have done better in a school that was strict.
>
> CLARICE (PR): At the beginning, I really liked this school, but now I'm at the bottom [failing]. There's too much freedom here, which is good if you can handle it, but I just end up bugging out.
>
> JW: What kind of freedom do you mean?
>
> CLARICE: Well, like they give you a lunch break and you can just hang out in the cafeteria and smoke. But I don't like the freedom.
>
> LUCY (LA): . . . Here it's mostly liberty. They give you the liberty to do everything you want here, but you're not allowed to take so much advantage of it. Then you're gonna mess up in your classes and everything. Then you're the one that's gonna suffer later on in life.

Here we can sense the dissonance these girls experience in adapting to a different disciplinary code. Their struggle with "freedom" is also germane to their role as Latina daughters, subject to parental constraints on their social lives. Noteworthy is Lucy's remark in which she links classroom performance and future life chances, a remark that reflects the school's attempt to foster an ideology of independence. The young women above, in critiquing the degree of independence expected, may also be voicing their discomfort at being positioned within contradictory sets of expectations.

Some of the teachers concurred with the students' assessment that lack of academic success can be attributed to the girls' inability to "discipline" themselves.

> Some of the girls can't deal with the freedom and lack of structure. They don't know how to discipline themselves.

It doesn't work for everybody. Some [of the young women] do need a more rigid atmosphere. They're not used to the freedom.

Her [referring to a girl who transferred out of A.H.S.] mother said it was too free. She said so herself that it was too free an atmosphere and she needed to be locked in and she wanted a prison.

[The girls who are not achieving] seem to be the girls who found our school to be confusing in some way and [are] mostly the ones who were unable to handle the degree of freedom and their mothers caught on and took them out. They were cutting and cutting and cutting.

TEACHERS AND STUDENTS

As Lois Weis (1990) has pointed out in *Working Class Without Work*, the teaching force helps to shape student identity in various ways. For example, the white working-class males, unlike those in other studies, expressed the value of gaining an education and mostly conformed to the norms of the school although their academic effort was minimal. Weis suggests that this response is shaped in part by teachers who articulate the instrumental importance of a high school degree over the substance and content of learning.

In this section, I will briefly focus on teachers' experiences inside the school which, in turn, appear to contribute to the shaping of young women's identities.

It is well documented that today, in most working-class and urban schools, teachers' sense of empowerment and optimism for the future are in serious decline. Despite the movement for teacher professionalism during the 1980s, many teachers now feel stymied in their attempts to "reach" kids. Teachers' lack of involvement with school policy decisions, their lack of control over their labor processes by rationalized administrative structures, the lack of occupational mobility—all contribute to the "disempowerment" felt by teachers (Fine, 1991). As Giroux warns, teachers lose their effectiveness with students when they do not feel respected by their administration or influential in their schools (1983). Wexler's portrait of a working-class school paints a dismal picture of the erosion of student-teacher relations. In Fine's (1991) ethnographic account of an urban school, she hears a popular refrain from teachers and staff that "nobody's listening to me," and she documents a pervasive and demoralized attitude among teachers. It is not surprising that troubled student-teacher relationships and a demoralized staff typify schools in which students feel that their faculty don't care about their well-being (McNeil, 1981). More to the point is Fine's findings (1991) that a significant relationship was found between educators who feel disempowered: "No one around here listens to me" and "School policy doesn't reflect what I think"; and those who disparaged students: "These students are bad kids" and "These students can't be helped." Fine suggests that empowered teachers may be more likely to view students holistically, optimistically, and compassionately, while disempowered teachers may be more likely to disparage, discredit, and further disempower their students. Moreover, she argues that teachers who feel they don't have a voice in the school's operations and policies may also be more likely to be strictly controlling, relying heavily on lectures, and encouraging students to remain passive.

That teachers felt relatively "empowered," viewed their students optimistically, and that students felt teachers cared about them were certainly in evidence at A.H.S. Wexler (1992) claims that "the pedagogic relation, the interaction between teacher and student, is the quintessential social relation. When this breaks down, it is a reinforcing relation of failure and withdrawal" (p. 32). Foley (1982) also documents in her research on alternative school students that the most salient difference between persisters' and dropouts' descriptions of their alternative school experience lies in the quality of their social relations. Foley also shows that exemplary teaching-learning relationships appeared to be an outgrowth of, among other things, diversification of teachers' roles to allow for more managerial participation, cooperative curriculum development, and built-in opportunities for teachers to counsel students.

Teachers at A.H.S. believe strongly that they have control over their own teaching practices, a belief reflected in some of their comments below:

> I particularly like having the flexibility and freedom to design my own class and to feel like I have control over my environment. . . . I like the idea that I don't have to do the same thing every year. No one is asking me, no one is demanding that I do the same thing and I can take chances. I can experiment and grow.

> The administration is very supportive, even given the political differences I have with them from time to time. I think in general they are supportive and they encourage creativity. . . . I like the administration, their flexibility in the sense of I get a class to teach and I know what the curriculum is, I know what needs to be learned, but I can do it any way I want to with any materials that I want to that are available and in my own style. I don't have to follow anything lesson plan by lesson plan which I just couldn't do. Realistically, you have a lot of room to be creative and you are supported.

> I think there's a tremendous amount of room to develop your own ideas and support.

I've had a free hand in pretty much everything I've done.

I have that ability here to create and to do things in my own way.

Clearly, these teachers feel empowered, deriving a sense of control not from the exercise of discipline but from the creativity, flexibility, and freedom this school supports. In reviewing field notes of my classroom observations during this year, I found that these teachers did indeed seem to hold high expectations that their students would pursue higher education. One teacher explained why she wanted to teach at A.H.S.:

> I like that A.H.S. is on a college campus. To me that seemed to be a very good idea for the kids who were bright, but nowhere, in no other school in their life, would they have a lot of influence to pursue college or an education.

During my first classroom observation, the teacher (female) asked me to tell the class about myself:

> Arlene asked me to put a few words on the board about myself. She explained that I was doing the highest degree (Ph.D.) and turned it into a mini-lesson on college degrees. She said, "here's a young woman, going to school for a doctorate, it's possible for you, too." (Field notes, 10/24)

Throughout the year, teachers routinely made references to the students about attending college, such as "You kids are gonna be in college some day"; "This is a skill that if you latch onto now, it will make college easier"; "The best model for learning is self-teaching and if you master it, you'll do fine in college." A teacher explained:

> The one nice thing about these kids, they all could see the possibility of passing, something I like to see. I like to have the kids feel that I can pass in class and once they knew [they] could pass this class, and really want to, then staying within the pale of possibilities in not getting completely put out, going to college. (Field notes, 10/24)

I do not mean to suggest here that teachers' expectations about students profoundly affect student behavior or mold or shape students' self-images simply because teachers believe one thing or another about them. Indeed, as previous research has shown (e.g., Fordham, 1988; Fuller, 1980; Mac An Ghaill, 1988; Mirza, 1992; Raissiquier, 1994), many working-class youth and youth of color do persist until graduation, despite their daily encounters with racism, sexism, and unequal class relations within the school, in order to use their secondary education to gain the credentials that might secure social mobility and economic well-being. But, given these girls' previous educational disengagement from the schooling process, obtaining a high school degree, let alone attending college, would most likely not have been options had they continued within a traditional educational system. What I am suggesting is that at an institutional level, the structure and functioning of the school have created conditions which provide students with opportunities to develop a sense of belonging to the school. A.H.S. is a place where teacher-student relations can and are expected to flourish. The young women clearly responded to this:

> CLARICE (PR): The teachers are nice here and you don't have to call somebody Miss so and so.

> TONI (LA): They treat you over here nicer. They listen to you and they help.

> CHRIS (WH): The teachers, they're more involved with you. There, they said they care but they didn't really. They're more open with you here. I like that.

> CAROLINA (LA): The teachers are nicer here. You know, like they are closer to the students, they understand you better.

> MARISOL (LA): Everybody cares, if you go to class they help you out with your problems and they really help.

> TINA (LA): They there for you. They listen, when you have a problem. And they keep on, 'cause you know, I wasn't coming and she [teacher] was, you know, she listened to me.

The point here is that in the absence of positive teacher expectations or "caring" relationships between teachers and students (in which pedagogic relations flounder) it is much more difficult for young women (and young men) to engage themselves in the schooling process and as such, use school as a tool in shaping their futures. As Ellsworth (1993) found in her research on high school dropouts, "a frequent criticism from many dropouts was a seeming lack of caring among teachers, administrators and counselors" (p. 264). The girls' comments above illustrate how the school provides opportunities for students to develop attachments with school adults who may ultimately see them through their high school years.

CONCLUSION

It was the purpose of this chapter to outline the salient features of A.H.S. that appear to impact on the girls' decisions to give schooling another try despite their negative past experiences. What I have tried to show here is that through the very act of attending A.H.S., the young women appear to be invested in obtaining educational qualifications. However, it was apparent from the interviews presented that Latina and African American young women, more so than the young white women, perceive A.H.S. as a school that, according to their specific rationale, will ultimately assist them in securing upward mobility.

I have also tried to show how the school attempts to promote certain behaviors (independence and self-control) in order to eliminate a disciplinary structure that negatively defines students' relationships to school. This cooperative environment enables young women to renegotiate their relationships to schooling and ultimately enables them to persist in school. And, finally, I have tried to illustrate that through the school's governance structure, which accords classroom autonomy to teachers, teachers feel empowered and view their students optimistically.

In the next chapter, I analyze aspects of the curricular form and content that may shed light on the role classroom knowledge plays in accounting for the kinds of identities outlined earlier.

CHAPTER 8

The Formal Curriculum

INTRODUCTION

In this chapter, I address the formal curriculum at A.H.S. Using Bernstein's (1975) framework of invisible pedagogy, I examine how both the pedagogical relationship, and the curriculum's form and content can produce changes in the way female student identities are constructed and shaped within school.

In particular I argue that through classroom practices and curricular knowledge young women

1. Learn skills that will benefit them in both their future workplaces and homes.

2. Are encouraged to work with peers collectively, which may later translate into future collectivistic struggle on behalf of women's interests, and heightened awareness of the value of women's autonomy, interdependence, and community.

3. Are exposed to curricular knowledge that promotes a critical understanding of the world and of young women's social positioning within it.

In addition, I suggest that the centrality of career education at A.H.S. underscores a serious concern for women's future employment; this emphasis and awareness importantly contribute to these young women's emergent identities.

I also consider how the school's curriculum addresses the needs, problems, and aspirations expressed by many of the Latina and African American girls, especially with regard to their future economic roles and their social status in a male-dominated culture. For white girls, however, the material in the classroom seems less pertinent to the future identities they envision.

BERNSTEIN'S THEORY OF PEDAGOGIC PRACTICE

Bernstein's (1975) analysis of the "microprocesses" of schooling—and how they relate to the social structure—is constructed around what he called the three-message systems in education—curriculum, pedagogy, and evaluation. Central to these message systems are the concepts of classification and framing.

Classification refers to the relationships between contents (areas of knowledge and subjects) and specifically refers to the "degree of boundary maintenance between contents" (p. 88). Strong classification refers to a curriculum that is highly differentiated and separated into traditional subjects; weak classification refers to a curriculum that is integrated in its contents and where the boundaries between subjects are "fragile" or less rigid. The concept of frame refers to the "context in which knowledge is transmitted and received"—in other words, the pedagogical relationship between teacher and taught. More specifically, framing gauges "the degree of control teacher and pupil possess over the selection, organization, pacing and timing of the knowledge transmitted and received in the pedagogic relationship" (p. 89). Strong framing occurs when there is a limited number of options available to teachers and students; weak framing implies more freedom (Sadovnik, 1995, p. 10). As Atkinson (1985) points out, framing also concerns the degree of insulation between what is defined as 'proper' educational knowledge and everyday common knowledge (p. 136).

For Bernstein, pedagogic practices can be viewed as class-related and class-based. He draws upon a distinction between invisible and visible pedagogies: invisible pedagogies are weakly classified and weakly framed, while visible pedagogies are strongly classified and strongly framed. Bernstein argues that invisible pedagogies are often found in schools with middle and upper class student populations whereas visible pedagogies are characteristic of schools with working-class populations.[1] To translate into a familiar American distinction, invisible pedagogies may be understood as "progressive" education and visible pedagogies as more conservative or traditional (Sadovnik, 1995).

Bernstein is careful to point out that unless certain conditions are met, both invisible and visible pedagogies may produce similar unequal outcomes, especially in the reproduction of power and symbolic control.[2] It is only when pedagogic practices seek to produce changes between groups rather than within individuals that educational practices can be transformative.

Alternative High School, with a predominantly African American and Latino poor and working-class population, has been established along the lines of invisible pedagogy. The success that A.H.S. has achieved suggests that invisible pedagogies do not work only with middle- and upper-class children. This matter calls out for further research, though it is beyond the scope of this study. My immediate and more spe-

cific concern is to examine how an alternative or invisible pedagogy contributes a change in the construction of how young working-class
women's identities are constructed and reconstructed in school.

TEACHERS, STUDENTS, AND CLASSROOM CONTROL

It was not difficult to recognize the "invisible pedagogical model" in
place in the two classrooms I observed.[3] Teachers and students stayed
together for two cycles. What follows is based on classroom observations of two "core" classes over two cycles.[4] One class consisted of a
white female/male teaching team and fifteen girls (seven Latinas, four
whites, two African Americans, and two Asians) and fourteen boys
(seven whites, six Latinos, one African American, and one Asian). An
African American female and white male comprised another team that
taught twenty-one girls (thirteen Latinas, six whites, and two African
Americans) and fourteen boys (seven whites, five Latinas, and one
African American).

Individual classroom practices and protocols reflect the hospitable
and innovative organization that characterize A.H.S. as a whole.[5] Just as
vertical relations of formal authority play a diminished role in exchanges
between administrators and teachers at A.H.S. (there are, for example,
no academic departments or deans), so too between teachers and students.[6] By changing the hierarchical structure of educational relations,
the school teaches students, in the course of their day-to-day dealings
with teachers and administrators, that power relations are neither natural nor inevitable; they learn, rather that the structure of authority is
negotiable (Anyon, 1981).

In contrast to the pedagogical arrangements at more conventional
schools, teacher control in these two classrooms was usually much more
a matter of discussion and negotiation between student and teacher than
teachers simply wielding power as amply illustrated in both Anyon and
Weis in their descriptions of working-class schooling.[7] For girls whose
previous experience of school was largely one of conflict, this model of
implicit teacher control has significance. In the previous chapter, I
described how girls resisted authority with strategies that were ultimately self-defeating (resulting in suspensions, course failures, etc.). At
A.H.S., students find that authority is not absolute or natural, but subject to negotiation. Such a lesson may later yield useful applications,
both at work, in dealing with bosses, and at home in negotiating a more
equitable division of labor with one's mate.

In the following, I describe what this implicit classroom control
looks like in practice.

Because classroom instruction centered in cooperative learning (discussed later), individual desks were replaced with rectangular or round tables. Teachers' desks, used generally for storage, were shoved in corners. Boys and girls arrived for class wearing Walkmen and often bringing food and drinks. Teachers themselves often had snacks. (Occasionally students not assigned to the particular class came and were allowed to stay.) Such a convivial atmosphere could be thought to represent an idiosyncratic instance of teacher indulgence, but this would be to misconstrue what has been, to a significant extent, consciously engineered. This classroom atmosphere reflects the teachers' belief that, in the absence of explicit teacher control over students' movements and activities (talking, eating, etc.), students will be more motivated to work and less likely to challenge teachers. As Arlene, one of the teachers put it, "Tony [her co-teacher] and I never cared about having a quiet class. We were more interested in finding the best ways kids learn."

Because of the seating pattern and nature of cooperative learning (described in the next section), communication between students was an accepted part of classroom routine and students could generally interact at will. Students moving around the classroom and students speaking to each other were regarded as not only acceptable but necessary. Such tolerance is characteristic of invisible pedagogy and encourages students to regulate their own movements and social relationships. I observed many occasions when girls and boys appeared to regulate their own time by arriving late to class or leaving early, usually without demur from the teachers:

> Clarice and Betty walked in at 10:10, forty minutes late. (Field note, 11/9)

> Saw Jackie and Betty in the hallway during class right before I went in. They showed up thirty minutes late and then both left before the period ended. (Field note, 12/8)

> Cheryl walked in at 10:00 (thirty minutes late). Then she left and came back again. She stayed until 10:45 and walked out again. (Field note, 1/19)

> I noticed Jackie waiting outside the door for Walter (in class). He got up, said he was going to the bathroom. (. . .) Ken also walked in halfway through the class. He went over to the group of four guys, played with one by wrapping the sweatshirt around his neck, then sat down. About ten minutes later Ken stood up, asked to borrow fifty cents from Walter and left saying, "I'm going on my lunchbreak." (Field note, 5/18)

Increased student interaction meant, of course, higher levels of noise. While noise was an acceptable part of classroom behavior, teachers tried to control excessive noise, employing various strategies, sometimes as simple as a "silence sign" (a two-finger peace sign), but very rarely issuing direct orders.

Team teaching carried with it a degree of observability (of students' activities) not enjoyed by a single teacher in the classroom. Teachers routinely roamed around the classroom, sometimes one teacher sitting the whole period with one group of students, while the other moved from table to table. Tony's comment below illustrates the increased level of control facilitated by moving about:

> TONY· I feel the best way to deal with these kids in the classroom is to not pull the schoolteacher game. You know, I never, I myself never liked a teacher who sat back of the desk and said, "Here, Jeanne [observer], you come up to the desk." I like fooling around and moving around class. I actually think I have more control when I move around. (Field note, 11/9)

At the beginning of the class each day, teachers wrote the classroom agenda on the board. Students always knew the class content for the day, but the order of activities on the agenda often changed according to student interest. Sometimes, alternative assignments were negotiated with students, as the following field note describes:

> Teacher explains to Liza that she won't receive credit for the class unless she hands in her missing essay assignments. Liza explains that she doesn't like to write, it is easier for her to draw her dreams than to write about them. (The series of essays centered around dreams.) A compromise was reached where the teacher agreed to accept a series of drawings but Liza had to provide brief written descriptions of the drawings. (Field note, 1/26)

I observed other instances where students were able to secure for themselves more favorable outcomes, for example on tests:

> There was test today with five separate skill areas. Subject covered Latin America. One section asked students to write short answers. Ramona called Tony over and explained she was having some difficulty and asked Tony whether she could write the answers in Spanish. Tony responded, "Sure, anything that shows me you know what you're talking about." (Field note, 1/16)

These weakly framed authority relations helped students learn alternative ways of relating to teachers that were not counterproductive (as many oppositional strategies can be). Young women may be able to draw on these lessons in the future in their negotiations for better working conditions or for more egalitarian domestic responsibilities. More immediately, the classroom "ethos," both friendly and permissive, fostered a recognition that learning need not be a highly routinized, strictly regulated process.

COOPERATIVE LEARNING

There is evidence to suggest that a classroom structure based on individualism and competition may be detrimental to young women's academic achievement (Fine and Zane, 1989). Girls perform better and are more engaged in tasks that require cooperative learning. However, collectivity or collaboration in the classroom can also encourage the development of a collective identity. Learning to depend on group members for success can teach girls the value of concerted action, of particular importance should they join in collective struggle against oppressive work conditions or male dominance. We saw in previous chapters that many of the young women's identities, particularly Latinas and African Americans, suggest "a moment of critique" (Weis, 1990) that could at some point be linked to a broader struggle. But unless young women develop a consciousness that these are shared issues and unless they have the skills to organize, their individual solutions may in the end work against them (a point to which I return in the conclusion).

At the beginning of the year, according to my field notes, there was strict adherence to a cooperative classroom structure centered in groups. Each group was composed of a manager, recorder or secretary, interpreter, and occasional floaters (those who joined different groups for various reasons). Teachers generally started off a class by directing managers to get their groups' work folders. Groups, however, shifted a great deal in response to changes in friendship alliances or student absences. By the second cycle, despite the clear intention of the teachers to foster a cooperative environment, the model proved extremely vulnerable to racial conflict introduced into the classroom by several white working-class boys and girls. As a teacher explains:

> TONY: We gave up on the group because of group conflicts. They [students] brought in a very high percentage of racial prejudice, higher than I've seen before. There was just too much violence going on in the groups. (Field note, 1/26)

Groups also broke up under the pressures of individualism:

> We used groups a lot less the second time than we did the first time. I think that what we came to realize is that these kids needed not just to

have allegiance as a group, they had that, but in some groups that wasn't working as well in terms of kids who were doing individual work. . . . Debbie (WH) and the others in that group never pooled their efforts in terms of work, ever. They talked and blabbered and finally I split them up because I saw they weren't really dependent on each other in terms of work, but each one did his own, each one was responsible for his own. (Field note, 1/26)

We see here the difficulty for many students in adapting to a different educational code, one emphasizing collective development rather than the individualism and competition characteristic of more traditional modes of schooling.

Although most groups broke up, teachers nevertheless organized their classes around cooperative task structures. Typical assignments required students to work in pairs or threesomes. For example, a work task might go as follows:

In groups of three work on the answer sheet. Put your name on your paper with a star and then write down the names of two people you are working with. All three of you must have the same answer for each question, so be sure to discuss your answers and come up with the best answer. You will all receive the same grade.

Here we see the deployment of cooperative incentive structures, where grades depend upon the performance of their group (Slavin, 1985).

The altered social organization of learning, stressing cooperation instead of individualism and competition, seemed to benefit a group of six or seven girls (white, Latina, and African American). Over the first and second cycles, they formed a relatively unchanging and cohesive group. While not necessarily friends outside of class, the girls attended class regularly, engaged in classroom activities, and generally performed well academically. The following field note illustrates how teachers provided a "safe space" for this group to work through a conflict:

When I entered class after the break, the girls in the "girls' group" were holding a serious discussion. No other students were allowed in the room. Something about C's sister getting mugged and the guy held a screwdriver to her throat. Discussion was about Y telling everyone about the incident, C feeling that this was family problems and shouldn't be discussed with everyone. She was furious with Y. The whole group was involved in expressing their feelings of sympathy for C's sister and whether or not Y had a right to tell others. I made a move to leave the room out of respect, realizing that no one else was being allowed in the room. C told me to stay. Teachers were on the other side of the room talking quietly with each other. (Field note, 11/29)

The teachers here deliberately structured the situation to allow the girls to attempt to resolve the conflict themselves. This particular incident also afforded an opportunity for the girls to discuss a socially significant issue, namely violence against women. The fact that no other students were allowed in the room underscored the importance the teachers assigned to the situation. In an exploration of how a small group of young women of different ethnic/racial and class backgrounds discuss, understand and negotiate "difference," MacPherson and Fine (1995) cite the critical need for creating safe spaces for female adolescents to "'play with' notions of gender, race and sexuality, to try on ideas, test themselves and each other, without suffering the more typical silencing of women's talk" (p. 183). Moreover, by having so structured a space in which to safely congregate, the girls had a chance to *collectively* engage in discussion in order to hash out a problem.

Despite the breakup of the group-centered classroom discussed above (except for the one group of girls just mentioned), cooperation was often conspicuous and seemed especially to benefit several Latina students. For example, I observed one girl who often appeared to be teaching the other girls around her. I commented on this to the teacher, who concurred:

> She, left to herself, would very frequently say, "I don't know what's going on." Yet when she was in a teaching situation, she always made sure that she understood and she would extend herself to not only do her work, but she would do Evette's work, and pretty soon the others [girls] started coming to her for help. (Field note, 1/19)

Reorganizing the scene of instruction from a structure of individualism and competition to one of cooperation appeared to benefit many of the girls in the classroom. The academic ability of the girl above was reinforced through tutoring her peers. This group of girls developed a peer culture that not only redounded to their academic advantage, but also represented a "safe space," granted legitimacy by the teachers, where they could voice concerns and work out serious conflicts arising in their lives. Such opportunities that foster collectivistic values and solutions may, in the long run, lead the girls to seek out more collective strategies for dealing with oppressive forces in the workplace or stressful experiences in the home. As one teacher put it, "when they rebel against us [teachers] *as a group*, that's great, we've done our job" (emphasis mine).

THE CURRICULUM

In this section, I explore classroom knowledge and speculate on the impact such knowledge has on the development of girls' identities as outlined in previous chapters.

Fine's (1989) concept of "silencing practices" in low-income urban public schools is useful in framing the following discussion of classroom curriculum. Silencing refers to "what doesn't get talked about in schools: how 'undesirable talk' by students, teachers, parents, and community members is subverted, appropriated, and exported, and how educational policies and procedures obscure the very social, economic and therefore experiential conditions of students' daily lives while they expel critical 'talk' about these conditions from written, oral, and nonverbal expression" (p. 153). Silencing then keeps intact the ideologies of equal opportunity and outcomes of schooling, while at the same time obscures the unequal distribution of resources and outcomes in society. This discrepancy between ideology and the actual material conditions of low-income students' lives characterizes low-income urban schooling. Students understand that such schooling neither provides them with an understanding of the social system and their place within it nor guarantees them commensurate returns for their educational degree as it usually does for members of the white middle and upper classes.

One of the most outstanding features of the A.H.S. core curriculum for ninth-grade students was its incorporating and accentuating the personal, social, and cultural histories of most of the students. African, Asian, and South and Central American histories, as well as these regions' contemporary relationships with the United States were examined through the lens of a critique of colonialism and imperialism, especially as represented in literature by members of the subordinated groups in question. As one teacher told the class, "We're only teaching from the point of view of the society we're teaching about. That means we read what people have to say about themselves" (from Field note, 10/19). The entire course was created by the teachers themselves, who used original handouts, school texts, various original works of literature, and student journals. Moreover, the subject matter cut across disciplines (geography, literature, history, science, etc.). In Bernstein's terms, classroom knowledge was weakly classified, with weak boundaries between subject contents, with an emphasis on everyday knowledge. Dependence on textbooks as authoritative sources of knowledge was minimized and student discussion was common and encouraged.

In presenting my data on classroom observations, I describe and analyze the kinds of topics, assignments, and discussions that took place in relation to the geographic region under study (i.e., Africa, Asia, South and Central Americas).

In both classrooms, teachers emphasized the primacy of students' personal knowledge and experiences, thus legitimating what students know and bring with them to the classroom. For example, at the beginning of the school year, all students were required to write their own life histories and make brief presentations to the class. In addition, students kept journals throughout the two cycles, recording their impressions and reactions to readings or class discussion; the journals were routinely collected by the teachers for grading.[8]

Each of the geographic areas was studied chronologically, from ancient history to colonial history to contemporary society and relations with the United States. In the following, I will highlight some of the patterns and practices characteristic of this school's alternative approach to pedagogy. I will begin with Africa, which was studied through a serial presentation of the historical themes of ancient greatness, slavery, colonialism, imperialism, independence struggle, and revolution.

During the study of ancient Egyptian civilization, which featured drawings of maps of cities and pyramids, students were asked to draw maps of their own homes, neighborhoods, and routes between home and school and present their own oral histories. Some homework assignments also called for interviewing family members to create life histories.

In the students' study of early African tribal and ethnic groups, teachers organized a video assignment. In groups, students researched and prepared reports on various African tribes and ethnic groups complete with maps and illustrations for a video presentation. Two students from each group sat on stools and a third filmed their presentation using a video camera. Although the experience was fraught with minor complications such as giggling, teasing from audience, and so on, the point was that students were provided opportunities to practice presentations of themselves and to manage situations (setting up, operating, and directing the video filming) where they were expected to be in charge. This sort of assignment offers a vivid contrast to what goes on in conventional working-class schools where students rarely have opportunities to actively learn how to manage situations, but instead are passively trained through tasks requiring and reinforcing skills like those needed for highly routinized working-class jobs (Anyon, 1981). In this classroom, students engaged in a range of activities where they controlled the conditions of their learning. In Anyon's framework, these skills (learning to present oneself, managing situations, self-directed research, etc.) closely resemble those skills needed for managerial or higher-status jobs.

The theme of slavery was initiated by reading an account by a young African who was kidnapped and sold into slavery. Students also read excerpts from the autobiography of the ex-slave and abolitionist Frederick Douglas; and they viewed parts of the movie *Roots*. In one class, students were asked to imagine they were slaves in the American South and to write a story describing their life. Here is an excerpt from a field note of the day these compositions were handed back to the students.

[T]he teaching intern, Charlie (Latino, wearing a black beret, and long lab coat), gave back the compositions. He cited Pam's (white) as being excellent (A+). Other grades were Bs and high Bs. Charlie talked about his impressions of their papers, making the point that many of them wrote as if being a slave was a bad, shit job when, as slaves they had no choice, they couldn't just find another "job." He talked about how it must have felt being forced away from family, put on a dirty stinking ship with starving people, and taken across the ocean to be a slave for some white guy. (The first time I've seen everyone in the classroom be *absolutely quiet*.) He went on to talk about civil rights in the United States, reminded them of the visitor from South Africa who spoke about apartheid and that things in South Africa weren't too different from the United States forty years ago. Still blacks and whites live apart from each other here, blacks are still discriminated against here. (Cheryl [African American] yells out, "Black people go to white neighborhoods and they get beat up.") Then he talked about Martin Luther King and asked Cheryl who he was. She says, "he was a man who died because he believed and fought for civil rights of BLACK people." (Field note, 11/23)

The teaching intern was able to link the historical circumstances of African Americans in this country with present-day inequality, and further drew a comparison to South Africa, thus linking similar struggles. At the same time, he was able to give voice to the experience of racism as expressed by Cheryl, and in the process affirm her personal history as an African American girl. Throughout the year, students were routinely provided with and encouraged to participate in such discussions, which shed critical light on the situation of dominated groups in the world, and brought to the surface various social struggles.

Another assignment centered on Leopold Senghor's poem, "Paris in the Snow." Background information about Senghor was provided and students were asked a number of questions about the poem; finally they were asked to write a poem expressing their feelings about slavery, and to present the poem to the class. In another assignment, students were asked to compare the text version of slavery, the TV version of *Roots*, the poem of Senghor, and the narrative by an African boy sold into slavery; and then discuss which rendition of the horror of slavery was the clearest. These exercises illustrate how students were taught to take into account a variety of sources and thereby actively construct their own interpretations rather than rely on a single "authority."

While studying colonialism and imperialism in Africa, both classes undertook a case study on Nigeria and its struggle for independence from Britain. In groups, students took on the roles of geographer, demographer, labor organizer, politician, and town planner in planning an independent Nigeria and answered various questions. They next studied the Biafran civil war, using Chinua Achebe's *Girls at War*.

As alluded to earlier, South Africa was also accorded significant time in the syllabus on Africa. Students read such works as *Kaffir Boy* by Mark Magubane, *Master Harold and the Boys* by Athol Fugard, and also watched the film *Cry Freedom*. A black South African visited both classes and discussed the structure of apartheid and its effects on the day-to-day lives of black people. Sitting in on both talks, I was impressed at the level of interest and personal involvement displayed by the students in their discussion. They were especially intrigued by matters concerning racial classification (i.e., white, Indian, "so-called Coloured"[9] or African); they wondered how they themselves would be classified. For example, several Latino boys asked if they would be classified as white or Coloured. A white male student (of Italian descent) argued that he shouldn't be classified white because he is Sicilian and "Sicily is an island where Africans came as slaves, so the people there have African blood." A white girl repeatedly asked questions about the Group Areas Act, which prohibited people of different racial groups from living in the same areas, finally asking, "If my husband was Puerto Rican and we had a baby, you mean he couldn't live with me?" An African American boy (who otherwise never spoke in class) asked such questions as, "Can a black policeman arrest a white person?" (No, usually black police are not in white areas), "Do black people carry guns?" (No, it's against the law; the government doesn't want blacks armed), and "Do blacks wear gold?" (No, they mine it but are usually too poor to buy it). Deciding he'd heard enough, this boy yelled out, "Dag, I wouldn't live there, I'd move as far away as I could get." The speaker replied, "Well, if it's your home, your country, why should you move? There're millions of blacks struggling now against the government." This led into a discussion about the African National Congress and the struggle against apartheid.

The themes of collective struggle and revolution recurred throughout the course. These themes were complemented by a cooperative learning pedagogy aimed at empowering students by encouraging cooperative, rather than individualistic and competitive behaviors. For example, during a class on Pan-Africanism, the students were given a copy of a speech made by Ngugi Wa Thiong'o in 1969:

> We want to create a revolutionary culture which is not narrowly confined by the limitations of tribal traditions or national boundaries . . . but looks outward to Pan-Africa, the Third World, and the needs of all [persons]. This national, Pan-African awareness must be transformed into a socialist program, or be doomed to sterility and death. Having decided on this, we can then utilize all the resources at our disposal—radio, television, film, schools, universities, youth movements, farmers'

cooperatives—to create such a society. . . . In this way we shall find new strength and a new dynamic . . . any true national culture, which can produce healthy, stubborn youths . . . such a culture will be best placed to contribute to the modern world.

As the students read the speech together and came to the part about the stubborn youths, the whole class exploded. Students started yelling, "That's us" and "Yeah, stubborn youths."

Shortly thereafter, students viewed a videotape about Africa, which took a look at most of its countries and interviewed a number of leaders and citizens. Each learning group had been assigned to draw a map of a particular country[10] and, during this film, they were to take notes on that country. A field note about this part of the class reads:

Video set up in front of class. Lights kept on during film. Arlene kept reminding each group to pay attention. Class was extremely loud, lots of commotion especially at the table in front of me—spitballs, balled-up paper, pens being thrown around by girls and boys. Settled down eventually. At beginning of video, not many paying attention. Barbara and Saundria (both African American) painting their nails. Emily and Delores (Latina) had their heads down, Linda (white) sat with her chair turned around, rest were drifting in and out of attention, chatting in low voices. Table of all girls (Jeannette, etc.) seemed to be watching and taking notes. Those closest to video seemed least disturbed. Teachers kept reminding students to take notes. When segment on Mozambique came on, teachers told everyone to pay special attention. The narrator was describing how farmwomen had organized a cooperative with no men involved. The women grew what produce they could and sold it in the city. At this point, the teacher stopped the film. He asked what these farming women had done. Someone called out "a cooperative." Teacher wrote the word cooperative on the board and asked what it meant. A few students said things like apartments. Teacher wrote on board "cooperative = a form of communism." Teacher then asked why this kind of cooperative could not occur in South Africa. Class started shouting out answers and finally came to conclusions that (1) blacks cannot own property, so therefore they wouldn't be free to do this; and (2) women were not allowed to work independent of men. Teacher went over this several times, said he was going to quiz them on this. After about the fourth time, kids started raising their hands and giving their own versions of this response. One girl (Latina), who hadn't appeared to be paying attention at all to the discussion, raised her hand and said, "This couldn't happen in South Africa because of apartheid and sexism!" (Field note, 11/16)

I include so much of this field note to impart some sense of the classroom dynamics, in this case involving a good deal of resistance or opposition from the girls. Most noteworthy, I think, is the demonstration that the "progressive" nature of the curriculum and the "relevance" of its topics do not guarantee that the students interpret them as such. As Cornbleth (1990) points out, a curriculum is a contextualized social process. Curricular knowledge is not simply presented to students who then internalize it and reproduce it on tests. Rather, the curricular process is much more complex. As Weiler (1988) writes, "the classroom is always a site of conflict and contestation, for the teacher trying to create a counter-hegemonic vision as much as for traditional or authoritarian teachers" (p. 120). This is because students are actively involved in creating their own meanings. As the field note describes, many of the girls were involved in resistant or oppositional behavior (throwing spitballs, painting nails, sleeping, etc.). However, when the film focused on women's cooperatives, the teachers insisted on the importance of this particular bit of information—that the women farmers of Mozambique organized themselves into cooperatives, independent of men, and were paid for their labor, thus highlighting women's economic activity and collective struggle.

The topic of revolutionary struggle was also prominent when the class focused on China. During a session on the Cultural Revolution, the teacher read the following poem (again I present the entire field note to illustrate how students actively incorporate, rework or reject classroom knowledge):

> Labor is joy; how joyful is it?
> Bathed in sweat and two handfuls of mud,
> Like sweet rain, my sweat waters the land
> And the land issues scent, better than milk
> Labor is joy; how joyful is it?
> Home from a night attack, hoe in hand,
> The hoe's handle is still warm
> But in bed, the warrior's already snoring. (Chinese poet)

When the teacher finished reading, a girl volunteered to read it again. Most of the class was quiet. The teacher started to ask questions:

TEACHER: Who is this poem about? What is it saying?
GLORIA: They have to work hard to get somewhere, it's about money.
TEACHER: Have you ever been on a farm? The smells on a farm?
Someone yells out: Smells like shit! (*lots of laughing from others*)
TEACHER: What is joyful? Walter?
(Christy is mouthing the word "labor" to Walter)
WALTER: Labor.

TEACHER: Very good, Walter, let's see if you're on a roll. Have any of you gone to bed feeling good?

(*Lots of hollering and laughing from students*)

TEACHER: What's important here? Silkworms, it all requires work.

(*Gina and Antonia walk out of the room*)

(*Charles walks out of the room*)

(*Betty, who is not enrolled in the class, stands in the hall in front of the classroom door. A girl in class says something to her. Betty replies, "Fuck you, bitch, you ain't never gonna be invited to my house."*)

TEACHER: Keep moving, Betty.

(*The teacher then gives a short assignment related to the poem. Gina and Antonia return to class; Jeanette leaves and then comes back.*)

The above highlights how students can inject humor into learning. It also illustrates how students can subvert a lesson (the teacher clearly changed her tack several times). While the underlying message of the poem was not lost on some students, others chose not to participate. The point is, however, that the teacher then continued with an exercise that held a powerful political message and that engaged most of the students. After a brief discussion of Chinese communism, the teacher made two lists on the board: One list was headed *Revolutionary (Communists)* and the other *Counterrevolutionary (Capitalists)*. Both teachers then solicited examples for each column. Students called out words such as, "students," "citizens," "workers," "party members," and, "proletariat" for the revolutionary column. The teachers asked, "Who are revolutionaries here?" Both teachers and several of the girls (mostly from the all girl group) raised their hands. One of the teachers asked, "How would you describe us?" The other teacher wrote on the board "useful," "kind," "loving," "caring," "respected," "intelligent," "freedom loving." Next, in the counterrevolutionary column students supplied words such as "uncivilized," "lazy," "drug dealers," "bosses," "politicians," "industrialists."

These examples illustrate the ideological nature of the curricular messages taught and received in the classroom, particularly when addressing the teaching of communism. In addition, the teachers revealed their own personal political commitment to revolutionary change and allied themselves with students similarly disposed.

I now turn to another discussion on communism but in a different class. The teacher was discussing a story narrated by a Central American Indian whose brother had been kidnapped by the rightist government's special forces to fight against the "guerilla."

TEACHER (*writes on board, "El Salvador"*): Where is it?

KEN: When's the fighting gonna stop there?

TEACHER: They say it won't be over for a while.

KEN: Why are they fighting anyway?

TEACHER: Change, reforms. (*Writes on the board, "Reforms"*) There are different sides. There are people who are happy with the way things are, for example the wealthy, the politicians and those who aren't happy like the poor people, the working people. Has anyone heard of Marxists before?

STEVE: There was a guy named Karl Marx.

TEACHER: His ideas led to communism. His idea is that workers should benefit from their labor. As it is now under capitalism, profits go to owners.

KEN: Why should he care?

TEACHER: If you're a working person you should care. For example, if Jeanne [observer] has a factory and we are workers making jeans, she pays us $10 and sells her jeans for $50.

TIMMY: She makes $40 profit.

TEACHER: That's right, it means we are exploited. We can say to her, you're an outsider, get lost, we want to control things so we get an equal share for our labor.

JEANNE: But I have the capital, I own the factory and the machines.

TEACHER: Yes, she owns the capital, she's the capitalist. She could fire us, but if we have a union she couldn't do it that easily. (Field note, 11/16)

This teacher proceeded to explain the Eastern Airlines strike then going on, describing how the union must negotiate with management. She then asked if any students had parents who were members of unions. The point of this classroom discussion is that inequality under capitalism and collective struggles against that inequality get talked about. Michelle Fine (1987) calls this process "naming." Simply defined, naming is identifying and defining those social and economic relationships that affect students' lives, particularly the inequitable distribution of power and resources.

I also observed occasions where teachers created situations for girls (particularly Latinas) to voice their personal experiences of oppression vis-a-vis gender identity. For example, during the unit on Latin America, teachers handed out copies of a poem entitled "Verses against the Inconsequence of Men's Taste and Strictures" by Sor Juana Ines de la Cruz. There was an English translation as well as the original Spanish version. Several questions were written on the board:

What kind of woman wrote this? How do you know a woman wrote this? What is she talking about? Do you agree with the writer?

Below is the field note describing the discussion:

Several girls with their heads down (two African American, two white), some boys talking, other boys reading and talking, table of girls, all six of them completely engaged in reading the poem, several other girls writing in their notebooks:

Teacher asks for volunteers to read in Spanish. Several girls raise their hands. L reads in Spanish, everyone claps when she finishes. Teachers ask for volunteers to read in English. About twelve hands go up (mostly girls, but a few boys). Tony says E had her hand up first so she can read. C (boy) yells out, "That's discrimination, why should only girls read?" E doesn't want to stand up and read, so M (girl) jumps up—reads with vigor. Whole class is dead silent. Y (girl) jumps up toward the end of the poem, breaks in, and finishes it. Also reads with great vigor. Teacher starts to ask questions. "What kind of woman is this?" Hands shoot up (I've never seen so many raise their hands. Mostly girls, boys are quiet.) Teacher calls on Y:

Y: This woman was used by a man. She wants to get back (*she and E shake hands*).

C (*boy*): Oh shit, oh shit.

M (*girl*): It's about time that women start expressing her feelings.

A (*boy*): This is the kind of woman who spends all her husband's money.

J (*boy*): Some men cause girls to do this.

(*Teacher wanders around class, stops behind A and reads from her notebook. Very strong comment about women always have their pride no matter what men make them do.*)

N (*boy*): A man wrote it.

I (*boy*): She is chauvinistic, she's stupid, one-sided

H (*a girl who had her head down earlier*): I think she was talking to a man. You know when you're talking to your husband, meaning *all* men.

R (*boy*): You're stupid. We're the ones that favor you!

(*Y lets out a huge laugh.*)

L (*girl*): The women are right.

(*Two girls and boy shooting spitballs across the room.*)

E (*boy*): Blame dumb men.

(The noise level starts rising considerably. Teachers tell students to answer questions on board.)

TEACHER: Sor Juana was one of the most brilliant women in Mexico. (Field note, 2/17)

By calling on a girl to read the poem first in Spanish the teacher legitimizes the use of Spanish in the classroom. (To digress a moment, I observed many occasions where the teachers encouraged Spanish, sometimes stumbling to speak Spanish themselves.) Moreover, as the above discussion illustrates, the poem seemed to speak to many of the girls, who visibly declared their alignment with the poet's point of view ("It's about time women started expressing herself" or "This woman was used by a man" and the handshake of solidarity between the two girls) or privately noted down their feelings (Tina's written comment that "women always keep their pride no matter what men make them do"). The passage also highlights the involvement of boys, who expressed resentment and seemed to feel personally under attack. (For example, Angelo's remark that "This is the kind of woman who spends all her husband's money," implies that in exchange for granting sexual favors, women take economic advantage of men.) Unfortunately, the dialogue ended when the teachers announced a written assignment. Clearly, this topic excited a tremendous amount of emotion and interest among both boys and girls, energy that could have been channeled into discussions about male power, sexuality, and equality. Nevertheless, this was an opportunity for the girls to get a hearing. The incident also seemed to signal among the Latina girls an emergent collective gender identity, something I never witnessed among the white or African American young women.

Finally, I would like to comment on the ways in which teachers linked subject matter to students' experiences, a characteristic of weakly classified curricula in which school knowledge and personal knowledge are not rigidly separated. During a Latin America period, for example, the teacher read aloud Garcia Marquez's *Eyes of a Blue Dog*. He introduced the story by saying to the class, "Your relations told you stories so you'd be tougher. They help you be you. Roots give you your identity." As a homework assignment, everyone was required to write down a story told to them by an older family member. Similar assignments, drawing on students' cultures and backgrounds, were common. The students' knowledge and experiences were often validated as "legitimate" input in the classroom—and were referred to in class as "prior knowledge" taken to mean what the students already know and may not even be aware of. As described earlier, another example of an assignment that drew on the students' experience included drawing a map of the route between home and school and reporting on what was seen, an exercise that led into a discussion about homeless people.

This discussion of school knowledge and classroom processes shows how alternative (i.e., invisible) pedagogical practices can encourage the formation of student identity in various ways. The most prominent feature of the classroom curriculum is the opportunity for students to confront their "own history," and thereby attain a critical understanding of the world and their own social positioning in it. Furthermore, respecting students' experience as a source of knowledge helps break down the barriers between formal "educational" knowledge and what Bernstein (1975) calls "everyday community knowledge of teachers and taught" (p. 89). This practice also calls upon students to develop skills that later may prove useful in negotiating better terms for themselves and others in the workplace. Finally, we see how the classroom creates an environment where girls can voice personal concerns and also engage in a collective critique of their gender oppression. In sum, these classroom practices, by stressing negotiation, collective development, and a sense of one's own history, may foster the development of a shared gender identity for young women of different backgrounds.

CAREER EDUCATION

In this final section, I briefly look at the potential influence of the school's career education program on emergent female identities. I suggest that the central position of the career education program[11] within the school curriculum underlines the seriousness accorded paid work as an element in the girls' future and as a source for their present self-definition.

The role of career education (and vocational programs) on the shaping of identity has been debated. For example, Willis (1977) criticizes those who suggest that career agencies (a form of career counseling and training) in school play a significant part in influencing young people's careers. As he explains,

> although the teacher's notion of the continuity between school and work is rejected by the "lads"; another kind of continuity is profoundly important to them. In terms of actual job choice it is the "lad's" culture and not official careers' materials which provide the most influential guides for the future. (p. 95)

Contrary to Willis's findings, many of the young women in this study, rather than creating and participating in a peer culture that reproduces their subordinate class, gender, and racial/ethnic locations, seem to be involved in a schooling process that will ultimately assist them in securing an economic future.

However, the contradictions that exist within the career education program are many, and mean that the outcomes for the girls are not "fixed." The program reflects an ideology that (too simply) assumes people can secure the job of their choice by demonstrating the requisite abilities. This assumption on the other hand, is challenged by a labor market where job "choices" are increasingly limited. This program, indeed like most career education programs, assumes that the labor market is relatively static and that one's occupational position is solely or primarily a matter of individual "choice." Another problem derives from a kind of stratification among students whereby some are deemed "ready" for the internship experience and others are not. The prerequisites for obtaining an internship were successful completion of the Professional Career Development class (required of *all* students) and the assessment by the student's supervisor as to his or her readiness to enter a worksite.[12]

Out of the thirty girls in this study, sixteen had been placed into internships and fourteen had not met the requirements. (One of three black girls, five of ten white girls, two of eight Puerto Rican descent girls, and six of the ten Latina girls had not been recommended for an internship.) In most cases, but not all, girls who did not participate in internships were those with the lowest achievement, in terms of poor grades and high rates of absenteeism. This relationship seemed to apply to all groups of girls. Moreover, these were girls whose future aspirations tended to center around traditionally "feminine" occupations such as secretarial work, dance, modeling, and child-oriented fields, girls who expressed either uncertainty or vagueness about their futures, or articulated close identification with future family responsibilities.

By mid-year, the girls had been officially sorted into two groups: those who were in internship positions full-time during the day, and girls who were not and thus required to attend school. This procedure reflects Sharp and Green's (1976) findings, in which a subtle process of sponsorship occurred that created classroom hierarchies in which some children were offered opportunities and others not. In this case, some girls had opportunities to develop relationships to wage labor and others did not. Moreover, there was clearly a stigma attached to having to attend classes while others were at their internships. Thus, the school sends the message that "if you don't do your schoolwork, you don't go on an internship, and if you don't go on an internship, you'll have difficulty getting a job." In other words, the emphasis is on a certain level of academic attainment to prevent future unemployment. We can thus see a strong ideological link, fostered by the school, between academic achievement and one's future position in the labor market. The emphasis on academic achievement and the future may partially account for the girls' commitment to obtaining qualifications in order to enhance their future job opportunities.

Another contradiction inherent in the career education program relates to the understanding of particular work relations. In general, younger male and female students (being less experienced) were placed in internship positions in which they were often expected to fulfill menial office-related tasks such as filing, typing, xeroxing, answering phones, and so on. Below several girls describe their responsibilities:

J: What kinds of things does she give you to do?

BARBARA: She tell me to do faxing, or go on errands, like take this some place to an office or something. And I do xeroxing, making copies, answer the phone, stuff like that, alphabetize something, put things in people's files, put in bills in the social worker's files and what else, if somebody need a name, like a patient's name, I get the patient's name and give it to the lady, stuff like that.

CYNTHIA: I go to Astoria General Hospital. I do medication forms, patient numbers, I send out the bills to the patient names, I work on the computer like counting numbers, make sure they have Medicaid numbers, Blue Cross, if not I write the numbers. I do typing. What else? I put paper in alphabetic order, like the patient names. I do photocopies. That's it.

J: When you go [to the police precinct] what do you do there?

CHRIS: I work with the detectives most of the time. Watch TV. I file, I make copies of things, I answer the phone.

MARTA: [In civil court] I put the docket numbers on client's files and I listen to the cases in the courtroom.

CAROLINA: I work across the street in the English department. It's OK, but sometimes I get mad because they treat me like a freshman who doesn't know anything. They know I type, but they won't let me do anything like that. I answer the phone, go to the printer for copies, file, that kind of stuff.

All of the girls indicated that these tasks, which they found boring, were the least desirable aspect of their "jobs." Presumably, boys would find such routine and unchallenging tasks boring as well. (I did not interview boys regarding their internship experiences.) But for girls, this drudgery takes on special significance. As Valli notes, a lack of correspondence between skill level and job requirements, such as Carolina complains about, can create a feeling of dissatisfaction that can result in low-quality work or a marginalization of wage labor identity. On the other hand, the work site itself offers opportunities for the girls to see the possibilities of engaging in different kinds of work and to meet women who may provide them with encouragement to pursue nontraditional or less sex-typed employment. For example, Chris explains:

> First I wanted to be a lawyer when I went to the [police] precinct and there was this one cop, I don't remember her name, she kept telling me cops do everything, and she changed my mind to want to become a cop.

Because the career education program curriculum requires students to participate in on-site job experiences and attend "career" courses, it encourages young women to identify with a future of waged work. Still, the program perpetuates the faith that jobs can almost automatically be obtained if one possesses ability, talent, and interest. Given the inequities of the labor market, this ideology needs to be seriously challenged. Furthermore, the program may actually reinforce the intransigence of young working-class women's social class position by channeling them into low-level jobs in which they perform traditionally feminine work, receive low pay, and can expect little opportunity for advancement. Nevertheless, given the nature of classroom pedagogy and curriculum in place at A.H.S., these young women may learn skills and gain the knowledge enabling them to more critically understand the circumstances they will face and perhaps, by so understanding, transform them.

CONCLUSIONS

This chapter, based on Bernstein's theory of pedagogical practices, has revealed how classroom processes and school knowledge can contribute to working-class female identity in various ways, particularly in relation to collective struggle and paid work.

Based along the lines of an invisible pedagogy, the weakly framed student-teacher relations promote an understanding that authority is neither natural nor inevitable—and that negotiation is possible. Implicit teacher control in the classroom provides young women with opportunities to negotiate with teachers. For the majority of these young women who have previously been in conflict with schooling and relied on oppositional behaviors or skills of resistance—which are ultimately debilitating both in school and in the workplace—learning to control the conditions of their own learning may provide them with skills to negotiate pay raises, better working conditions, or job enhancement. Furthermore, such skills may enable women to negotiate a more equitable division of labor in their own future households.

The chapter also illustrated how shifting the emphasis from individualism to collective development seemed to benefit young women in the classroom. Cooperative classroom strategies encourage collectivistic values, useful in improving working conditions. As Weis (1990, p. 206) points out, in order to truly press for change, individual problems must be seen as shared and as requiring collective action.

The chapter also revealed, through an analysis of the formal curriculum, how an integrated or weakly classified curriculum, which draws from students' experiences and "common sense" rather than from the authority of texts, promotes a more active relationship to ideas. Furthermore, a curriculum that embodies a critical perspective on the existing social, political, and economic order provides working-class women of various racial or ethnic backgrounds with a conceptual understanding of their positions within that order, and thereby equips them with knowledge that can be used to further the interests of their group in society.

The school then becomes an important context in which young women can explore their positions as women, develop critical insights, and learn skills to help them challenge their subordination in the workplace and home (Anyon, 1981; Weis, 1990).

CHAPTER 9

The Social Construction of Gender within the School

INTRODUCTION

This chapter explores how the school informally contributes to the formation of gender identity, how its gender code communicates to students "appropriate" ways of being feminine or masculine. These messages of gender appropriateness are often contradictory, as well as unintentional. They are usually conveyed through complex processes in dynamic settings—through, for example, the interactions between students and teachers in the classroom or the ways the school addresses students' sexuality and responds to male dominance (Kessler et al., 1985).

In addition to gender and class as components of the social interaction between female students and teachers, I also examine how race/ethnicity impact on teachers' assessments of and beliefs about their female students, thus revealing the multiple ways that adults make judgments about young women.

Arnot's theory of gender code, based on Bernstein's conceptual framework of educational codes, is employed in this chapter as a tool to analyze how messages concerning appropriate models of femininity and masculinity get distributed (Arnot, 1982). Bernstein's theory, which considers how symbolic messages get communicated through formal and informal structures (see chapter 8), is at the heart of Arnot's concept of gender code. The premise of her theory on gender codes is, of course, the notion that gender categories are socially constructed. Gender classification in industrial societies has been based on the strong sexual division of labor and the relationship of men and women to that division. Schooling not only reflects this division and helps constitute it, but, as Kessler and her colleagues (1985) point out, schooling can also enlighten young people about alternative gender relations. They suggest that, "the schools are an arena in which a complex often contradictory, emotionally, and sometimes physically violent politics of gender is worked out" (p. 35).

In analyzing how gender identities and the relations between masculinity and femininity are constructed and acquired through schooling, the teachers and their classroom practices are central. Since the structure of gender relations is one of the major social forces shaping education, patterns of femininity and masculinity form an important part of the context of teaching. Teachers, as Kessler and her colleagues (1985) suggest, do the main work of maintaining conservative gender codes and remaking or refashioning gender codes.

The next three sections—how gender shapes teachers' expectations of boys and girls, how race/ethnicity affects teachers' assessments of girls, and how gender impacts on student-teacher relationships—provide some evidence to suggest that teachers' views and practices regarding gender differentiation are often complex, contradictory, sometimes reinforcing and sometimes undermining social divisions and larger patterns of inequality.

TEACHERS AND GENDER DIFFERENCES

Teachers' beliefs about gender help to structure the way in which they respond to male and female students. Data from interviews with teachers[1] suggest that their views do confirm some generalized notions of stereotypical gendered behavior, but their views are not always consistent.

Teachers tended to consider gender itself to be an explanation for different educational skills and behaviors. With regard to academic ability, several teachers perceived girls as more teachable, more mature, and better or harder workers:

> EMIL: Girls seem to work harder and they don't challenge you like the guys do, especially at this age when they're caught up in all this image stuff. The girls definitely, they work better and they're better students [than boys].

> VINNIE: In terms of teaching, they're more mature. They pick things up quicker. . . . I would rather work with the girls instead of the guys.

> PETER: Well, I've had experiences with coaching. As far as that goes, the girls, I'm talking about coaching now, are much more coachable than the guys are. They're more dedicated, they tend to practice harder and are easier to teach.

> SUSAN: The top five students in terms of grade averages are females. They have the highest averages and tend to excel at school.

> ELIZABETH: Boys in general [are] more handicapped than girls. Their success rate is lower. When they get into trouble, they tend to get into more serious trouble.

Given this belief that girls fare better academically and are more motivated than boys, the teachers promote a kind of femininity in which academic achievement and mastery of knowledge is central to the school's construction (and restructuring) of gender. However, some teachers also express ambivalent attitudes toward their working-class female students that appear to support stereotypical notions of femininity. Two of the above teachers distinguish between their general impressions and specific examples from classes they teach (science and gym), in which girls are at a comparative disadvantage. This disadvantage is attributed to girls' internalized beliefs about their subordination as females:

> VINNIE: In science I still think it's part of the stereotype where girls are not encouraged in some ways to pursue math and science so when they do take them, they tend to find them a little difficult. They're not encouraged to because you're gonna get married anyway, you know, and let your husband take care of it. So, a guy tends to do a little better. I teach an electronics class and normally that's been true for the last three cycles that my class had been mostly males. That's part of the problem. Girls perceive science as being more male dominated, hard.

> PETER: A lot of the girls have a hard time in my class. They don't want to participate. . . . They don't want to change [clothes]. They don't want to run around. They don't want to get sweaty. They don't think it's ladylike. They're afraid that if they mess their hair up the guys won't look at them and they're very concerned about breaking their nails. Whereas the guys will just about go through a wall if I want them to. I guess that follows suit. I don't think that's abnormal. I think that's the norm in most cases.

Both teachers clearly believe that it is the girls themselves (because of internalized acceptance of gender subordination) who choose not to participate fully in science or physical education. As Vinnie posits, girls lack motivation because they themselves believe "you're gonna get married anyway . . . and let you're husband take care of it," and they "perceive science as being more male dominated, hard." Similarly, Peter states that "they're afraid that if they mess their hair up they guys won't look at them." By stereotyping girls' reasons for their disadvantage or disengagement, they rule out the role of the classroom or school structure in promoting inequality. Previous research regarding girls and their experiences in science classrooms (e.g., Mahoney, 1985; Kelly, 1981, cited in Wolpe, 1989) illustrates the very real oppressive conditions that girls must face in science classrooms; their passive behavior could be a deliberate attempt to retain their integrity and avoid being victimized by boys. In the case of the gym class, in order to participate in physical education class, girls must change into gym attire (in a room that serves as a changing room with no changing facilities) and walk through the school corridors into the gymnasium. This is especially embarrassing as other students make comments and males sometimes harass the girls. Nonetheless, the gym class is a school requirement that overrides students' attitudes.

Contradictory messages appear in the following remark where William asserts that girls need an education because "the female is ultimately the one who loses in this society." In his attempt to analyze gender subordination, he fails to distinguish class differences between girls:

> The male either has to get out and go work for a living or they have to go to college. The female should *have* to because the female is ultimately the one who loses in this society. When you talk about the haves and the have nots, the female's the loser. Because if you're a have-not, you got less chance. And the school's not answering this question at all. Not even addressing it. Now I say to my daughter just get the best education you can get and she wants to be a writer and I say write. She says she wants to be a musician, I said play the damn clarinet and get in the best school you can. You're the one who has to graduate from the Ivy not me. You have to go to the Ivy because you're female.

William correctly alludes to the increase in earnings attributed to post-secondary education ("the female should have to [go to college] because the female is ultimately the one who loses in this society"). However, in using as an example his daughter who wants to be a writer or clarinet player, he highlights the middle-class feminine search for self-fulfillment through paid work while downplaying the importance of economic self-sufficiency for women. (Clearly, it takes years of economic sacrifice to become a self-supporting musician or writer, making a woman's chances of becoming dependent on a male wage quite probable.) Working-class girls have neither the material resources to attend Ivy League institutions, nor the important personal connections (through parents, relatives, or friends) to such institutions; William's argument seems to apply only to middle- or upper-class girls. So, while one message is that girls do need to prepare for higher education because of their inferior social and economic status, the other message is for girls to seek careers that will bring self-realization but not necessarily economic self-sufficiency.

Below two women teachers discuss their views, also highlighting the girls' desire (and need) to attend higher education and obtain paid employment.

> CATHERINE: Boys can be a lot more academically handicapped than the girls. . . . The women seem to be a different matter altogether. First of

all, more of them are interested in going to college. I mean, you ask them and that is where they're going whether they think they have the brains, . . . college is something they are going to. It seems that expectation from family or peers is still there.

SUSAN: I do think they really have gotten the message from their parents, from their cohorts, that they need to go out and get their education and get good jobs, that they are smart, that they are not just baby factories.

These two teachers recognize the positive influence exerted by peers and family who emphasize going to college and getting "good jobs." Moreover, the teachers' observations accord closely with the attitudes expressed by African American and Puerto Rican girls who see themselves as future "career" women, and who therefore plan to postpone marriage or childbearing while they first continue their education and get settled professionally.

An interesting contradiction, however, emerges here. When asked about differences between boys' and girls' behavior in school, teachers perceive girls both as better students, more motivated to attend college, and as difficult students, as or more oppositional than boys in their classroom deportment:

JOE: In terms of discipline, . . . if a girl wants to be bad, she can be worse than the worst guy.

VINNIE: Girls can be in many ways worse than guys in many many ways, especially when they have personal problems they can be more vicious than guys. Guys tend to fight it out and it's over.

WILLIAM: Girls and boys both say they hate school or that it [is] boring, boring being the key word. Not much difference there.

SUSAN: If I was to take it from my own experience, I really couldn't say that the boys cut classes more. I would say that the girls are cutting classes more often or as often as boys. Suspensions, I'd say the same, too. You know, this one's looking at me. I mean certainly there's a difference between girls and boys. Sometimes their behavior, how they act is different. Boys may have more of a tendency to curse you out, or to throw things or punch things, but I've seen girls act that way too. Usually when girls get aggravated in class, they leave. The boys will stay out, too. If they don't like a teacher, they'll cut. All right? But some of the boys may have more words for the teacher than the girls. But I can't make a blanket statement like that because I know there are boys who will keep their mouths and just not go back to class. So it's very hard for me to differentiate here.

RICHARD: A general theory I've heard over the years is that the males tend to be more flexible or accepting or more resilient than females in any situation. If they have an argument with a teacher, with males, it's OK, it's over, let's move on. I can't say that I agree with that. I find males and females tend to behave in more similar ways.

Interestingly, the teachers use boys' behavior as the norm, so that the girls seem to be imitating boys' behavior. Teachers do not see girls' oppositional behavior as idiosyncratic expressions of femininity, but rather as deviancy from a white middle-class standard about what constitutes "proper" female classroom behavior. While girls may have high academic and career expectations (which are compatible with the school's model of femininity), they can still challenge dominant views of how a "proper girl" should behave (Weiler, 1988).

My classroom observations confirm that girls' behavior can occasionally be extremely oppositional, though such antagonism does not imply that they are not dedicated to school and academic achievement. In general, it is not possible to point to a particular group of young women (i.e., white, Latina, or African American) and describe them simply as either conforming to or conflicting with school norms. The situation is far more complex. What can appear to be conformist, female behavior—a quiet and seemingly passive demeanor—may actually be a deliberate coping strategy to "avoid trouble."

As my data show, girls can demonstrate antischool behavior while still aspiring to college and a career. Similarly, girls can attend school regularly and therefore seem interested in their education, but still perform badly academically and care little about a future career. The range of girls' reactions to schooling has been well documented. For example, Fuller (1983) argued, in the case of black British girls, that they could be both critical of school and able to manipulate and succeed within the school's system of examinations and certification. Classroom observations by Wolpe (1988) and Davies (1984) also illustrate wide-ranging and variable behaviors, including girls who appeared to do no work at all and girls who engaged in a number of counterschool activities such as "excessive use of body language, verbal wrangles, and wandering about the classroom" (p. 46). Similarly, Davies (1984) describes in detail how day-to-day classroom styles differed among a group of "deviant" girls whose "scripts" ranged from manipulation to withdrawal to helplessness, depending on the classroom situation.

Based on my observations, the group of girls who was failing or most in danger of failing academically seemed to be most in conflict with school and included a group of counterschool white girls and several immigrant Latina girls. For the most part, these girls expressed their rejection of school by chronic absenteeism (forty or more unexcused absences over the year). As a consequence of their truancy, they received failing grades. White girls generally remarked that school was "boring" and "a waste of time." The desire to spend time with boyfriends accounted for some of the time girls spent outside of school during the day. The two Latina girls attributed their chronic absence to a combination of personal problems (such as depression), heavy domestic responsibilities, and part-time employment.[2] It is interesting that a rejection of the school itself did not figure in their explanations as it did for the white girls. When these girls attended class, they were usually quiet and withdrawn, often sleeping, avoiding doing any work. Lucy (a Latina), who appeared quiet in class and rarely interacted with the teachers, explained her behavior in these terms: "I see how he [teacher] is with other students, so I don't talk to him. I don't want any trouble." There was also the matter of her previous experiences with teachers:

> I used to get in trouble a lot 'cause the teachers used to get on my nerves and they used to push me, and I don't like that. Once I pushed a teacher back and he fell and they got me in trouble. Then I had to do something. Once I had this fight with the principal and I threw an ashtray and they called the security guards and that went on my record. So, you know, I got a bad record now. I don't want to keep on making any trouble, so I'm trying my best.

Sadly, in Lucy's case, "trying my best" meant withdrawal from her classmates and teachers and a minimal engagement in classwork. On the surface, Lucy's reserve could be construed as typically feminine behavior, suggesting conformity. (One teacher described her as a "an okay student when she comes, a little on the quiet side.") But the above passage reveals something quite different—an active (and ultimately self-defeating) strategy to protect herself from a potentially hostile environment.

Another group of girls (African American, Latina, and white), also doing poorly academically, although not failing (receiving Ds and NCs, i.e., no credit), came to school regularly. While they maintained a minimal level of achievement, they were extremely oppositional in their school and classroom behavior. For example, two of the girls (one African American and one white) were suspended for fighting (not with each other) and causing physical injury to their opponents. Their typical classroom styles were equally disruptive as they danced, sang, and moved around the classroom. Importantly, their female teacher did not necessarily view their behavior negatively, claiming, "They really wanted to be here. This is really big for them to be in the classroom and be noisy."

Emily, on the other hand, could be disruptive without moving around:

> Emily kept her head down throughout class. Several girls kept walking over to her to ask her what was wrong. An argument started between Delores and Antonia about who Emily was closer to and would tell what was wrong. Finally the teacher walked over to Emily and asked her to come outside. Emily protested in a loud voice refusing to go. Everyone in the class was focused on the situation. (Field note, 2/2)

Sometimes girls could be verbally disruptive, like Betty (Latina), whose name recurs in my notes accompanied by such comments as:

> Betty screams and curses all the time, throws makeup back and forth with Clarice, calls everyone a fucking bitch or "puta" (Spanish for whore), complains endlessly how stupid class is, how she hates the teacher, calls some of the students fucking nerds. (Field note, 2/4)

In addition to being disruptive, some girls could also be aggressive toward teacher or school authority. Below, Jackie (white) defiantly and condescendingly ridicules Tim (teacher) to neutralize his conciliatory attempt to get her to come to class:

> Tim [teacher] gave me a nice long speech in the cafeteria today. B and I were sitting there, buggin' out, we didn't go to class. He comes up, he goes, "Can I talk to you a minute?" I looked at him, I go, "Go ahead." . . . He's sittin' there, "Why don't you come to my class anymore? Did I do anything that bad to you that you don't come?" I just looked at him and I'm sittin' there laughing and laughing. And he's sitting there, "Do you hate me that much?" He was like what's wrong with you and I'm like oh, shut up, just shut your fat mouth. I mean the day he kicked me out of class, that was it. I mean, I didn't do anything. I walked in late, everyone walks in late. He goes, get out, and I was like, "What are you crazy?" I said, "What the hell's wrong with you?"

Some of this was indeed corroborated by Tim. Jackie, however, ultimately returned to Tim's class, explaining she needed the credits.

It would be easy to categorize these young women as being anti-school. However, their attendance was good, and while they did not do schoolwork regularly, they always made up the assignments before the end of the marking period.

The group of girls of average academic ability (which included girls from all backgrounds) also engaged at times in oppositional behavior, but were generally very pro-learning, pro-credentials, and articulated strong college and career orientations. What is interesting about this group of girls is that, though they could be as oppositional and confrontational as the previous group, they expressed, for the most part, a commitment to gaining qualifications through higher education.

Then there were those girls (all Latina) at the top of the academic scale, receiving mostly As, never or seldom absent, and cooperative, generally getting down to work when expected to. Without exception, these girls displayed a strong labor market identity during formal interviews. They were certainly not passive, indeed at times assertive and dominant in the classroom. Two of the girls were described by a (male) teacher as "future revolutionaries" because of their outspokenness in class and superior writing skills. These girls as a group performed better than any of the boys in class, dominated classroom activity, and exacted more of the teachers' time and attention.

The variation in girls' classroom behaviors represents some of the ways that young women interpret the school's gender code and also bring with them into the classroom competing gender codes derived from their peer and family cultures (Arnot, 1984, p. 19). Teachers can encourage or inhibit particular aspects of these reworked gender codes. For example, while quiet girls may be left alone, thus reinforcing the notion of good student as quiet girl (and thereby abetting a girl's disengagement from classroom learning), girls who dominate classroom activity may similarly be rewarded for their outspokenness and academic achievement.

I have tried to uncover some of the complexity in teachers' attitudes toward gender differentiation in order to shed light on the kinds of messages that may be transmitted from teacher to female student and may be implicated in the ongoing process of gender identity construction. In the next section, I turn to the subject of teachers and how their own versions of femininity and masculinity impact on their classroom authority and methods of control and through which particular models of femininity and masculinity get transmitted. As an aspect of a school's gender code, gender relations between teachers and students can either promote or inhibit certain forms of feminine or masculine identities among students (Kessler et al., 1985).

TEACHERS' ASSESSMENTS OF THEIR FEMALE STUDENTS: THE INTERSECTIONS OF RACE/ETHNICITY, GENDER, AND CLASS

As discussed above, teachers generally identified females as better students than their male counterparts. However, when teachers were asked to talk about differences between groups of girls (i.e., black,

Latina,[3] and white), interesting distinctions emerged. This suggests that teachers do not relate to female students in a monolithic way, but that perceived racial or ethnic differences can powerfully influence the ways in which teachers differently evaluate and assess black, Latina, and white female students. This is not to suggest that teachers' expectations are necessarily accepted and internalized by students as part of their ongoing self-definition. Teachers' expectations or beliefs can, in fact, have quite contradictory effects. As Fuller (1980) found among a group of West Indian schoolgirls in England, an increased consciousness of their racial and gender subordination propelled them to academic success, despite the British school system's imputation of "underachievement" to West Indian students. In other words, students actively accept or reject various definitions or labels applied to them. I suggest only that processes of differentiation (in this case, teachers' different expectations of female students) may subtly prod some students toward future stereotypical roles while encouraging others to press toward greater academic achievement and more fulfilling work (Grant, 1992, 1994).

Teachers' Beliefs about Latina Students

Several teachers concurred that Latinas are good students, motivated to do well, and share a strong collective identity:

> TIM: Hispanic girls generally seem to be more motivated [than other groups of girls]. Hispanic girls . . . can be very on the ball and have been my best students. . . . Hispanic women seem to have a sense of their own unity as Hispanic women.

> SUSAN: I would say that our Hispanic population by and large tend[s] to be very bright. I think if you look back, you'll see that there are a lot of school valedictorians, salutarians. I'm talking about our female Hispanics, not necessarily our male Hispanics. We've had a lot of dropouts in the male Hispanics.

> RICK: . . . Probably the three greatest minds in our class are Hispanic females.

In chapters 4 and 5, I presented excerpts from Latina and Puerto Rican girls' interviews to show that most have as a primary aim, upon graduation, the pursuit of a college education as preparation for a career. It was noteworthy that for Puerto Rican girls, higher education as a primary goal held even for those girls whose low academic achievement might disqualify them from finishing high school. Furthermore, many of the girls emphasized postponing marriage and childbearing until they were "settled" in high-paying jobs. Significantly, still others approached the subject of marriage with more reservations, hoping to maintain emotional and financial independence from husbands by not marrying. These girls clearly did not want to be financially dependent on a man's income. Below, several teachers discuss Latina girls' orientations toward futures of paid labor and independence from men:

> LAURA: They are more oriented, I think, toward, more career oriented. . . . For some reason, in general, they have more of a sense of what they want to do or to be—lawyers, nurses, whatever and they tend to be a little more in a peculiar sort of way, more independent of men.

> SUSAN: I believe that many of the females are going on to higher education and looking for jobs. They see children in their futures, in many cases in their near future but don't necessarily feel as though they need a man around.

> TONY: I see a lot of our Hispanic girls doing well. For example, I see Gloria going out there and selling, having her own business and really excelling.

The model of Latina femininity here presented is one of high achievement, career orientation, and independence from men. But other models exist; for example, Latina girls who were failing courses, disruptive in class, and had vague aspirations, at the most envisioning marriage and children soon after high school. It is uncertain whether peer pressure and teacher expectations will move this group of girls toward a more career-oriented femininity and, if so, it is not clear what conflicts the girls may face. What is important is that for the group of Latina girls who envision higher education and careers, their own and their teachers' expectations are clearly in synchrony.

Teachers' Beliefs about African American Girls

As for their female African American students, teachers emphasized the struggle of these girls' lives (due to racism and early childbearing) and their autonomy. Regarding African American girls' relationships with men, teachers remarked upon their dependence on males; but as one teacher suggested, "[they are] not necessarily looking at marriage":

> MARY JANE: I think that the black women that I've seen here are many times dependent on their mates, but not necessarily looking at marriage. Many of them have had children, are taking care of children, are going back to school and thinking about college. Those of them that

make it through do think along the lines of higher education or working or having some type of career, and not necessarily with the father of their child.

ARTHUR: Black girls seem to depend a lot on black men even when they are deceiving them. It is strange to find for example a black girl who is doing really really well in school choose to be around a guy who is not achieving at all.

TOM: . . . There is this sort of black girl who is incredibly supportive and strong and exceeds beyond expectations which is a characteristic largely absent from black males in my experience. . . . A good portion of our black girls seem to really know the barriers they are up against culturally and racially and since A.H.S. gives the opportunity to exceed them, they seem to gain some amount of self-dignity and pleasure in exceeding them, especially some of the black women who have had it really difficult. At the age of fifteen or sixteen have had a child or whatever and some of them can come back remarkably aware and together.

CARL: The black girls have to be more an island unto themselves or maybe with their group for survival. They are much more independent, but there's a tragic sense about them. There are very few options because of the color of their skin. That's the sense I get. I think it's still a white male–dominated society in spite of the gains. The black person knows in society that they're losing. . . . I tell them, you have to get out of here with a diploma, go through that maze of the white world and if you come out at the other end, you're gonna be infinitely more successful than anyone.

The overriding image here is of independent and hard-working young women who are acutely aware of racism. In addition, early childbearing and emotional (though not necessarily economic) dependence on males are also emphasized. There is also the assumption that they, unlike Latina students, may not all make it through the educational pipeline.

The model of black adolescent femininity suggested by the teachers differs somewhat from the black girls' own perceptions and projections. They expressed determination to complete higher education and pursue a career. They eschewed serious relationships with boys and avoided sex, recognizing pregnancy would abort their aspirations. However, in their long-term projections, marriage and children figure prominently into their futures alongside careers.

Teachers' Beliefs about White Girls

Teachers had much less to say about the white girls in their classes. In fact, several white female teachers responded with brief comments that implied a mutual understanding between us (I am also white and female). This is an important point in that it conveys a "normative" or "typical" standard of behavior and attitude that requires no elaboration:

> KAREN: Jackie, for example, would be the typical white girl with us. . . .
>
> SUSAN: Our female white population is our typical middle-class female, white kind of mores, values.

Joe comments that the white girls are "practically invisible in the school," although white students make up almost one-half of the student population:

> In A.H.S., the type of white girl we get face a very interesting problem. I see the white girls as practically invisible. I think that in many ways they are suffering from the most acute sense of identity problem of any of the girls because they are not in the majority.

One male teacher spoke at length about white girls. Here he discusses the girls' future attachments to men and sexuality:

> SAMUEL: The white girls have gotten from their mothers, they still have this suburban, "if I attract a guy, I won't have to go to work." Those patterns are there. It's been in this school the three years I've been here. . . . The white females that seem to be doing the best in this school are the Greeks, because I think the parents own a business, the kids have a part in it.

Of the group of white girls (ten) who were interviewed, several had high or average grades, and some expressed intentions of attending college and engaging in paid labor. What distinguished the white girls from the Latina and black girls was their emphasis on marrying and having children and their weaker attachment to paid work. This image mirrors the teachers' comments that allude to white working-class women's economic dependence on men. And indeed, most of the white girls seemed to aspire toward more "traditional" roles in the family, seeking economic security through marriage.

These images of white girls (invisible, weak identity, and economically dependent on men) present a remarkable contrast to the images of Latina girls (strong sense of identity, bright students, career-oriented, and independent of men) and those of African American girls (strong, independent, hard working, and racially aware). The effect of teachers' perceptions can be subtle but profound, influencing how the girls perceive themselves, their potential, and their opportunities.

TEACHERS, GENDER, AND CLASSROOM CONTROL

In the previous chapter, I discussed how teacher-student relations were weakly framed and teacher control appeared to be more a matter of negotiation than one of power and status. What is missing from the discussion (and from Bernstein's framework of pedagogical relationships) are the ways in which gender can profoundly shape those relationships.

Below I will discuss how teachers' gendered patterns of classroom control appear to replicate a traditional sexual division of labor, in which female teachers discipline and nurture and male teachers are "soft" and not likely to intervene with female students. These versions of teacher femininity and masculinity thereby become the adult models (of femininity and masculinity) that constitute the school's gender code.

The following discussion draws on observation data from two classrooms—one taught by a middle-aged teaching team composed of a white male (Tony) and an African American female (Arlene) and the other classroom taught by a younger teacher team (each thirty years old) composed of a white male (Joe) and white female (Patty).

Depending on their age, women teachers draw on different aspects of their own femininity to construct and maintain their authority in the classroom. For example, Arlene drew on her role as a mother (and indeed I often heard female students call her "mom"):

> As an older female, see, I have to take a lot of things into consideration. I think in part, the girls related to me as an older woman. I found the girls tend to relate in whatever ways they tend to be relating to an older woman, to their mothers for example.

This representation of herself as a "mother" figure implies a familial relationship with her students,[4] and even a certain kind of "matriarchal" (see Davies, 1984) force that elicits the students' grudging obedience:

> A lot of times I seem to take on the disciplinarian role more so than Tony, which doesn't always happen in a family situation. But in a way, it was like a family in here. Mom, pop, and the kids. In some families mom hands out the punishment and some families it's dad and in our family it was mom because I had the [grade] book (*laughs*). And I did the grading. So in the final analysis, I think the girls, and probably the fellows too, kind of grudgingly obeyed me and just generally loved Tony, which is not to say that I don't think they are fond of me, I think they are.

Tony, however, does not see himself occupying a parental role:

> The eternal battle of the mother-daughter thing was acted out with Arlene. I mean Arlene got all the crap from them. You know, the good

old my mother, myself really carrying through here. Whereas with me, my father myself doesn't wash. There's a different mystique between the mother and daughter and the father and son which we saw in the classroom. There really wasn't a single guy in the class that was really after me, except for when I played schoolteacher and they didn't want to do their work.

As Tony describes it, Arlene's role as a mother in their teaching dyad is virtually guaranteed to produce both love and hostility on the part of the students, both male and female. Thus, student relationships with "maternal" teachers are likely to be highly ambivalent. In Tony's case, however, his relationships with students, particularly the male ones, are not structured by a parenting role and hence are less ambivalent—he does not become the "target of all the crap." This structure, in a sense, mirrors a conventional mother-father-child triad in which most of the parenting is done by women; as Tony puts it:

They [female students] would tend to perceive the male as softer and the woman commanding the male, especially among the Hispanic women, which I was always conscious of. Um, I feel the best way to deal with the kids is to respond that way and not pull the schoolteacher game. . . . They perceived Arlene as a much more traditional teacher.

Tony here alludes to the combination of power and powerlessness that often characterizes Latina women's experiences with men. As Brown (1975) describes, it is not uncommon for Latina women to have power within the household to decide whether or not a man is going to live with her. She may choose to put him out if he is not a good provider. Tony clearly has chosen this posture of male "powerlessness" in dealing with his female, particularly Latina, students.

Tony was highly popular among his students, particularly with the girls. Not having to take on a "parent" role, he was able to cede more explicit control to Arlene and adopt a less-threatening ("softer") "fooling-around" role that, nevertheless, gave him control. Tony's style of classroom control, cajoling and humoring, is often used by male teachers (see Riddell, 1992) as a way of avoiding confrontation with female students. The following excerpt from my field notes illustrates this last point:

The classroom was organized in smaller groups today, about three to each table. The topic was Latin America. It was small group work, drawing maps, answering some questions. Most of the class seemed to be working while Tony and Arlene circulated around the room. Usually when someone calls out, it's for Tony. He walks around joking, cajoling, trying absolutely any way he can to get them to do some work. He pays a lot of attention to Hillary and Alicia and to the table of girls. . . . He was really prodding Debbie to do the work, making jokes. She was groaning about the assignment, was tired, hated maps, etc. But at the end of the period, she had finished everything. (Field note, 2/17)

Rather than threatening students with failing grades or other disciplinary techniques, he jokes and cajoles.

The following incidents, taken again from fieldnotes, both involve the same girl and underline the difference in meaning between a male teacher–female student relationship and a female teacher–female student one:

Arlene had to leave early today. After she left, incident occurred with Tony and Gladys. Tony sits down next to Gladys. I don't know exactly what was happening. Gladys got up to leave the room and Tony said, "Gladys sit down." She got up and said, "No, I'm not sitting down, you sound like my father." She gets up and walks behind Tony. He pushes his chair back as if to block her. She yells loudly, "LET ME GO" and pushes by him, leaving the room. Tony turned it into a joke, and said something like "OK, you're learning." (Field note, 1/18)

Lots of commotion in class, Gladys and Cam left the room. Arlene jumps over chairs to get them and runs out of room after them. Comes back holding onto both, all seem breathless. Gladys was excited and jumps up on a chair imitating to the whole class how Arlene came running after them, flying up the stairs, how fast she runs, then she comes in the office and yells, GET BACK TO CLASS NOW! (Field note, 2/16)

In the first incident, we see Tony's inability to prevent Gladys from physically exiting the classroom. (He uses his chair to block her rather than physically restrain her.) In order to diffuse a tense situation and to avoid confrontation, he jokes about the situation as she leaves the room. In the second situation, Arlene aggressively runs after the two girls and physically returns them to the classroom, an option available to her as a "matriarchal" force.

So far, we have seen a sexual division of classroom labor where Arlene assumes the role of disciplinarian while Tony figures as an easygoing "soft" ally. This meant that it was Arlene's duty to reprimand girls. She also set rules, such as forbidding magazine reading in class as well as overt displays of femininity such as use of makeup, hair styling, spraying perfume, polishing nails, and so on. Tony generally ignored these behaviors. What was not tolerated by either teacher were overt displays of aggression or hostility between girls:

Terry and Linda (white) were going at each other all morning. Terry shoved the table at Linda, Linda took Terry's notebook and flung it across the room. Terry went over and grabbed Linda's hair. Arlene yelled at them to stop and kicked them both out of the classroom, told them not to come back until the break. . . . After break, both came back. Linda sat in doorway looking out into the hall. Terry sat in usual seat, but didn't talk the rest of the period. (Field note, 2/28)

Lots of fooling around between Delores, Emily, and Marta (all Latina) in class today. Marta reached over and grabbed Emily's breast. Emily lets out *loud* scream, yelling she's in pain. Starts swinging at Marta. Delores rushes over to placate Emily. Arlene yells at them to stop it or they'll all get zeros. (Field note, 1/18)

Underlying the various prohibitions Arlene enforces is the effort to transform the girls' working-class femininity into one oriented toward higher education, academic achievement, and career attainment.

Younger teachers, closer in age to their students, could not as easily assume a parental role and, therefore, drew on other aspects of their femininity or masculinity in relating to girls and boys in the classroom.[5] For example, Patty tries to appeal to girls through their common experience as women. In aligning herself with the girls in her classroom, she felt a measure of control over them, which her male partner was unable to cultivate:

I feel that the girls might feel a little more clubby with me than they did with Joe and I encouraged that. . . . I guess I can reason with girls better than he can. At least I think so. I'm just more comfortable with girls. I can't imagine having a room of thirteen-year-old boys. It's just a gut thing.

As an example, Patty related an incident that occurred in the cafeteria with one of her female students, Betty. Betty had approached another girl aggressively and a fight was about to break out. Witnessing the incident, Patty called to the security guards to intervene, and Betty was taken to the principal's office. As Patty explained:

She [Betty] was looking at me like I was betraying her and actually that was a very important point for us because I had taken her upstairs to the office and we talked about how she had a lot more going for her than this kind of empty behavior that is negative. I think from that time she took me a lot more seriously and if I said something to her she would really listen to it. . . . I felt like with her maybe because she was a girl I was successful.

Several times I observed Patty talking with groups of girls after class, in hallways or empty classrooms. She reported that girls sometimes solicited her opinion or advice about personal problems or boyfriends. Patty's close alignment with these girls had several implications for her male partner's (Joe's) ability to assert control. For example, I observed occasions where girls would turn to Patty to verify something Joe had told them, thus undermining his authority. In the following incidents, we can also see how Patty mediated conflict between Joe and female students:

> Cheryl walked in second half and like she always does when she comes late, starts quietly copying things off the board. When she appeared to finish the assignment, Joe went over to her and said, "Let me see what you're doing." Cheryl flips through the pages of her notebook too quickly for Joe to see what it was:
>
> JOE: Cheryl, you can't work on that now, you have to work on the assignment.
> CHERYL: I finished already.
> JOE: Well, let me see it then.
> (*Cheryl refused to show Joe her notebook again and he grabbed it. She yelled, "Give me back my book." There was a tug of war over the book and Cheryl was angry. Joe let go of the notebook.*)
> JOE: You can either do the work or leave. (*Cheryl starts to leave*) No, you can't leave.
> CHERYL: But you said I could leave, so I'm leaving.
> (*They both go out in the hall and Joe calls Patty. All three come back several minutes later. Joe and Cheryl do not talk during the remainder of the period. Patty goes over to Cheryl several times.*) (Field note, 12/7)

When Joe's attempt to negotiate with Cheryl failed, he was forced to relent and assert his authority physically (grabbing the book); failing in that, he had no option but to call in Patty to resolve the situation for him, thus himself undermining his control. Unlike the other classroom, there was no clear-cut "disciplinarian" in this team, although by default, Patty assumed most of the responsibility. A very strong gendered division of labor assigned Patty the roles of conflict mediator and counselor to "upset" girls:

> During class Clarice seemed visibly upset with the boy next to her. She was yelling at him, "Fuck you, asshole, fuck you." Then she jumped up, pushed a few chairs and stormed out of the room. Joe smiled at me and said, "She'll get over it." Patty left class and went after her. (Field note, 2/1)

> Aurea complained to me today that Joe [teacher] had called her a bitch in class and she ran up to the vice principal's office to complain. She was told she didn't have to go back to class and that Patty would tutor her in the missed work. (Field note, 11/9)

Both teachers and the vice principal felt that girls are best dealt with by women. In both cases, Patty has the ultimate responsibility for dealing with "upset" girls.

The following field note exemplifies Patty's role as disciplinarian in the sexual division of labor:

> I'm beginning to see a change in the frequency of the makeup sessions in class. Only occasionally now do I see someone put on lipstick or, for example, Betty took out a bottle of hairspray and surreptitiously started squirted it. But Patty will tell them immediately to put the stuff away as soon as she sees it. I have never once seen Joe tell the girls to put away their makeup even when Patty wasn't in the room. (Field note, 2/5)

This example of Patty's action and Joe's nonintervention is similar to the division of labor displayed by the previously discussed team where Arlene had the responsibility for prohibiting the use of makeup in class. Interestingly, both male teachers never reprimanded girls for engaging in feminine activities that mimicked women's stereotypical attempts to make themselves desirable for men (Raissiguier, 1993).

Sexuality also plays a role in teacher-student relations and holds implications for classroom control. Below, Patty recounts her relationship with a male student:

> Something that I have always worried about with boys is, like Jay is a good example of a female teacher/ troubled boy relationship. What he did with me was he got the distinct . . . impression that he was really pissed off that he was supposed to listen to what I had to say and he didn't think he had to give that to me, and that if I wasn't as thrilled with him that he could just say "Fuck her, I don't need her either" and he very much took it as a relationship [with a woman] and if I wasn't giggly with him and happy with him then he was going to be angry at me. That can happen with boys.

Teachers bring to class—and exhibit through their interactions—gendered patterns of behavior (or models of femininity and masculinity) that students either accept or reject. For example, the sexual division of labor in the classroom suggests that it is "women's work" to nurture and discipline. Furthermore, the male-female dynamics of the teaching team (i.e., the sexual division of labor) make up and reinforce the school construction of a particular form of femininity and heterosexual sexuality (e.g., married couple; female teacher as nurturer and confidante; male teacher as remote, "soft," or likely to intervene negatively). Thus, we see how teacher gender relations conform to the larger societal structure of the sexual division of labor and provide models of appropriate gender behavior for girls and boys (regardless of background) to both observe and participate in. At the same time, however, the school and its teachers attempt to address some aspects of young working-class women's gender identity—overtly feminine behavior such as prominent displays of using makeup as well as aggression and neglecting schoolwork—and transform these behaviors into a model of femininity oriented toward learning, higher education, and careers.

SEXUALITY IN SCHOOL

Sexuality plays an important part in all girls' identity formation, but has been underresearched.[6] As Wood (1984) has observed:

> The whole sexy atmosphere of the period [of his research] led me to reflect on the absence of any real work on sex as it manifests itself in schools. . . . I mean, particularly, how sexuality manifests itself in school as an axis of power relations and as a locus of social orderings. (p. 56, cited in Wolpe, 1989, p. 97)

I have found quite useful the concept of "social scripting" originated by Simon and Gagnon (1971) in analyzing students' sexual behaviors in school and here described by Miller and Fowlkes (1980):

> They [Simon and Gagnon] view sexual behavior as social behavior entered into and endowed with meaning by social actors whose interpersonal relationships are bound together by common and shared understandings and communications that are the product of their common and shared social and cultural worlds. Sexual behavior is above all learned behavior; sexual conduct is "neither fixed by nature or by the organs themselves." Social scripts organize an understanding of the particular in social activity. (Miller and Fowlkes, 1980, p. 262, cited in Wolpe)

I observed such social scripting both in the classroom and in the school as a whole, as well as in my formal and informal discussions with students and teachers. The following discussion illustrates the "dragging in" of elements of sexuality that get replayed and reconfigured within the school.

In the course of my observations during the school year, I witnessed many instances of girls and boys kissing, hugging, and caressing each other in public spaces such as the hallways, cafeteria, and outdoor patio. (This held for girls and boys of all backgrounds.) Examples from field notes are illustrative:

> Saw Eve (PR) and her boyfriend (PR) (both fourteen years old) in hallway between classes. They were standing in the doorway, he behind her with his arms around her, slightly bending down, kissing her neck. (Field note, 5/24)

> One area of the cafeteria seems to be demarcated for couples only who sit and kiss, appear to be sleeping with their arms around each other, etc. (Field note, 11/20)

> Saw Brendan (WH) in the cafeteria (during class time) with his girlfriend (WH). She was sitting on his lap, they were kissing and hugging each other. (Field note, 10/31)

My field notes from classroom observations also illustrate girls and boys in cross-sex friendships (none of them were involved with each other as "girlfriend" or "boyfriend") that appeared to mimic adult sexual behavior. I witnessed many instances where girls and boys demonstrated affection (always within their racial or ethnic group):

> Tanya (LA) and Raphael (LA) sat close together watching the film. Raphael was lying on Tanya's arm, and she was leaning on him. (Field note, 2/20)

> Jill (WH) and Richie (WH) were affectionate with each other today. She was putting her head down on his arm and he had his other hand on her head. (Field note, 1/18)

> Michael (AA) and Samantha (AA) seem to be close in class, affectionate with each other especially when the lights go out for a video when they appear to be snuggling against each other. They whisper and giggle with each other constantly. (Field note, 2/2)

Aside from individual displays of sexualized behaviors conducted in public spaces within the school and classroom (and never reprimanded by adults), the school appeared to promote the "normality" of heterosexuality through activities that encourage heterosexual pairing, such as the school prom.[7] Throughout the year, pictures of the previous year's prom were prominently displayed in the hallways. Closer to the event itself, students signed up for various committees. Valentine's Day also represented an important occasion to celebrate romance:

Valentine's Day: My immediate impression on walking into the school was how many girls were walking around with either a single red rose or a bunch of carnations wrapped in cellophane. I walked into cafeteria. Saw a few of the girls, one got a stuffed bear and box of chocolates; another got a nameplate necklace from boyfriends. Later in class, Tom had a stuffed bear that was being passed around the room. Mona sat most of the hour cradling it like a baby, rocking it, etc. Trish also spent a lot of time cuddling it. Cheryl and Sandra were extremely dressed up. . . . The topic for class today also centered on Valentine's Day. Tony introduced Marquez's book, *Love in the Time of Cholera* and had kids come up with words having to do with love. (Field note, 2/14)

Even the school newspaper ran two pages of Valentine's Day love greetings, such as "Doreen, I love u forever, marry me"; "To Rose, stay sweet and always keep looking good"; "To Sheila, a girls who is sweet and caring and please never change"; and "My Sweet Susan, keep on smiling, mi amor." Messages from girls to boys were conspicuously absent, as if it were the boys' prerogative to send Valentine's messages—not unlike the stereotypical assumption that it is the male's role to make romantic advances (whether asking for a date or initiating sex).

These are but a few examples of how a particular form of sexuality—heterosexual pairing—gets promoted and sanctioned in the school and thus appears as "normal." Such activities coach students in appropriate gender behavior, in what Rich (1980) calls "compulsory heterosexuality," a systematic set of institutional and cultural arrangements that reward people for appearing to be heterosexual. This ethos creates tremendous pressure for all girls to participate in the culture of romance, which may ultimately direct them into domesticity and motherhood. There are many more examples demonstrating how girls are familiarized with social scripting relating to sexual interactions. As other studies on working-class girls have shown (Davies, 1984; McRobbie, 1978; Riddell, 1992; Raissiguier, 1994), girls often emphasize their sexuality as a form of opposition. As Raissiguier (1994) points out, "it has been argued that working-class females introduce overtly feminine and sexualized selves into the classroom to displace dominant expectations of how they should behave and respond in educational settings" (p. 79). An exaggerated feminine script can be recognized in girls' use of makeup, in their concern about fashion, in talk about boyfriends (sexual signaling), and in flirtations with male teachers. Davies makes the point that these kinds of scripts reflect working-class girls' low-status position. Similarly, Skeggs (1991) argues that female students are able to use their own sexuality as a tactical resource to "challenge directly the legitimacy of masculine regulative power" (p. 132). Skeggs furthermore argues that female sexuality can be "experienced as fun, empowering and pleasurable, and it is these contradictory aspects, which momentarily escape regulation that they [girls] are able to use in the classroom" (p. 133).

I would like to point out, however, that the above studies focus, for the most part, on white working-class female adolescents (except for Raissiguier's, in which she also discusses working-class girls of Algerian descent). During the course of my classroom observations, I never once observed "flirtatious" interactions between African American females and male teachers. This might suggest, although the subject needs much more attention, that perhaps African American females employ different strategies, such as confrontation and withdrawal, to counter (white) masculine power or to displace notions of "proper" (white middle-class) feminine behavior. Fuller, for example, describes the black girls in her study as engaging in various antischool behaviors (although the girls were unwavering in their commitment to obtaining educational qualifications), none of which included introducing overtly feminized and sexualized selves into the classroom. Below, a white male teacher describes his difficulty in interacting with African American females:

> Katrina [an African American female] and I did fairly well in class, way better than probably any of the other black girls I've had [in class]. . . . From my experience teaching in Brooklyn and my teaching here [at A.H.S.], I have never been able to really get the black girls to open up in the classroom. I find them sharp enough and they can deal with the material, but the tendency is to play dumb. . . . They get really upset with me when I say to them, I know what you're doing. Maybe that's a control thing, too, from a white male, the whole interplay there.

The flirtatious behavior of some of the white and Latina girls, however, was a common theme remarked on by several of the male teachers, and clearly represented a source of considerable difficulty for them:

> HARRY: The girls knew exactly all the moves, where to put their bodies. They're the ones that grab me from behind, and all that stuff with the touching the breasts that went on. Did you catch that? They would come up and grab me, and my response would be "Look, you can grab me and you don't go to jail. I grab you and I go to jail."

> JOHN: I think some of the girls tend to flirt a bit and it's always a test. You're always being tested.

> ANTON: One of the biggest things that struck me when I came to A.H.S. or teaching high school in general, was the degree to which there was a very playful kind of teasing, a kind of sexual rapport which goes on with the girls. And I don't think it is motivated by me entirely (*laughs*).

Anton further explains that such behaviors might best be seen not as a matter of power but as one of practice:

> I think the girls are kind of looking for that—the ability that they can flirt and do it in a safe way and that they won't be put into any difficult position because of it. They can play out their flirtations and know, like a workshop, like a flirtation workshop, they can play out certain whatever and they don't have to really deal with the consequences of it.

All three men allude to the problems and dangers represented by the girls' sexuality ("I grab you, I go to jail," "it's always a test, you're always being tested," "they [girls] don't have to really deal with the consequences of [their flirting]"). As Lees (1993) has observed, males often fear girls' sexuality because of its allegedly dangerous potential to entrap them. Aside from what Anton describes as flirting as "practice," there are real benefits girls derive from using their sexuality, as Bev (WH) explains:

> [I]f the girl's pretty and acts nice, the guy teacher will like treat her better. Girls can get away with a lot more than guys.

The following excerpts from my field notes illustrate how girls can use their sexuality to their advantage:

> Maryann walked into class as I was interviewing Daniel [teacher]. She went over to him and hugged him, then stood with her arms around him (he was sitting down and she was standing behind him). There was lots of kidding on his part and hugging on her part. She wanted to know why (pouting) she hadn't passed his class. Daniel promised if she came to class regularly next cycle, she would definitely pass. (Field note, 3/3)

> Charlene walked into class today and went over and kissed Stuart [teacher] hello and squeezed his waist. She walked over to a desk, sat down, and promptly pulled out a magazine and read it behind her bookbag. Stuart never said anything to her (and there were only seven students in class). (Field note, 4/18)

> William asked students to write a brief paragraph. . . . Hillary got up from her seat and wandered over to William's desk where he was sitting, pulled up a chair, leaned back, threw her leg up on his desk and whispered to him. She never did the assignment. (Field note, 4/19)

Despite the humiliation of failing the class, Marta hugs and kisses Daniel, perhaps highlighting her sexual appeal to compensate for her failings. Bev is able to resist doing the assignment by coyly approaching the teacher and chatting with him. Through the use of body language and affected "coquettish" speech, the girls appear to gain their (male) teachers' favor. Clearly manipulative, the girls also seem to be rehearsing a particular kind of adult feminine sexual behavior. Adopting such scripts momentarily gives them power, but ultimately perpetuates their subordination. Given the inequalities that define male-female relations, relying on sexuality as a mode of relating to others may reproduce aspects of male superiority (Holly, 1989). Furthermore, flirting is an option available only to girls who conform to conventional standards of female behavior and physical attractiveness, as Bev points out; to reward flirtation can ultimately pressure girls into conforming to those standards.

GIRLS AND SEXUAL HARASSMENT

Throughout the year, I observed numerous occasions during which male students attempted to dominate or harass females. This also conforms closely with Deirdre Kelly's (1993) findings in which she documented a range of male behaviors intended to dominate or harass girls. Mahoney (1989) observes that sexual harassment functions as a reminder to girls of the intimate connection boys make between sex and power, and also reminds them that they are defined primarily in sexual terms.

Instances of physical abuse were always met with immediate reprisals by the teachers:

> FEMALE TEACHER: That boy, Arthur, I really had it out with him not to touch anybody in class any more, ever, ever, ever, because . . . he had thrown Dawn down on the floor and was pretending to strangle her and calling her a "bitch." I had to immediately take him to guidance counselors and they called his parents. (Interview)

> The boys in front of me were constantly throwing spitballs at the girls. Sheila's high moussed hair was on the receiving end of most. She was getting upset, shouting, pushing the table. Other projectiles flew past me. More pushing tables and Sheila finally got pissed off at Randall and she pushed his notebook and it fell on the chair. He got mad at her and went over and pushed her very hard so that she fell over in her chair. The teacher (male) went over to them, grabbed Randall and said, "out of here." He later said to me, "I've never done that before [throw someone out of class], but when I see a guy start shoving a women, he's outta here." (Field note,11/16)

In these two instances, physical harassment of female students was addressed at once. On the other hand, verbal harassment in class was rarely or only summarily dealt with:

Students volunteered to read their dream pieces. [The written assignment asked students to write about a dream they remembered.] Henry
read what sounded like a rap piece about Judy being a "hoe" [whore],
how she fucks three guys at once, she's a slut, etc. There was a vicious
tone to it. (I felt like it was written previous to class and he had mem-
orized it.) The teacher said something like, "OK, Henry, that's it right
now." (Field note, 2/2)

Tamara and Michelle came back to class with cans of soda. Michelle
opened hers and it squirted all over, dripping down the front of her
shirt. Andy laughed and said, "Take your shirt off and [show] what's
underneath." Michelle said, "Shut up, that's not nice" and left the
classroom. Tamara who was witnessing this declared in a loud voice
that she hated Andy, "He's so disgusting." Andy glared at her. Clarice,
sitting next to Andy said, "Let me tell you something about Andy. He
has a mean temper, don't mess with him." Andy was shaking his head,
affirming this and said, "That's right, and if I don't get you then I send
somebody." (Field note, 4/18)

In both instances, the teachers did not intervene (or only marginally).
The second instance shows how harassment can pressure some girls into
aligning themselves with boys in order to protect themselves from abuse.
As above, rather than siding with Tamara, who expressed her dislike of
Andy, Clarice takes up Andy's defense and leads him into his threaten-
ing posture.

Although I never witnessed classroom discussions on sexual harassment, the college with which A.H.S. was affiliated was making an
attempt to educate students and staff about this issue by launching a
Sexual Harassment Awareness Week during the last month of school.
The schedule included entertainment, movies, panels, and workshops
such as "For Men Only, the Politics of Sex," and self-defense workshops
for women. Several Latina girls in this study participated by staffing
tables around the main lobby, distributing literature and large colorful
buttons that read, "SEXUAL HARASSMENT IS NOT OK."

During the same week, however, an incident occurred that was
reported in the student newspaper. A fourteen-year-old female was
attending an afterschool basketball game and was attacked by a male in
his twenties as she went to a water fountain in the hall. She was able to
fight off her attacker and called security. The director of security was
quoted in the paper, saying that "girls should not walk alone under any
circumstances," adding, "She was too attractive, and she was in a position where she wasn't protected, she wasn't with someone, she was by
herself." One might interpret such comments as conveying the message
that the victim invited the attack because she was attractive and alone,
thus shifting the responsibility of the attack onto the young women her-

self. Despite attempts to explore and critique male dominance through the Sexual Harassment Awareness Week, widespread beliefs about the origins of harassment or violence against women (that women invite abuse or harassment) remain and are incorporated into the school's gender code.

DISCUSSION AND CONCLUSION

To sum up, this chapter has focused on the ways in which the school becomes a space for all young women to observe and rehearse various aspects of adult femininity and sexuality. Many of the ordinary social interactions that take place in school and within the classroom mirror the social situations common among adults. During this period when gender identity is being strengthened, these encounters and situations influence their understandings of themselves as young women.

I have argued that within the classroom, all girls are unconsciously absorbing lessons about gender through their teachers' behavior, especially the traditional division of labor (woman as nurturer and disciplinarian, man as "soft" and remote). In addition, I argue that many of the girls were learning and participating in "scripts" relating to adult sexual behavior and embodied in the school's gender code, which sanctioned peer-initiated sexual behavior and sponsored activities such as the prom. What the girls experience in school conforms to present-day cultural formations that define gender appropriate behavior and dictate the protocols of heterosexual relations. Participation in such conventional cultures of femininity may ultimately direct and limit girls to future roles of domesticity and motherhood, and may also consign them to the sectors of the lowest-paying labor market as they cope with the dual burden of paid work and family.

As we saw in this chapter and previous ones, however, the school, does attempt to reorient working-class girls, through classroom practices and the academic and career education curricula, toward the production of a femininity that includes a professional work life. I have tried to show that these forces exist simultaneously—on the one hand, conventional models of femininity persist, as in the gendered divisions of labor in the classroom, the encouragement of girls to relate to male teachers through sexuality, the inevitability of heterosexual pairing in the school; on the other hand, an alternative model of femininity that promotes academic achievement, career attainment, and a challenge to male dominance.

As I argued in earlier chapters, U.S. Puerto Rican, African American, and many Latina girls present strong labor-market identities; they plan to postpone marriage and childbearing until they are established financially. Nevertheless, they still express strong orientations toward marriage, domesticity, and children, despite their own personal experiences with parental divorce or absent fathers. I believe that this model of womanhood, articulated by many of the Latina and African American girls, has some of its roots within the school's gender code as outlined above.

The Latina and African American girls' understandings of themselves in the future seem quite attuned to the kind of feminism promoted by the school. Many of these girls come from families where economic dependence on men is less pervasive and the experience of women as the major earner in the family is not unfamiliar. On the other hand, the school's gender code, which promotes academic mastery and economic self-sufficiency through paid work, appears to have totally failed to influence the white girls' aspirations. Perhaps, as I will later elaborate, the experience of having employed fathers, brothers, and uncles has exempted them from the disruptions that generally prompt changes in working-class girls' identities. For these girls, their best chances of economic security still lie in attaching themselves to men. Schooling and qualifications are simply not the dominant foci in the construction of their futures. In this case, the school's gender code has failed to connect (Connell et al., 1982).

CHAPTER 10

Conclusions

This book has examined the ways in which thirty young working-class women of African American, Dominican, South American, U.S. Puerto Rican, and white European backgrounds, enrolled in an alternative high school for "at-risk" students, anticipate their future lives as adult women and the role of the school's gender code in shaping those expectations. The gender code of the school, through various processes, promoted at times a contradictory version of femininity that on the one hand, emphasized academic mastery and economic self-sufficiency and on the other, condoned "traditional" patterns of gendered cultural and social interaction.

The chapters on girls' visions for their futures illustrate the differences in expectations for variously constituted groups of girls (the variables including race, ethnicity, immigration experience, family form, etc.). While some girls held more progressive conceptions of their future lives, embracing a version of femininity that emphasized the importance of educational and career success, and challenging the sexual division of domestic labor, others displayed more conservative and "traditional" notions of femininity.

An examination of the processes of identity formation among diverse young women alerts us to significant differences within the category of young women, suggesting the possibility of the emergence of multiple femininities. Recall how the young white women articulated a future identity that, for the most part, revolved around marriage and family with little orientation toward paid employment. Although they perceived that they would most certainly have to enter the labor market at some point in their adult lives, their identification with domestic concerns was still primary. For all these young white women, romance played a central role in their lives. Many were involved in long-standing, monogamous relationships, and spent a great deal of leisure time with boyfriends. They also provided much of the household labor for their families. Their probable adult lives will mirror their present and preparatory circumstances, lives constructed around domestic responsibilities and relationships with men.

On the other hand, the young women of African American and U.S.

Puerto Rican descent, given the long histories of female participation in the labor market and the reality of economic discrimination against men, expressed a primary identification with obtaining jobs or "careers," desiring a family life after establishing themselves economically. While most envisioned the domestic sphere as their future responsibility, they also clearly wished to negotiate more equitable terms in the division of labor with their mates. With regard to romance, it appeared much less a concern than it did for the white girls. While many in this group expressed interest in boys and in dating, they did not enter into the type of intense involvements typical of the white girls.

The group of immigrant Latina girls, whose family experiences of immigration have created ruptures in traditional gender consciousness, reflected a range of future expectations that are both consonant with the new possibilities presented by the school, and at the same time, reflect some of the cultural prescriptions of gender within their families or communities. Most of these young women intended to pursue jobs or careers in the hope of maintaining some economic independence and control over their domestic lives. Education is recognized as valuable by these girls; this sense of value is greatly reinforced by their families, who view education as a primary vehicle for social mobility. Yet for some, their academic performance was barely passable and higher education not a realistic goal. While all the immigrant girls envisioned getting "good" jobs, marrying, and having children, the girls most engaged in school anticipated getting settled first economically before marriage, and those less engaged in school planned on entering into emotional attachments with men or early childbearing before a period of independence. Many of these girls found themselves struggling to redefine gender boundaries, just as their mothers had to adapt to new gender codes after settling in the United States.

Several aspects of this alternative school emerged as significant in shaping various aspects of the young women's identities. These included a school ethos that embodied the belief on the part of the staff and students that graduating from high school was a realistic goal, a disciplinary structure that served as a corrective for the girls' previously negative attitudes toward school, a pedagogic relationship in which teachers view students optimistically and students feel teachers care, and a curriculum that emphasized career preparation and helped students develop skills necessary to examine critically aspects of the unequal social structure in which they live.

One element that appears to influence the young women's attachment to schooling is the disciplinary structure. The discipline code at A.H.S. attempted to promote self-regulation and self-control rather than distribute punishment and flex authority. Previously defined by their

relationship to a punitive disciplinary structure (discipline deans, detention, suspensions, etc.), the students entered a more hospitable environment without such threatening structures. Thus, students had the opportunity to recreate alternative self-images vis-à-vis school (Wexler, 1992).
For many of these young women, school had meant containment, punishment, and condescension. A.H.S. on the other hand, provided a more
constructive atmosphere: the students spoke appreciatively of "freedom" and of being treated as adults. Such conditions take on special significance for young women from family cultures that greatly curtail their
social freedom.

Another factor that surfaced as particularly pertinent to the formation of an academic identity, is the young women's connection to significant adults in the school. This has special meaning for young women in
their first year of high school. As Taylor and her colleagues (1995)
found, it is during the early high school years that many of the girls in
their study began to experience a kind of psychological isolation (frequent losses of relationships, self-imposed silencing, disconnection from
themselves and others). The authors describe girls in their study who,
during the transition from elementary school to ninth grade in high
school, begin to feel "unmoored, lost in the shuffle from one classroom
to the next and missing the teachers whom they knew and who knew
them since they were young" (p. 197). They quote a young women who
describes feeling "unwanted" in high school because of the lack of attention from overburdened counselors and teachers. For the young students
in my study, establishing attachments with significant school adults
appeared to help "moor" the girls in their first year of high school and
contributed to the sense of possibility that they might indeed graduate
from high school. Although I described in detail many instances of the
girls' opposition and resistance to individual teachers, these same girls
often expressed the sentiment that at A.H.S. "teachers are there for
you."

The curriculum-in-use at A.H.S. was another factor that emerged as
significant in the production of girls' identities. Using Bernstein's framework of visible and invisible pedagogies, I examined how elements of the
curricular form and content signaled changes in the way female student
identities are constructed and shaped within school. In particular, I
argued that through classroom practices and curricular knowledge
young women learned skills that will benefit them in both their future
workplaces and homes; they were encouraged to work with peers collectively, which may transfer to future collectivistic agitation on behalf
of women's interests and may promote a deeper sense of women's
autonomy, interdependence and community; and they were exposed to
strategically selected educational materials that refined their critical

understanding of a socially stratified world and their location within it. In addition, the importance assigned to career education at A.H.S. signaled how seriously the school regarded the future employment for women. I also speculate that the school curriculum fostered a work ethic and a critical awareness of male domination, thus taking into account the particular sensibilities and experiences of many of the Latina and African American girls. White girls, on the other hand, appeared to find the curriculum's contents less resonant or less relevant to their future identities.

IMPLICATIONS AND ISSUES

The above findings lead to several theoretical implications and also pose some concerns. First, this work has contributed empirically to new directions in feminist theories that challenge the notion of a unified or essential gender identity among women. The findings in this study suggest that we simply cannot assume that the identities of all young women of a particular social class or racial/ethnic group are unitary and homogeneous (Roman, 1988) as illustrated by the differential importance young women attach to schooling, future employment, marriage, and children. I have attempted to press beyond merely acknowledging the differences among the young women in the study to look at the ways in which their differences are socially, historically, and materially constructed. This study also lends empirical support to the new thrust in feminist theories that examine the importance of race/ethnicity in the social construction of gender. This text has illustrated how race, ethnicity, social class, and so forth are not simply individual attributes that account for the variation of a universal experience of being female; rather, as Erkut and her colleagues contend, these factors are interconnecting and mediate gender in ways that produce qualitatively different female experiences for girls and young women (Erkut et al., 1996, p. 53).

Throughout this book, my purpose has been to demonstrate the fluidity of gender identity and the differential impact of schooling processes on female student identities. Such a focus goes beyond explaining only in terms of their social class or racial/ethnic group status, young women's school behavior, the importance they place on educational qualifications, and, ultimately, their expectations and aspirations for the future, but looks at the interplay of school processes, young women's race, social class locations, and the economic environments in which they live in shaping identities (Davidson, 1996).

This has particular relevance with regard to the relationship between identity and academic engagement. Ogbu (1989), for example, has argued that "involuntary" minorities such as African Americans or U.S. Puerto Ricans, construct an oppositional identity in which school success is equated with "acting white," in response to the historical inequalities experienced in U.S. society. As I have shown, however, "involuntary minorities" such as the young African American and U.S. Puerto Rican women in this study within a nontraditional school setting, clearly attached importance to gaining qualifications. Because their day-to-day classroom behavior, at times oppositional and challenging to adult authority, was generally not interpreted by school adults as being antithetical to their academic success, they were able to experience generally positive outcomes. There were many times I observed girls who engaged in oppositional behaviors such as disrupting class, dominating classroom activity, and exacting more of the teachers' time and attention, and teachers responded with comments like "they really wanted to be here [in the classroom]. This is really big for them to be in the classroom and be noisy." I would argue that this factor, adults' positive interpretations of oppositional behaviors, that in more constraining settings such as in traditional schools would be condemned or viewed negatively, emerged as extremely relevant to the formation of young women's pro-academic identities despite their "minority" group status. Thus, under such circumstances, a girl could simultaneously engage in oppositional practices yet excel academically and find relevance in gaining educational qualifications. The range in the young women's (both "involuntary" and "voluntary" minorities) responses to their schooling experiences challenges Ogbu's notion that meanings attached to schooling and actual school experiences are more or less fixed for students depending on the status of their racial/ethnic group (Davidson, 1996).

In an alternative schooling environment, (in which teachers are responsive to students, a less punitive discipline structure is in place, etc.), contrary to Ogbu's view, most young women of African American or U.S. Puerto Rican descent ("involuntary minority" youth) have been able to find meaning in gaining educational qualifications and have reworked their previously negative relationship to schooling. On the other hand, many of the ("voluntary") immigrant Latinas exhibited a range of academic identities from not attending school at all to becoming valdictorians of their classes and envisioned future family and work lives spanning from "traditional" to more radical conceptions. Perhaps this is reflective of what Portes (1996) calls "segmented assimilation"— that is, different groups of second-generation immigrant youth (even individuals within the same ethnic group) will take different pathways to adulthood depending on a variety of conditions, contexts, and resources. Thus, ideologies regarding schooling, classroom behavior, and so on for "voluntary" immigrant youth such as the young Latinas in this study, are similarly not predictable or fixed.

In the same way that Ogbu's theory of academic engagement and minority status needs "broadening" to incorporate the interactional effects of schooling processes, gender, "minority" status, and social class, my examination of the curriculum using Bernstein's framework of invisible pedagogy also points to its limitations and the need to understand better the complex interplay between the curriculum and how students' responses to the curriculum are influenced by factors such as race/ethnicity and gender in addition to social class background. Clearly, the evidence from A.H.S. suggests that a more invisible pedagogy (weakly classified, integrated curriculum) is as effective in urban schools with low-income working-class students of color as it is in private or suburban schools with white upper-middle-class youth, typically associated with invisible pedagogy. The contradictory evidence, that working-class youth of color succeed with this particular pedagogical method usually reserved for more privileged youth, argues for a "broadening" of Bernstein's theory that takes into consideration race/ethnicity in addition to his focus on social class. Moreover, the fact that so many of the young women of color succeeded academically and responded so positively to a less rigidly defined curriculum and pedagogical style also argues for a much more multidimensional theory that takes account of gender (Semel, 1994).

Throughout the pages of this text, I have attempted to bring to the surface the complexity of identity formation—how the particular practices and messages conveyed by this school's gender code (both the emphasis on academic mastery and economic self-sufficiency and the condoning of "traditional" patterns of gendered cultural and social interaction) interact with the young women's beliefs and behaviors that they bring to school with them. It is this interaction that helps to shape aspects of the young women's identities outlined in this book. And, at the same time, this study has shown that as the young women negotiate an identity that is shaped by their schooling experiences, they must also negotiate an identity between the culture in which they live, and particularly in the case of Latinas, the cultures in which their parents were raised.

In addition to the theoretical implications just mentioned above, there are several concerns, some of which are troubling, that this study raises. These concerns center around the transitions from an alternative school to traditional higher education settings, the personal costs involved in success, future economic prospects for low-income young women, and prospects for equitable relationships with males.

As Fine (1989) has argued, there is evidence that a classroom structure based on individualism and competition may be detrimental to young women's academic achievement. Girls perform better and are more engaged in tasks that require cooperative learning. This has even more resonance for Latina students. Cooperative learning is entirely consistent with the kinds of cultural beliefs and practices common among Latino families; as Carrasquillo (1991, cited in Taylor et al., 1995) explains, interdependence and cooperation are cultural values that strongly influence the socialization and identity formation of Latino children. These beliefs, therefore, are likely to produce ways of learning that are nonindividualistic and more cooperative in nature and hence more likely to engender success among Latina students. But the question arises to what extent will the young women be prepared to negotiate more conventional patterns of learning in individually based, traditional classrooms that are characterized by competition with classmates and where success is based on individual assertiveness, reflecting the competitive individualism of a capitalistic society. As the young women move to more individually structured environments such as college classrooms or job settings, the question will be whether they can initiate cooperative ways of learning with peers or organize collectively around demands to improve job conditions.

There is also the troubling concern about the cost of success for these young women if they do "make it." For most, if they do enter higher education, they will be the first in their families to do so. Improving their lives through advanced schooling and good jobs will in many cases be fraught with conflict. Signithia Fordham (1997) eloquently describes the costs of academic success for the young African American female students who are socialized to silence and invisibility in school, and as a result are isolated and alienated from their more communal, underachieving peers. This painful situation sometimes leads high-achieving girls to give up their efforts to succeed. Perhaps more painful is the perception that their mothers and teachers are less than supportive of their pursuits. Fordham writes, "what they do not discern is that their mothers and seemingly unsupportive teachers are unconsciously preparing them for a life away from the black community . . . the African American female's survival 'out there' is largely dependent upon her ability to live a life saturated with conflict, confusion, estrangement, isolation, and a plethora of unmarked beginnings and endings, jump starts and failures" (p. 103).

For Latina women, success can be equally costly. As Gloria Anzaldúa (1987) describes, "the welfare of the family, the community . . . is more important than the welfare of the individual. The individual exists first—as sister, as father, as padrino—and the last as self" (p. 19). The pursuit then of individualistic goals of entering higher education to prepare for a career can similarly cause dissonance in Latina women where "self" must be first in order to succeed.

In a related way, the costs for white working-class women are also high. Although historically a large proportion of white working-class women were forced to work outside the home because of economic necessity, the ideal was to have a non-income-earning wife at home supported entirely by a man's wage. Although some changes over the decades have occurred in part due to the demise of the family wage ideology, the ideal of a stay-at-home wife remains. Working-class families still value this concept mainly because the jobs available to working-class women are often limited by their education and socialization (Carter, 1994, p. 74). For a young white working-class woman to believe that her independence and self-worth is related to her economic production, is to break from the cultural pressure to conform to the dominant working-class ideal of the stay-at-home wife whose primary identity is centered around husband, home, and children. This break can also be painfully isolating and alienating.

Many of these young "at-risk" women, especially the young women of color, are attempting to contradict society's assumptions about the value low-income young urban women attach to schooling and about how they think about the future. The stereotypical assumptions about young working-class or poor women (all assumed to be "at risk" educationally) encompass beliefs about their lack of motivation for academic achievement and lack of incentive to plan for the future (Taylor et al., 1995, p. 176). Clearly, the majority of these young women presented in this book do not fit such stereotypes. However, there is the concern that although many of the young women articulate future hopes of continuing their education, obtaining decent jobs, and finding loving husbands, these desires may be extremely difficult to fulfill. Although A.H.S. provides students with the tools and information to negotiate entry into college, these working-class girls will need much more in terms of social and financial support to persist in higher education and to make important career connections (Taylor et al., 1995). As Taylor and her colleagues point out, for low-income and working-class young women, already at the margins in the larger world because of their social location, there is little room for error and there are few resources (p. 199).

Another unsettling issue raised by this study is the way in which race and ethnicity will eventually mediate the opportunities of young working-class and low-income women despite the best intentions of the school and the girls themselves. Although white working-class women appeared less interested in pursuing higher education and paid work than the African American, U.S. Puerto Rican, and some of the Latina girls, it is more likely that they (white working-class girls) will receive higher returns on their education, experience less unemployment, be less likely to have to support families alone, or live in poverty. Race, ethnicity, and class form critically important determinants of women's economic and social well-being. For example, in New York City, while 9.3 percent of all white families were headed by a female, 42.2 percent of Puerto Rican families, and 39.2 percent of African American families were. Because female-headed households tend to have considerably lower income than other (usually more "traditional") domestic arrangements, Puerto Rican and African American families are likely to suffer higher levels of poverty. However, this is also true for two-parent African American and Puerto Rican families. Moreover, white women with only a high school diploma are much more likely to be employed in high-paying or middle-level occupations than African American or Latina women. On the other hand, African American clerical workers are more likely than white or Latina women to have four years of college, thus illustrating the variable worth of educational qualifications. It is this reality that the young women face when leaving A.H.S.

This particular alternative high school appears to succeed in reestablishing these young women's interest in education, helping them to see how schooling can be instrumental in their later pursuit of economic security. Certainly, with a high school diploma, and with some degree of on-the-job experience through the career education program, these young women stand a better chance in the labor market. For those who seek higher education, access will be even greater. However, it is a mistake to assume that higher educational attainment and achievement will *necessarily* lead to decent jobs, given the persistent inequalities in the labor market, particularly in New York City. Yet there is some evidence that a high school diploma makes some difference for women. As Fine (1986) points out:

> While it is easy to be cynical about the economic advantage gained by a high school diploma, for women in particular, the relative advantage gained by a high school diploma is substantial. . . . [I]t is the difference between a 31 percent chance of living in poverty for black female graduates and 62 percent for black dropouts . . . an 11 percent chance for white female graduates and 28 percent for white female dropouts.

The fact that the young women in this study who graduate will hold a diploma from an alternative high school will also increase their chance for success in the labor market. An article by Catterall and Stern (1986) provides evidence, based on data from the High School and Beyond study (Jones et al., 1983), that students who had attended alternative schools generally had higher employment rates and occasionally received higher wages than comparable students from standard institutions. This finding is confirmed by A.H.S.'s own followup study of 1988 graduates. Of 137 graduates who were randomly contacted by telephone, 95 (69 percent) reported a full-time job and 50 percent of them were employed in a skilled position as defined by the Department of Labor. An analysis of graduates' income suggested that A.H.S. graduates fell within a substantially higher-income range than other high school graduates. Nevertheless, while having a high school diploma, especially one from an alternative high school, may mitigate some of the effects of persistent labor market discrimination, the school itself cannot entirely eradicate the influences of race, class, and gender in the labor market success.

This study has also raised the issue of the girls' desires for more equitable relationships with males. The discrepancy between what they desire in a partner and what probably lies ahead with regard to women's subordination in the home will be difficult for these young women to reconcile. One concern lies with the economic experiences of working-class men and men of color and how their situation will affect women in the future. Although the experience of wives working outside the home can lead to renegotiation of more equitable gender roles within the family, as seemed to be the case in the families of some of the Latina girls, it remains to be seen whether such rearrangements have staying power; it may happen that, with the decline in real wages, job instability, underemployment, or long-term unemployment, men will attempt to reassert their patriarchal privilege within families. While female identity is continually being reconstituted, the constitution of masculinity and male identity has changed very little (Lees, 1993; Weis, 1990; Connell, 1996). This could, as Weis speculates, put men and women on a collision course. In fact, Stafford (1991) has found that in the presence of long-term unemployment, young men retreat into an aggressive sexism that could well lead to an increase in the level of domestic violence (cited in Lees, 1993).

For the young women who articulate a gender identity that emphasizes their dependence on males and downplays their own participation in waged labor, the future looks grim. Although they most probably will have to engage in some form of waged work, this will not be sufficient to modify their dependence on spouses principally because of low pay, low mobility, and constant job instability, leaving them extremely vulnerable in the event of divorce. Furthermore, a primary identification with domestic concerns over paid work puts them in a precarious labor market position where they may not be motivated to struggle for adequate wages, quality child care, or job advancement opportunities because of the jobs' relative lack of significance in the young women's lives.

For those women who do aspire to economic autonomy and some kind of family life, the fact that they do work will probably do little in and of itself to alter the unequal division of labor within the family. Generally, there has not been a positive correlation between women's increased participation in the workforce and men's increased participation in household labor (Carter, 1994). As Carter points out, working women continue to do the lion's share of domestic labor while men's contribution remains unchanged when their wives work. What does seem to affect the unequal division of labor is how much a woman contributes to the family income. The greater her share of income, the less disproportionate is her involvement in household labor. Similarly, the greater her control over the family income, the greater her increase in self-confidence, leverage over fertility decisions, and her overall voice and vote in the marital relationship (Blumberg, 1991). This suggests an urgency for women to prepare for and demand certain types of jobs that provide adequate wages and security, which might enable them to better control the conditions of their lives.

RECOMMENDATIONS

The recommendations I propose here address the concerns I have raised above. While the recommendations are specific to A.H.S., young working-class and poor women in all urban schools would also benefit. However, without concurrent changes in school structure and curriculum, these interventions obviously will have limited effectiveness. Nonetheless, the recommendations I put forth make up a wish list for *all* young working-class and low-income women.

The importance of future employment and economic independence for women is actively embodied in the school's gender code, which emphasizes paid work and careers, and which is embraced by many of the girls. There is little emphasis at A.H.S., however, on the relationship between working and the family. Domestic labor is taken for granted and is rarely spoken of as "work"; it is not part of the agenda in discussions about training students for the future. The stress is almost exclusively on career preparation. Yet most girls envision having a family, and it is the family that will throughout their lives absorb most of their time and effort. The school should, therefore, examine more carefully the relationship between family and work, and take seriously the potential conflicts between and the multiple demands of women's domestic and economic roles. In particular, curriculum topics for both girls *and* boys could focus on family and work, and help the students develop a critical understanding of both the domestic division of labor and the local labor market. Discussions might center around questions such as those that Carter puts forth (1996, p. 75): How does the family perpetuate the biases and assumptions about the limits on women's work? What part does childhood socialization play in our expectations about adult family roles? Why are women expected to work a double shift—one on the job and one at home? Such a pedagogical strategy assumes particular importance in light of recent research that demonstrates the "intransigence" of male culture (e.g., Connell, 1993; Weis, 1990).

The school should also recognize and redress its failure to understand the femininity of white working-class girls. Although many of these girls do anticipate being employed, much more needs to be done to encourage a *primary* identification with waged labor. As I discussed, in viewing economic production as a primary aspect of their gender identity, women might be more motivated to struggle for decent wages, affordable high-quality daycare, and job mobility. Furthermore, identification with workforce participation might provide working-class women with more leverage within the home. However, an emphasis on career training itself does not alter a version of femininity that makes women's security and economic opportunities rely entirely upon the economic status of the men with whom they are affiliated. This suggests adding an additional layer to the career education piece that provides young working-class women with opportunities throughout their high school years to connect with adult women who are employed in various kinds of jobs requiring different levels of education. In particular, working-class or poor women who have successfully completed high school or college and are working in middle-class professions would provide these young women with alternative models of working-class femininity (Carter, 1994).

It is important not to downplay the significant lack of social support that many young working-class women of all backgrounds may encounter as they negotiate entry into college or the workforce. One aspect is the substantial psychological and emotional costs to young women of color as they try to improve their lives. Thus, it is critical to help such young women understand and identify racism, sexism, and discrimination and to develop effective coping strategies for dealing with these barriers that can limit their education and career development. Hackett and Byars (1996) have suggested that the most effective kind of role model intervention for young girls of color is often exposure to models similar in age and social background. Research has shown that similar-age peers are more effective in teaching and developing the kinds of coping behaviors young women will need. Because of the unique relationship A.H.S. enjoys with a community college, college students could be recruited and supported by the school to provide the girls with successful role models or mentors close in age. In addition, teachers need to help the young women identify resources within their communities such as girls' clubs or organizations, or civic/business organizations that provide mentoring or community activities for young women.

Finally, in order for these girls to press for better standards of living and more equitable relationships with mates, A.H.S. needs to more actively promote the development of the girls' sense of a collective or social identity as women. All girls need to be guided toward a critical understanding of how social structures of domination affect their lives and how these impact differently on different groups of girls; with such an understanding, these structures may be challenged collectively. For girls who belong to oppressed groups, it is important to develop and encourage this sense of cultural and collective identity if they are to successfully challenge their social subordination both as females and as members of a racial or ethnic minority, particularly within work settings. This calls for an emphasis within the career education curriculum that critically analyzes the role of organized labor in improving working conditions and traces historically the changes in labor movements. This curriculum should trace the historical exclusion of women and people of color from organized labor and how this has impacted on women's lack of control in the workplace to the present-day movements of women workers pressing for change, and in particular the role of women of color taking on important leadership roles.

The school's structure and the faculty's willingness are conducive to making these things begin to happen. Faculty, staff, and students at A.H.S. have been pushing and continue to push forward in many positive directions.

POSTSCRIPT

In 1994, I wrote to the principal at Alternative High School to follow up on the girls with whom I had not remained in contact to find out what had happened to them educationally. Of the thirty girls in the study, over one-half (sixteen) graduated from Alternative High School, all of them graduating in 1992. (One young woman of Colombian descent graduated a year earlier as class valedictorian.)

The young women in the study who graduated from A.H.S. were: Terry, Cynthia, Laura, Jeanette, Beth, Debbie, Saundria, Barbara, Anglea, Delores, Aurea, Antonia, Ana, Carolina, Paula, and Marlissa. Four girls transferred before graduation to their neighborhood schools or moved from the New York area and it is unknown if they completed high school (Jackie, Gloria, Marta, and Magda); five others transferred to local area G.E.D. (General Education Development) programs and it is also unknown if they entered their programs or passed the G.E.D. (Doreen, Clarice, Lucy, Maria, and Marisol); and five young women were discharged from A.H.S. for being over seventeen years old and unable to complete required classes or New York State standardized exams (Linda, Kerry, Marta, Cheryl, and Marissa).

After a visit to the school in 1997, counselors informed me that the following girls had attended college: Antonia, Toni, Carolina, Saundria, Barbara, and Terry. Others may have also attended college, but at the time it could not be ascertained.

APPENDIX A

Methodology

SAMPLE SELECTION

At the start of the school year, after receiving permission from the principal to conduct my study at A.H.S., I sent letters to all the ninth-grade teachers explaining who I was and briefly stating my research intentions; I asked to meet with them individually to discuss observing their classes. Four out of six teachers responded positively and agreed to have me sit in on their classes as often as I liked. (There were three "core"[1] ninth-grade classes, each taught by a team of two teachers—I received permission from two teams.) The only remaining qualification was that the ethnic and race composition of those two classes provide me with the three groups of girls I had targeted for the study. Teachers reviewed their class lists with me, "roughly" indicating what they believed to be the ethnic origin of their female students. This was mainly based on the students' names, their appearance, and autobiographies they had written. However, it was not until the young women had completed my questionnaires that I could be certain that they satisfied the requirements of the study.

During the first classroom visits, I asked girls to fill out the following background questionnaire:

1. Name

2. Birthdate

3. How would you describe yourself?
    a. African American/black
    b. Asian American
    c. Latina/Hispanic
    d. White/Caucasian
    e. Other:

4. Where were you born?
    If not in the United States, when did you come to the United States?

5. Where was your mother born?
    If not in the United States, when did she come to the United States?

6. Where was your father born?
   If not in the United States, when did he come to the United States?
7. What classes are you taking this cycle?

I derived my sample of thirty girls based on these questionnaires.

DATA COLLECTION

Interviews

After the initial three months I spent establishing familiarity with the students, I began conducting interviews in January with the girls and the teachers whose classes I had been observing. Interviewing continued until April. Since the school followed a trimester system (based on three "cycles"), the two classes I had been observing ended in March after two cycles. The internship program began in late March and fourteen of the girls who participated were no longer attending classes. However, several girls were assigned internships within A.H.S. or in the college offices, so I did occasionally see them and was able to set up interviews. The girls not participating in the internship program were required to attend classes. I observed one class (three times a week) for the remainder of the school year. For the most part, I first scheduled formal interviews with the girls slotted for internships.

I conducted, in a variety of settings, formal interviews with thirty female students. I approached each girl individually to arrange for an interview and would say something like:

> I would like to interview all of the girls in both classes for my study that I hope will be a book someday. I'd like to know if you would be willing to speak to me sometime. I'd like to ask you about some of your ideas about school, your ideas about the future. We won't talk about anything you're not interested in or don't want to talk about. It is very confidential, your name will never be used. So, if you agree, the principal says that your parent or guardian has to sign this permission slip first.

After a girl agreed to an interview (and returned a consent form), we would decide upon a convenient time and place to meet. While many girls did appear at the arranged time for an interview, just as many did not. I often spent considerable time trying to track down a "no show," checking the cafeteria and neighborhood restaurants, consulting friends and teachers, and so on. Eventually, I was able to obtain each girl's class schedule and made it a point to confirm an interview, waiting for each girl outside her classroom door. In addition, one teacher made a "deal" with those girls who were chronic absentees and hard-to-arrange interviews: that if they came to his class, they could be excused to talk to me. These various strategies proved successful.

Interviews were usually conducted in empty classrooms; however several took place in neighboring restaurants. All interviewees (female students and teachers) were asked questions conforming to a semistructured interview schedule. Responses were followed up with further probe questions. Generally interviews were individual, but some were conducted as groups when girls expressed the desire to be interviewed together.

To record formal interviews, I asked interviewees' permission to tape the interview with a small, microcassette recorder; I also took notes during the interviews, the recorder failing to work on occasion. The formal interviews lasted between 30 and 90 minutes; on average, they were 60 minutes long.

The interview protocol:

School-Related

1. Can you tell me why you came to A.H.S.?

2. Can you tell me what some of the differences between your old school and A.H.S. are? (students? teachers? amount of schoolwork? curriculum content? classwork? homework? fights? rules?)

3. What are some of the things you like/dislike about A.H.S.?

4. Do you think that teachers treat girls and boys the same way or differently? Can you give me some examples?

5. A.H.S. has students from a lot of different backgrounds like Latino, African American, white. Do you see any differences between different groups of people in the school?

6. If you could change anything at A.II.S., what would you change?

7. Do you think you'll go on an internship in the spring? If so, what job will you do? Why did you choose this?

8. Because I only go to "core" class, I don't have any idea what the rest of the day is like for you. Could you tell me what a typical day in school is like for you?

Outside School

9. I'd like to ask you some questions about your life outside of school. What is a typical week day like for you? (What did you do yesterday?) What is a weekend day like?

10. Do you have a boyfriend?

11. Can you describe him?
12. Does he go to school?
13. Who lives at home with you?
14. Do you have any chores (housework) at home that you are responsible for?
15. What kinds of chores (housework) do your brothers/sisters do?

After High School

16. I'd like to ask you some questions about after high school. What would you like to do when you graduate?
17. What if you could do anything you wanted to what would you do?
18. Do you think you'll do that?
19. How do imagine your life in five years? In ten years?
20. What is the ideal husband?
21. Would you work if you had children? If yes, how will you arrange child care?

Background Questions

22. Does your mother/father work? What type of employment?
23. How much education has your mother/father/brother/sister completed?
24. Where was your mother born? Where was your father born? Where were you born?
25. If not in the United States, what were the circumstances of your mother/father/you coming to the United States?
26. How does your mother feel about the job she is working at?
27. What kind of life would your mother/father like you to have?

I also conducted formal interviews with eight teachers. In addition to the four teachers whose classes I was observing, I interviewed four other teachers who taught courses for ninth-graders. These interviews took place in empty classrooms, outside on the patio, or in restaurants. They were also taped with the permission of the interviewees.

Teacher interview protocol:

1. How did you come to teach here?
2. Did you have any difficulties orienting yourself to A.H.S.?
3. How would you define success in teaching here?
4. Is there anything that prevents you from being as successful as you would like?
5. Is there anything you especially like about teaching at A.H.S.? Anything you dislike or would like to change?

6. Would you say there are any notable differences between boys' and girls' reactions to school? In what ways? Why do you think this is? Any differences between students of different racial or ethnic backgrounds?

7. Would you say that girls and boys respond to you as a female/male teacher the same way as to a male/female teacher?

8. If you had to teach only girls or only boys, which would you choose and why?

All interviews were transcribed onto computer. Once printed out, each interview and accompanying notes were placed in the individual folder that maintained other relevant data on each girl and that contained such data as my observation notes or informal interviews, questionnaires, class schedule, and records of type of internship, grades, and attendance.

Observations

Depending on the situation in the classroom, I constantly shifted between being an observer to participant observer. I sometimes sat unobtrusively off to the side and at other times sat with a group of students or attempted to do the classroom assignment. It was apparent to me after the very first classroom visit that I would need to be flexible. As discussed in the text, the classroom pedagogy was based on cooperative learning. This meant that students sat in groups of two to six at large tables, not at individual desks. Interaction between students was encouraged as classroom assignments called for cooperative work. The team of two teachers circulated among the groups of students. I cannot begin to capture the noise, activity, and what sometimes appeared as sheer chaos that prevailed in the classroom. I usually sat (or, on particularly good attendance days, stood) wherever there was available space. In one classroom, I often sat cross-legged on top of the teacher desk, which was shoved in a corner. In another classroom I usually sat on a high stool that students always left unoccupied. My first field notes were filled with references to the noise and commotion and my inability to record anything. I was simply unprepared to systematically observe a class which did not fit a traditional model of classroom conduct and interaction. After my initial confusion and floundering, I decided to focus on one group of girls during each class. I worked out a system whereby I collected all handouts, copied notes and homework assignments for each class, and either sat with or observed one group of girls.

During class I recorded various activities of the girls, their reactions to classwork, interactions with peers or teachers, their comings and goings in and out of class. After classroom observations, I sat in the college library to review my notes, fill in sketchy recordings, and note my reactions. These reactions were marked off with parentheses within my observation notes. I kept a separate notebook for recording informal observations or discussions conducted in the cafeteria or around school grounds. All observation notes were typed on the computer and compiled chronologically. Headings for each note consisted of the date, teachers' names, place and time of observation. Once printed out, I kept the observations from both classrooms separate and numbered each page consecutively. Other observation data was treated similarly. By the end of the year, I had amassed hundreds of pages of observation data.

Data Analysis

I read through all field notes several times, jotting down ideas, themes, and insights. I was able to identify broad categories for coding purposes and developed a list of codes. For broad categories I used numbers; subcategories were coded with letters. Next, I marked off relevant chunks of data by typing the code number above the marked-off chunk. I was then able to do a computer search for each code, which I then highlighted and moved to another document. I gathered all commonly coded bits of data together, careful to type in the page number of the original field note next to each passage. This method was like cutting (with scissors) coded passages and placing them in folders.

I handled interview data in a similar way, although I employed a software program intended for bibliographic use. The program projected a kind of index card on the computer screen enabling the user to enter subject terms on top of the "index card." On the "index card" itself, I entered each girl's response to core questions (future paid work; further education; marriage; children); labeled the subject term under such headings as work, family, education; and I entered the girl's name and ethnic background. For example, the "card" on the screen might look like the following:

Paid Work/Susan/Puerto Rican//p. 23/mother employed/father absent/ internship/ etc.

What kind of work would you like to do . . . ?
"I always wanted to . . ."

The computer program allowed me to sort the responses by any subject heading I wished, thus allowing for greater breadth of analysis by grouping interview responses according to various subject headings.

However, I only used this method for analysis of the "core" interview questions. I used a similar approach to the remaining interview data as I did with observation data—that is, combing the interviews for common themes and creating coding categories.

Research Role

With many of the girls (both white and Latina) I developed a comfortable and friendly relationship. They shared their problems with me, discussed their boyfriends, asked me for academic help. In one class, I often was the subject of sexual chaffing, with some of the girls teasing me about the [male] teacher's supposed interest in dating me or with them offering to arrange a date. This easy relationship was sometimes understood or manipulated by the girls as an alliance against the classroom teachers. Sometimes, girls would comment loudly to me about how much they hated the class or the teacher, or sometimes they would engage me in conversation, show me notes from boyfriends or poems they were writing, at clearly inappropriate times, to avoid classwork. The teachers would ordinarily respond by reminding students that I was "invisible" and not to be talked to during class.

Because I was dealing with so many girls (thirty) whose friendship alliances were constantly shifting, I wanted to avoid becoming associated with any one particular group of girls to the exclusion of others. To maintain the appearance of impartiality, I had to pay particular attention to such details as with whom I sat in the cafeteria or classroom and to whom I talked in the hallways, always making sure I rotated among different groups or individuals. I always tried to respect the right of the girls to decide whether and to what degree they were willing to allow me into their lives. I kept in mind a passage by McRobbie and Garber: "girl culture is so well insulated as to effectively exclude not only other undesirable girls—but also boys, adults, teachers, and researchers" (1976, p. 222). While there were various and varying limitations the girls set on my involvement with them, many of the young women did permit me significant access to their lives.

APPENDIX B

Girls' Educational Profiles

Girl's Name	Achievement*	Internship	College	Desired Career/Job
White European				
Terry	High pass	Hospital	Yes	Sports medicine, occupational therapy
Cynthia	High pass	Hospital	Yes	Secretary, fashion design, clerical, accounting
Beth	Pass	Police station	No	Writer, lawyer, clerical
Chris	Pass	Police station	Yes	Police woman, lawyer, clerical
Jeannette	Pass	High school	Yes	Hotel manager, clerical
Laura	Pass	None	Yes	Child psychologist, secretary
Debbie	Low pass	None	No	Dance studio owner
Linda	Low pass	None	No	Secretary
Doreen	No credit	None	No	Lawyer
Jackie	No credit	None	No	Model
African American				
Saundria	High pass	Teacher assist	Yes	Broadcaster, lawyer, nurse
Barbara	Pass	Hospital/clerical	Yes	Social worker, lawyer, doctor
Cheryl	Low pass	None	No	Writer/lawyer

(continued on next page)

Girl's Name	Achievement*	Internship	College	Desired Career/Job
Puerto Rican				
Angela	High pass	High school/clerical	Yes	Business manager, clerical
Marta	High pass	Civil court/clerical	Yes	Businesswoman, clerical
Delores	Pass	Civil court/clerical	Yes	Lawyer
Aurea	Low pass	Teacher assistant	Yes	Teacher, lawyer, army, doctor
Emily	Low pass	Politician office/clerial	Yes	Lawyer
Gloria	Low pass	None	Yes	Teacher
Clarice	Low pass	None	Yes	Choreographer, dance
Latina				
Toni	High pass	Architect assistant	Yes	Industrial design
Carolina	High pass	Administrative assistant	Yes	Fashion design
Paula	High pass	None	Maybe	Executive secretary
Antonia	High pass	Computer	Yes	Computers
Magda	Pass	None	Yes	Bilingual secretary
Marisol	Low pass	Office assistant	Yes	Teacher
Marlissa	Low pass	None	Yes	Corrections officer
Berta	Low pass	None	Yes	Housewife
Lucy	No credit	None	Yes	Pediatrician
Tina	No credit	None	No	Housewife

* High pass means mostly As and Bs; Pass refers to low Bs and Cs. Low Pass means low Cs and Ds and no credit resulted from failing the course and not receiving any credits.

NOTES

1. All names of individuals and institutions have been changed.

CHAPTER 1. INTRODUCTION

1. During the time I conducted my research, The New York City Board of Education operated approximately fifteen alternative high schools that serve youth at risk of dropping out of traditional or regular high schools. (The number of alternative schools and programs, many selective and theme-based, grew to fifty-six by 1996.) The original alternative high schools, most founded in the 1970s, are typically small in size and flexible with regard to rules and regulations; they generally serve students with histories of poor attendance and low academic achievement.

2. The term racial/ethnic (which refers to all groups of girls) is to be understood as socially constructed categories of group and individual identity (see Omi and Winant, 1986).

3. Fine and Weis (1998) provide a rich discussion of the economic decline of working-class and people of color in urban regions during the last twenty years. They also provide rich data on the differential impact of this economic downturn on African American, Latino/a, and white men and women in the last two decades. See also Ortiz, 1994; and, Eitzen and Zinn, 1989.

4. There were thirty-two licensed faculty members at A.H.S. Ninety-four percent of the faculty held master's degrees and 31 percent were enrolled in doctoral programs.

5. Students wishing to enroll in A.H.S. are required to go through a selection process. Approximately 600 applications are received each year and only 150 students are selected. Every year, guidance counselors from seven junior high schools are asked to gather together a group of students they believe could benefit from the A.H.S. program. A.H.S. staff and students visit the junior high schools to talk to students and answer questions. The criteria for selection include a high rate of absenteeism, three or more subject area failures, identified social and emotional problems stemming from the home environment, student interest in attending A.H.S. as evidenced in an essay and interview. Staff also take into consideration whether an applicant has a family member who attended or is attending A.H.S., a factor that would indicate a potential student's famil-

iarity with the goals and structure of the school. No applicant is turned down because of academic deficiency. Students with limited English proficiency and special education students are not accepted.

CHAPTER 3. STATUS OF AFRICAN AMERICAN, LATINA, AND WHITE WOMEN IN THE UNITED STATES

1. Families below the poverty level are defined as those whose income is below a minimum threshold level that the Census Bureau considers essential for family members to be able to buy the food necessary to maintain appropriate nutrition levels.

2. More than a third (35 percent) of the females in the sample never passed Algebra or its equivalent. Less than two-thirds (61.6 percent) completed biology and less than a quarter (24.5 percent) completed chemistry.

CHAPTER 4. YOUNG WHITE WORKING-CLASS WOMEN

1. Throughout this book, I have referred to the young women as "girls." Most referred to themselves and others as "girls."

2. Appendix B enumerates salient characteristics of this group, including academic standing, internship, and future education and work intentions.

3. All students are required to complete a full- or part-time cooperative education internship during three of the four years in high school. The internship positions are nonpaying and typically in the area of community service (e.g., hospitals, schools, police stations, social service agencies). The students receive academic credit for working.

4. Cynthia's use of the term "career" seems to imply not necessarily the attainment of a professional job, but rather a strong emotional attachment to paid work (Gersen, 1985).

5. Ironically, as Kathleen Gersen (1985) points out, working-class jobs which typically entail close supervision and little personal control, are often more demanding timewise and consequently more in conflict with domestic commitments.

6. African American women of all classes have always worked outside the home because of persistent labor market discrimination faced by African American men (see hooks, 1989; Davis, 1981; Weis, 1990).

7. Fine (1988, 1991) cites the Hispanic Policy Development Project (1987), whose findings, based on data from the *High School and Beyond* study, demonstrated that low-income female sophomores, who in 1980 expected to be married or have a child by the age of nineteen, were disproportionately represented among nongraduation rates. Moreover, attitudinal data, again based on the *High School and Beyond* study (Ekstrom et al., 1986), concluded that young women who ultimately dropped out of school were more likely to agree that "most women are happiest when making a home" and that it is usually better if the man is the achiever and the woman caretaker of the home.

8. One girl has a brother who vacuums the house every other weekend.

9. Generally as younger sisters grow older, they acquire a greater share of domestic labor. This is not the case with brothers, however.

10. This is significant because much of the other girls' household work revolves around food preparation, especially evening meals.

11. To "mess around" refers to engaging in sexual activity.

12. I never witnessed this ritual performed by a boy. Boys, on the other hand, make their exclusive "right" over a girl public by walking into a classroom to pick up their girlfriend, a proprietary arm around a girl's shoulder, hugging and kissing in the hallways or cafeteria (discussed more fully in another chapter).

13. Based on 1990 Census data, Rivera-Batiz estimates that 7.5 percent of all white families lived below the poverty level in New York City. While this masks important differences within the white population, it is considerably lower than for any other racial/ethnic group in New York City.

CHAPTER 5. YOUNG WOMEN OF AFRICAN AMERICAN AND PUERTO RICAN DESCENT

1. The term U.S. Puerto Rican is used throughout this text to differentiate from those Puerto Ricans living on the island of Puerto Rico and individuals of Puerto Rican descent born in the continental United States.

2. Although U.S. Puerto Rican women's labor market participation declined during the 1970s, Cooney et al. (1982) did not find "traditional" sex roles to be an important reason for the decline. More important factors were declining job opportunities and low educational attainment.

3. It is interesting to note that 18 percent of island Puerto Rican women over the age of twenty-five have completed four or more years of college.

4. Amott and Matthaei note that when class background is taken into account, low-income white women are more likely to drop out of school than low-income African American women. They suggest that the higher dropout rate for African American women is the result of their greater concentration in conditions of poverty.

5. U.S. Puerto Rican women continue to be underrepresented in teaching.

6. At the time of the interview, Aurea's uncle was incarcerated.

7. Gloria's mother and father had divorced, and the father remarried.

8. Written communication with Michelle Fine.

9. It must be noted that not all girls had relations with males of the same age. In particular, three girls of Puerto Rican backgrounds described relationships (not necessarily sexual) with older males in their neighborhoods. What is common to these three girls is their relative lack of academic achievement compared to the others in the group. See Sharon Thompson (1995) for an analysis of relationships between young teen women and older males.

10. This is an area that needs much more exploration—looking at mothers' relationships and the role of daughters. It reminds me of a researcher friend who asked a girl if she ever talked to her parents about AIDS. The girl replied, "All the time—I keep warning my mother to be careful with all her boyfriends." In other words, how do mothers' romantic relationships play into girls' understandings about gender relations?

11. The proportion of African American women and U.S. Puerto Rican women in the labor market has historically been much higher than the proportion of white women in the labor market. For example, in 1950, 38.9 percent of Puerto Rican women (in the United States), 37.4 percent of African American women, and 28.0 percent of white women participated in the labor force (Cooney and Colon, p. 60).

CHAPTER 6. YOUNG WOMEN OF DOMINICAN AND SOUTH AMERICAN DESCENT

1. The girls' countries of origin are: Colombia (4); Dominican Republic (4); and, Ecuador (2). All but two girls (born in the United States) were born in their country of origin.
2. Antonia's mother died after arriving in the United States in 1980 and she is a dependent of her married brother employed in a hospital as a maintenance worker.
3. This is an important point. Many girls show responses that seem to be fundamentally contradictory to each other, for example, "for sure I'll be married . . . I won't really want to be married." This ambivalence (or conflicting feelings) sometimes is lost when we try to force girls' responses into definite categories of either paid work or family (Gersen, 1985).
4. Toni was born with a cleft palette.
5. Estimations of the number of hours of housework range from a few hours to over twenty hours per week.
6. The children's mother (Tina's sister) lives in a shelter for homeless women.
7. Her mother was on an extended visit in Colombia.

CHAPTER 7. REDEFINING RELATIONSHIPS TO SCHOOLING

1. LA refers to immigrant Latinas of non–Puerto Rican origin, including, Colombian, Dominican, and Ecuadoran.
2. AA refers to girls of African American descent.
3. See chapter 2 for a description of the career education/internship program.
4. PR refers to girls of Puerto Rican descent
5. WH stands for girls of white European descent, including Greek, Italian, Romanian, German, and English.

CHAPTER 8. THE FORMAL CURRICULUM

1. An excellent example of the social class differences in classroom pedagogies can be found in Anyon (1981).
2. Bernstein claims that the roots of both pedagogies are based on middle-class assumptions; and that poor and working-class children, without access to the codes (or regulative principles underlying various message systems) that underlie

these pedagogies, are therefore at a comparative disadvantage. Such practices create and perpetuate stratified groups in schools and ultimately in society.

3. All incoming freshmen were required to take the team taught interdisciplinary (combined social studies/English) "core" course, which focused on the areas of Africa, Asia, and South and Central Americas through the "themes of repression, revolution, colonization and imperialism."

4. I observed two of three "core" classes of ninth-graders over the course of the school year.

5. It is important to note that not all classes at A.H.S. follow an invisible pedagogy model, thus supporting Bernstein's claim that invisible pedagogy often exists within visible pedagogy. More traditional classroom practices do take place at A.H.S. However, all students are required to take the interdisciplinary English/Social Studies "core" course that is the focus of this chapter.

6. For example, the school constitution (written by students) states that if students can be brought up on charges of misconduct, so too can teachers. In daily practice, teachers did not enjoy special privileges—teachers and students ate and smoked in the same cafeteria and shared the same bathrooms. One of the more popular measures for minimizing the differences in age and status is the acceptability for students to address teachers by their first name.

7. These accounts of working-class schooling indicate a preoccupation with classroom order and teacher control.

8. Traditional evaluative mechanisms such as grades, quizzes, midterms, and finals were still in place and all students were assigned final grades for Social Studies and English. However, no students received failing grades. Instead, students who did not meet the requirements for passing the courses received "no credit" for the course and had to complete additional coursework in order to receive a grade and credits.

9. "Coloured" was a classification used during apartheid to refer to individuals of mixed racial heritage or individuals of Malay background.

10. Students also engaged in an independent research assignment where they called the United Nations Mission of a chosen African country and requested various kinds of information.

11. At A.H.S. all students are required to complete three ten-week internships as well as five ten-week quarters of classroom study that include Personal and Career Development I and II and Career Decision-Making. Internships, generally unpaid, are typically in an area of community service such as in hospitals, schools, police stations, and social service agencies. All students in internships are monitored by instructors and evaluated by employers.

12. The internship selection and allocation processes could not be explored sufficiently. While certainly an important aspect of identity formation, it was not possible within the constraints of a doctoral thesis to investigate these processes.

CHAPTER 9. THE SOCIAL CONSTRUCTION OF GENDER WITHIN THE SCHOOL

1. As part of the interviews with teachers, teachers were asked to respond to the questions (1) whether they see any differences between girls' and boys'

responses or attitudes to school, and (2) if they had to teach only girls or only boys who would they choose and why.

2. See Deirdre Kelly (1993, pp. 125–163) for an in-depth discussion on low-income girls' disengagement from an alternative high school.

3. In general, teachers did not differentiate between Latinas of Puerto Rican, Caribbean, South and Central American descent. In many cases, teachers did not know the country of origin of Latina girls.

4. Deirdre Kelly (1993) classifies teachers in her study undertaken in an alternative school as being developmentalists or traditionalists—the former group being mostly female teachers who frequently compared teaching to parenting.

5. It is interesting that these two teachers did not talk about their classroom relationships with students and each other as a family (as the other teachers did); however, both teachers in this team did invoke the metaphor of their "divorce" when their differences compelled them to abandon team teaching and teach on separate days.

6. A few notable exceptions include Ann Marie Wolpe's *Within School Walls*, Michelle Fine's *The Missing Discourse of Desire*, and Catherine Raissiguier's *Becoming Women, Becoming Workers*.

APPENDIX A. METHODOLOGY

1. The ninth-grade program centered on an interdisciplinary "core" course that integrated English and Social Studies. This course was required of all ninth-grade students.

BIBLIOGRAPHY

Acker, Sandra. 1987. "Feminist Theory and the Study of Gender and Education." *International Review of Education* 33 (1987): 419–435.

Acker, Sandra. 1991. "Critical Introduction: Travel and Travail." In J. Gaskell (ed.), *Gender Matters from School to Work*. Milton Keynes and Philadelphia: Open University Press.

Acosta-Belén, Edna (ed.). 1986. *The Puerto Rican Woman: Perspectives on Culture, History and Society*. New York: Praeger Press.

Alba, Richard. 1990. *Ethnic Identity: The Transformation of White America*. New Haven: Yale University Press.

Alcoff, Linda. 1988. "Cultural Feminism Versus Post-Structuralism: The Identity Crisis in Feminist Theory." *Signs* 13.3 (1988): 405–437.

Althusser, L. 1985. "Ideology and Ideological State Apparatuses." In V. Beechey and J. Donald (eds.), *Subjectivity and Social Relation*. Milton Keynes and Philadelphia: Open University Press.

American Association of University Women (A.A.U.W.). 1992. *How Schools Shortchange Girls*. Washington, D.C.: American Association of University Women and Educational Foundation.

Amos, V. and Parmar, P. 1982. "Resistances and Responses: Experiences of Black Girls in Britain." In A. McRobbie and T. McCabe (eds.), *Feminism for Girls: An Adventure Story*. London: Routledge and Kegan Paul.

Amott, Theresa. 1993. *Caught in the Crisis: Women and the U.S. Economy Today*. New York: Monthly Review Press.

Amott, Teresa and Matthaei, Julie. 1991. *Race, Gender and Work: A Multicultural Economic History of Women in the United States*. Boston: South End Press.

Andersen, Margaret L. and Collins, Patricia Hill. 1992. *Race, Class and Gender: An Anthology*. Belmont, Calif.: Wadsworth.

Anyon, Jean. 1981. "Social Class and School Knowledge." *Curriculum Inquiry* 11.1 (1981): 3–42.

Anyon, Jean. 1983. "Workers, Labor and Economic History, and Textbook Content." In M. Apple and L. Weis (eds.), *Ideology and Practice in Schooling*. Philadelphia: Temple University Press.

Anyon, Jean. 1984. "Intersections of Gender and Class: Accommodation and Resistance by Working-Class and Affluent Females to Contradictory Sex Role Ideologies." *Journal of Education* 166.1 (1984): 25–48.

Anzaldúa, Gloria. 1987. *Borderlands la Frontera*. San Francisco: Aunt Lute Books.

Apple, Michael. 1982. *Education and Power*. Boston: Routledge and Kegan Paul.

Apple, Michael. 1983. "Curricular Form and the Logic of Technical Control." In M. Apple and L. Weis (eds.), *Ideology and Practice in Schooling.* Philadelphia: Temple University Press.

Apple, Michael. 1990. *Ideology and Curriculum.* New York and London: Routledge.

Apple, Michael and Weis, Lois. 1983. *Ideology and Practice in Schooling.* Philadelphia: Temple University Press.

Archer, Sally. 1985. "Career and/or Family: The Identity Process for Adolescent Girls." *Youth and Society* 16.3 (1985): 289–314.

Arnot, Madeleine. 1982. "Male Hegemony, Social Class and Women's Education." *Journal of Education* 164.1 (1982): 64–89.

Arnot, Madeleine. 1984. "A Feminist Perspective on the Relationship between Family Life and School Life." *Journal of Education* 166.1 (1984): 5–24.

Arnove, Robert and Strout, Toby. 1980. "Alternative Schools for Disruptive Youth." *The Educational Forum* 44.4 (May 1980): 453–471.

Asher, Carol. 1984. *Helping Hispanic Students to Complete High School and Enter College.* New York: ERIC Clearinghouse on Urban Education.

Atkinson, Paul. 1985. *Language, Structure and Reproduction: An Introduction to the Sociology of Basil Bernstein.* London: Methuen.

Baker, Maureen. 1985. *What Will Tomorrow Bring? A Study of the Aspirations of Adolescent Women.* Ottawa, Ont.: Canadian Advisory Council on the Status of Women.

Barrett, Michele. 1980. *Women's Oppression Today: Problems in Marxist Feminist Analysis.* New York: Schocken Books.

Beneria, Lourdes and Stimpson, Catherine (eds.). 1987. *Women, Households, and the Economy.* New Brunswick, N.J.: Rutgers University Press.

Bernstein, Basil. 1971. *Class, Codes and Control.* Vol. 1. London: Routledge and Kegan Paul.

Bernstein, Basil. 1975. *Class, Codes and Control.* Vol 3. *Toward a Theory of Educational Transmissions.* London: Routledge and Kegan Paul.

Bluestone and Harris, 1982. *The De-Industrializing of America.* New York: Basic Books.

Blumberg, R. L. 1991. "Income Under Female Versus Male Control: Hypothesis From a Theory of Gender Stratification." In R. L. Blumberg (ed.), *Gender, Family, and the Economy: the Triple Overlap.* Newbury Park, Calif.: Sage. Cited in Patricia Carter, "Women's Workplace Equity: A Feminist View." In R. Lakes (ed.), *Critical Education for Work: Multidisciplinary Approaches.* Norwood, N.J.: Ablex.

Bogdan, Robert and Biklen, Sari Knopp. 1982. *Qualitative Research for Education.* Boston: Allyn and Bacon.

Bourdieu, Pierre. 1977. "Cultural Reproduction and Social Reproduction." In J. Karabel and H. H. Halsey (eds.), *Power and Ideology in Education.* New York: Oxford University Press.

Bowles, S. and Gintis, H. 1976. *Schooling in Capitalist America.* London: Routledge and Kegan Paul.

Brah, Avtar. 1988. "Extended Review: Gender and the Politics of Schooling." *British Journal of Sociology* 9.1 (1988): 223–245.

Brah, Avtar and Minhas, Rehana. 1985. "Structural Racism of Cultural Difference: Schooling for Asian Girls." In G. Weiner (ed.), *Just a Bunch of Girls: Feminist Approaches to School.* Milton Keynes and Philadelphia: Open University Press.

Brown, S. 1975. "Love Unites Them and Hunger Separates Them: Poor Women in the Dominican Republic." In R. Reiter (ed.), *Toward an Anthropology of Women.* New York: Monthly Review Press.

Buswell, Carol. 1984. "Sponsoring and Stereotyping in a Working-Class Comprehensive School in the North of England." In S. Acker et al. (eds.), *World Yearbook of Education 1984: Women and Education.* London: Kogan Page.

Carrasquillo, Angela. 1991. *Hispanic Children and Youth in the United States: A Resource Guide.* New York: Garland Publishing. Cited in Taylor et al., *Between Voice and Silence: Women and Girls, Race and Relationship.* Cambridge: Harvard University Press, 1995.

Carby, Hazel. 1982. "Schooling in Babylon." In Centre for Contemporary Cultural Studies, *The Empire Strikes Back: Race and Racism in Seventies Britain.* London: Hutchinson. Cited in H. Mirza, *Young Female and Black.* London: Routledge, 1992.

Carter, Patricia. 1994. "Woman's Workplace Equity: A Feminist View." In R. Lakes (ed.), *Critical Education for Work: Multidisciplinary Approaches.* Norwood, N.J.: Ablex.

Castro, Mary Garcia. 1982. "'Mary' and 'Eve's' Social Reproduction in the 'Big Apple': Colombian Voices." Occasional Paper No. 35. New York University, Faculty of Arts and Sciences.

Catteral, James and Stern, David. 1986. "The Effects of Alternative School Programs on High School Completion and Labor Market Outcomes." *Educational Evaluation and Policy Analysis* 8.1 (Spring 1986): 77–86.

Christian-Smith, Linda. 1988. "Romancing the Girl: Adolescent Romance Novels and the Construction of Femininity." In L. Roman, L. Christian-Smith, and E. Ellsworth (eds.), *Becoming Feminine: The Politics of Popular Culture.* London and Philadelphia: The Falmer Press.

Christian-Smith, Linda. 1990. *Becoming a Woman Through Romance.* New York: Routledge.

Collins, Patricia Hill. 1990. *Black Feminist Thought.* London: Unwin Hyman.

Connell, M., Davis, T., McIntosh, S., and Root, M. 1981. "Romance and Sexuality: Between the Devil and the Deep Blue Sea?" In A. McRobbie and T. McCabe (eds.), *Feminism for Girls.* London: Routledge and Kegan Paul.

Connell, R. W. 1985. *Teachers' Work.* Sydney: George Allen and Unwin.

Connell, R. W. 1993. "Disruptions: Improper Masculinities and Schooling." In L. Weis and M. Fine (eds.), *Beyond Silenced Voices: Class, Race, and Gender in United States Schools.* Albany: State University of New York Press.

Connell, R. W., Ashenden, D. J., Kessler, S., and Dowsett, G. W. 1982. *Making the Difference: Schools, Families and Social Division.* Sydney: George Allen and Unwin.

Cooney, Rosemary Santana, and Colón, Alice. 1984. "Work and Family: The Recent Struggle of Puerto Rican Females." In C. Rodríguez, V. Korrol, and

J. Alers (eds.), *The Puerto Rican Struggle: Essays on Survival in the United States*. Maplewood, N.J.: Waterfront Press.

Cooney, R., Rogler, L., Hurrell, R., and Ortiz, V. 1982. "Decision Making in Intergenerational Puerto Rican Families." *Journal of Marriage and Family* 44 (August 1982): 399.

Cornbleth, Catherine. 1990. *Curriculum in Context*. London and New York: The Falmer Press.

Coultas, V. 1989. "Black Girls and Self-Esteem." *Gender and Education*, Special Issue: "Race, Gender, and Education" 1.3 (1989): 147–161.

Crenshaw, Kimberle. 1989. "Demarginalizing the Intersection of Race and Sex: A Black Feminist Critique of Antidiscrimination Doctrine, Feminist Theory and Anti-racist Politics." *The University of Chicago Legal Forum* (1989): 139–167.

Crenshaw, Kimberle. 1991. "Mapping the Margins: Intersectionality, Identity Politics, and Violence against Women of Color." *Stanford Law Review* 43 (July 1991): 1241–1299.

Crump, S. J. 1990. "Gender and the Curriculum: Power and Being Female." *British Journal of Sociology of Education* 11 (1990): 365–387.

Darabi, Katherine and Ortiz, Vilma. 1987. "Childbearing among Young Latino Women in the United States," *American Journal of Public Health* 77.1 (1987): 25–28. Cited in V. Ortiz, "Women of Color: A Demographic Overview." In M. B. Zinn and B. T. Dill (eds.), *Women of Color in U.S. Society*. Philadelphia: Temple University Press, 1994.

Davidson, Ann Locke. 1996. *Making and Molding Identity in Schools: Student Narratives on Race, Gender, and Academic Engagement*. Albany: State University of New York Press.

Davies, Lynn. 1984. *Pupil Power: Deviance and Gender in School*. London: The Falmer Press.

Davies, Lynn. 1987. "Gender and Comprehensive Schooling." *Comparative Education* 2.26 (1987): 47–66.

Davis, Angela. 1981. *Women, Race and Class*. New York: Random House.

de Lauretis, Teresa. 1986. "Feminist Studies/Critical Studies: Issues, Terms, and Contexts." In T. de Lauretis (ed.), *Feminist Studies/Critical Studies*. Bloomington: Indiana University Press.

Del Castillo, A., Frederickson, J., McKenna, T., and Ortiz, F. 1988. "An Assessment of the Status of the Education of Hispanic American Women." In T. McKenna and F. Ortiz, *The Broken Web*. Claremont, Calif.: The Tomas Rivera Center and Floricanto Press.

Delamont, Sara. 1980. *Sex Roles in the School*. London: Metheun.

Dill, Bonnie Thornton. 1983. "Race, Class and Gender: Prospects for an All-Inclusive Sisterhood." *Feminist Studies* 9.1 (1983): 23–40.

Dill, Bonnie Thornton. 1987. "The Dialetics of Black Womanhood." In S. Harding (ed.), *Feminism and Methodology*. Bloomington: Indiana University Press, and Milton Keynes: Open University Press.

Earle, Janice, Roach, Virginia, and Fraser, Katherine. 1987. *Female Dropouts: A New Perspective*. Alexandria, Va.: National Association of State Boards of Education.

Eckstrom, R., Geertz, M., Pollack, J., and Rock, D. 1986. "Who Drops of Out of High School and Why? Findings from a National Study." In G. Natriello (ed.), *School Dropouts, Patterns and Policies*. New York: Teachers College Press.

Eisner, Elliot and Peshkin, Alan (eds.) 1990. *Qualitative Inquiry in Education: The Continuing Debate*. New York and London: Teachers College Press.

Eitzen, Stanley and Zinn, Maxine Baca. 1989. "Structural Transformation and Systems of Inequality." In S. Eitzen and M. Zinn (eds.), *The Reshaping of American: Social Consequences of the Changing Economy*. Englewood Cliffs, N.J.: Prentice Hall.

Ellsworth, Jeanne. 1993. "The Social Construction of Dropouts." In L. Weis and M. Fine (eds.), *Beyond Silenced Voices*. Albany: State University of New York Press.

Erkut, S., Fields, J., Sing, R., and Marx, F. 1996. "Diversity in Girls' Experiences: Feeling Good about Who You Are." In B. Leadbeater and N. Way (eds.), *Urban Girls: Resisting Stereotypes, Creating Identities*. New York: New York University Press.

Espín, Olivia. 1992. "Cultural and Historical Influences on Sexuality in Hispanic/Latin Women: Implications for Psychotherapy." In Margaret L. Andersen, and Patricia Hill Collins (eds.), *Race, Class and Gender: An Anthology*. Belmont, Calif.: Wadsworth Publishers.

Fine, Michelle. 1985. "Dropping Out of High School: An Inside Look." *Social Policy* 16 (Fall 1985): 43–50.

Fine, Michelle. 1987. "Silencing and Nurturing Voice in an Improbable Context: Urban Adolescents in Public School." In H. Giroux and P. McLaren (eds.), *Schooling, Politics, and Cultural Struggle*. Albany: State University of New York Press.

Fine, Michelle. 1991. *Framing Dropouts: Notes on the Politics of an Urban Public High School*. Albany: State University of New York Press.

Fine, Michelle and Weis, Lois. 1998. *The Unknown City: Lives of Poor and Working-Class Young Adults*. Boston: Beacon Press.

Fine, Michelle and Zane, Nancie. 1989. "Bein' Wrapped Too Tight: When Low-Income Women Drop Out of High School." In L. Weis, E. Farrar, and H. Petrie (eds.), *Dropouts from School: Issues, Dilemmas and Solutions*. Albany: State University of New York Press.

Foley, Eileen and McConnaughy, Susan. 1982. *Toward School Improvement: Lessons From Alternative High Schools*. New York: Public Education Association.

Fordham, Signithia. 1988. "Racelessness as a Factor in Black Students' School Success: Pragmatic Strategy or Pyrrhic Victory." *Harvard Educational Review* 58.1 (February 1988): 54–85.

Fordham, Signithia. 1997. "Those Loud Black Girls: (Black) Women, Silence, and Gender 'Passing' in the Academy." In M. Seller and L. Weis (eds.), *Beyond Black and White: New Faces and Voices in U.S. Schools*. Albany: State University of New York Press.

Fordham, Signithia and Ogbu, John. 1986. "Black Students' School Success: Coping with the Burden of 'Acting White'." *Urban Review* 18.3 (1986): 176–206.

Fuller, Mary. 1980. "Black Girls in a London Comprehensive School." In R. Deem (ed.), *Schooling for Women's Work*. London: Routledge and Kegan Paul.

Fuller, Mary. 1983. "Qualified Criticism, Critical Qualifications." In L. Barton and S. Walker (eds.), *Race, Class and Education*. Beckenham, England: Croom Helm.

Gaskell, Jane. 1983. "The Reproduction of Family Life: Perspectives of Male and Female Adolescents." *British Journal of Sociology of Education* 4.1 (1983): 19–37.

Gaskell, Jane. 1985. "Course Enrollment in the High School: The Perspective of Working-Class Females." *Sociology of Education* 58 (1985): 48–59.

Gaskell, Jane. 1987. "Gender and Skill." In D. Livingstone (ed.), *Critical Pedagogy and Cultural Power*. South Hadley, Mass.: Bergin and Garvey.

Gaskell, Jane. 1991. *Gender Matters from School to Work*. Milton Keynes and Philadelphia: Open University Press.

Georges, Robert A. and Jones, Michael O. 1980. *People Studying People*. Berkeley: University of California Press.

Geronimus, Arline. 1992. "Teenage Childbearing and Social Disadvantage: Unprotected Discourse." *Family Relations* 41 (1992): 244–288.

Gersen, Kathleen. 1985. *Hard Choices: How Women Decide about Work, Career, and Motherhood*. Berkeley: University of California Press.

Giroux, Henry. 1983. *Theory, Resistance, and Education*. South Hadley, Mass.: Bergin and Garvey.

Giroux, Henry. 1992. *Border Crossings*. New York and London: Routledge.

Gitlin, Andrew. 1983. "School Structure and Teachers' Work." In M. Apple and L. Weis (eds.), *Ideology and Practice in Schooling*. Philadelphia: Temple University Press.

Glenn, Evelyn Nakano. 1985. "Racial Ethnic Women's Labor: The Intersection of Race, Gender and Class Oppression." *Review of Radical Political Economics* 17.3 (Fall 1985): 86–108.

Goldstein, Beth. 1988. "In Search of Survival: The Education and Integration of Hmong Refugee Girls." *Journal of Ethnic Studies* 16.2 (Summer 1988): 1–27.

Grant, Linda. 1992. "Race and the Schooling of Young Girls." In J. Wrigley (ed.), *Education and Gender Equality*. London and New York: The Falmer Press.

Grant, Linda. 1994. "Helpers, Enforcers, and Go-Betweens: Black Females in Elementary School Classrooms." In M. B. Zinn and B. T. Dill (eds.), *Women of Color in U.S. Society*. Philadelphia: Temple University Press.

Grant, Carl and Sleeter, Christine. 1986. "Race, Class, and Gender in Education Research: An Argument for Integrative Analysis." *Review of Educational Research* 56.2 (Summer 1986): 195–211.

Griffen, Christine. 1985. *Typical Girls? Young Women from School to the Job Market*. London: Routledge and Kegan Paul.

Gurak, Douglas. 1987. "Family Formation and Marital Selectivity among Colombian and Dominican Immigrants in New York City." *International Migration Review* 21.2 (Summer 1987): 275–298.

Gurak, Douglas, and Kritz, Mary. 1982. "Women in New York City: Household Structure and Employment Patterns." *Migration Today* 10.3–4 (1982): 15–21.

Hackett, G. and Byars, A. M. 1996. "Social Cognitive Theory and the Career Development of African American Women." *The Career Development Quarterly* 44.4 (1996): 322–340.

Hall, Stuart. 1985. "Signification, Representation, Ideology: Althusser and the Post-Structuralist Debate." *Critical Studies in Mass Communication* 2 (June 1985): 91–114.

Halperin, Samuel. 1988. *The Forgotten Half: Pathways to Success for America's Youth and Young Families.* Final Report, Youth and America's Future. Washington, D.C.: The William T. Grant Foundation Commission on Work, Family and Citizenship.

Harding, Sandra. 1987. "Introduction: Is There a Feminist Method?" In S. Harding (ed.), *Feminism and Methodology.* Bloomington: Indiana University Press, and Milton Keynes: Open University Press.

Harding, Sandra (ed.). 1987. *Feminism and Methodology.* Bloomington: Indiana University Press, and Milton Keynes: Open University Press.

Hartmann, Heidi. 1987. "Changes in Women's Economic and Family Roles in Post–World War II United States." In L. Beneria and C. Stimpson (eds.), *Women, Households, and the Economy.* New Brunswick, N.J.: Rutgers University Press.

Higgenbotham, Elizabeth. 1994. "Black Professional Women: Job Ceilings and Employment Sectors." In M. B. Zinn and B. T. Dill (eds.), *Women of Color in U.S. Society.* Philadelphia: Temple University Press.

Hispanic Policy Development Center. 1984. *Make Something Happen: Hispanics and Urban School Reform.* Washington, D.C.: Hispanic Policy Development Project.

Holland, Dorothy and Eisenhart, Margaret. 1990. *Educated in Romance.* Chicago: University of Chicago Press.

Holly, Leslie. 1989. "Introduction: The Sexual Agenda in Schools." In L. Holly (ed.), *Girls and Sexuality.* Milton Keynes, England: Open University Press.

hooks, bell. 1984. *Feminist Theory: From Margin to Center.* Boston: South End Press.

hooks, bell. 1989. *Talking Back: Thinking Feminist Thinking Black.* London: Sheba.

hooks, bell. 1990. *Yearning: Race, Gender, and Cultural Politics.* Boston: South End Press.

Hudson, Barbara. 1984. "Feminity and Adolescence." In A. McRobbie and Mica Neva (eds.), *Gender and Generation.* London: Macmillan.

Hurst, Marsha and Zambrana, Ruth. 1982. "Child Care and Working Mothers in Puerto Rican Families." *Annals of the American Academy of Political and Social Science* 461 (May): 113–124.

Irvine, Janice. 1994. "Cultural Differences and Adolescent Sexualities." In J. Irvine (ed.), *Sexual Cultures and the Construction of Adolescent Identities.* Philadelphia: Temple University Press.

Johnson, Colleen. 1985. *Growing Up and Growing Old in Italian Families.* New Brunswick, N.J.: Rutgers University Press.

Jones, Alison. 1989. "The Cultural Production of Classroom Practice." *British Journal of Sociology of Education* 10.1 (1989): 19–31.

Jones, C., Clarke, M., Mooney, G. McWilliams, H., Crawford, I., Stephenson, B., Tourangeau, R., and Peng, S. 1983. *High School and Beyond 1980: Sophomore Cohort First Follow-Up.* Chicago: National Opinion Research Center.

Joseph, Gloria and Lewis, Jill. 1986. *Common Differences: Conflicts in Black and White Feminist Perspectives.* Boston: South End Press.

Kelly, Deirdre. 1993. *Last Chance High: How Girls and Boys Drop In and Out of Alternative High Schools.* New Haven, Conn.: Yale University Press.

Kelly, Gail and Nilhen, Ann. 1982. "Schooling and the Reproduction of Patriarchy: Unequal Workloads, Unequal Rewards." In M. Apple (ed.), *Cultural and Economic Reproduction in Education.* London: Routledge and Kegan Paul.

Kessler, S., Ashenden, R., Connell, R. and Dowsett, G. 1985. "Gender Relations in Secondary Schooling." *Sociology of Education* 58.1 (1985): 34–48.

Kessler-Harris, Alice and Sacks, Brodkin Karen. 1987. "The Demise of Domesticity in America." In L. Beneria and C. Stimpson (eds.), *Women, Households, and the Economy.* New Brunswick, N.J.: Rutgers University Press.

Komarovsky, Mirra. 1967. *Blue Collar Marriage.* New York: Vintage Press.

Korrol, Virginia Sanchez. 1983. *From Colonia to Community: The History of Puerto Ricans in New York City, 1917–1984.* Westport, Conn.: Greenwood Press.

Kuhn, Annette and Bluestone, Barry. 1987. "Economic Restructuring and the Female Labor Market: The Impact of Industrial Change on Women." In L. Beneria and C. Stimpson (eds.), *Women, Households, and the Economy.* New Brunswick, N.J.: Rutgers University Press.

Ladner, Joyce. 1971. *Tomorrow's Tomorrow: The Black Woman.* Garden Ciy, N.Y.: Doubleday.

Lees, Sue. 1986. *Losing Out: Sexuality and Adolescent Girls.* London: Hutchinson.

Lees, Sue. 1993. *Sugar and Spice: Sexuality and Adolescent Girls.* New York: Penguin.

Lesko, Nancy. 1988. "The Curriculum of the Body: Lessons from a Catholic High School." In L. Roman, L. Christian-Smith, and E. Ellsworth (eds.), *Becoming Feminine: The Politics of Popular Culture.* London and Philadelphia: The Falmer Press.

Mac an Ghaill, Mairtin. 1988. *Young, Gifted and Black: Student Teacher Relations in the Schooling of Black Youth.* Milton Keynes, England: Open University Press.

Mac an Ghaill, Mairtin. 1989. "Coming-of-Age in 1980s England: Reconceptualising Black Students' Schooling Experience." *British Journal of Sociology of Education* 10.3 (1989): 273–286.

MacDonald, M. 1980. "Socio-Cultural Reproduction and Women's Education." In R. Deem (ed.), *Schooling for Women's Work.* London: Routledge and Kegan Paul.

MacPherson, Pat, and Fine, Michelle. 1995. "Hungry for an Us: Adolescent Girls and Adult Women Negotiating Territories of Race, Gender and Class Difference." *Feminism and Psychology* 5.2 (1995): 181–200.

Mahony, Pat. 1989. "Sexual Violence and Mixed Schools." In C. Jones and P. Mahony (eds.), *Learning Our Lines: Sexuality and Social Control in Education.* London: The Women's Press.

Matthaei, Julie. 1982. *An Economic History of Women in America: Women's Work, the Sexual Division of Labor and the Development of Capitalism.* New York: Schocken Books.

Matute-Bianchi, Maria Eugenia. 1986. "Ethnic Identities and Patterns of School Success and Failure among Mexican-American and Japanese-American Students in a California High School: An Ethnographic Analysis." *American Journal of Education* 95 (November 1986): 233–255.

McCarthy, Cameron. 1990. *Race and Curriculum: Social Inequality and the Theories and Politicsw of Difference in Contemporary Research on Schooling.* London and New York: The Falmer Press.

McCarthy, Cameron. 1993. "Beyond the Poverty of Theory in Race Relations: Nonsynchrony and Social Difference in Education." In L. Weis and M. Fine (eds.), *Beyond Silenced Voices: Class, Race and Gender in U.S. Schools.* Albany: State University of New York Press.

McCarthy, Cameron and Crichlow, Warren (eds.). 1993. *Race, Identity, and Representation in Education.* New York: Routledge.

McClaren, Peter. 1989. *Life in Schools.* New York: Longman.

McKenna, Teresa and Ortiz, Flora. 1988. *The Broken Web: The Educational Experience of Hispanic American Women.* Claremont, Calif.: The Tomas Rivera Center and Floricanto Press.

McNeil, Linda. 1981. "Negotiating Classroom Knowledge: Beyond Achievement and Socialization." *Journal of Curriculum Studies* 13.4 (1981): 313–328.

McRobbie, Angela. 1978. "Working-Class Girls and the Culture of Femininity." In Women's Studies Group, Centre for Contemporary Cultural Studies, *Women Take Issue.* London: Hutchinson.

McRobbie, Angela. 1980. "Settling Accounts with Subcultures: A Feminist Critique." *Screen Education* 34 (1980): 37–49.

McRobbie, A. and Garber, J. 1975. "Girls and Subcultures: An Exploration." In S. Hall and T. Jefferson (eds.), *Resistance through Rituals: Youth Subcultures in Post-war Britain.* London: Hutchinson.

Medrano, Luisa. 1994. "AIDS and Latino Adolescents." In J. Irvine (ed.), *Sexual Cultures and the Construction of Adolescent Identities.* Philadelphia: Temple University Press.

Mickelson, Roslyn Arlin. 1990. "The Attitude-Achievement Paradox Among Black Adolescents." *Sociology of Education* 63 (1990): 44–61.

Mickelson, Roslyn Arlin. 1992. "Why Does Jane Read and Write So Well? The Anomaly of Women's Achievement." In J. Wrigley (ed.), *Education and Gender Equality.* London and New York: Falmer Press.

Miles, Sheila. 1987. "Asian Girls and the Transition from School to . . . ?" *Comparative Education* 26.2 (1987): 107–129.

Miller, R. Y. and Fowlkes, M. R. 1980. "Social and Behavorial Constructions of Female Sexuality." In C. R. Stimpson and E. S. Person (eds.), *Women, Sex and Sexuality*. Chicago: University of Chicago Press.

Mirza, Heidi Safia. 1992. *Young, Female and Black*. London: Routledge.

Moore, Helen. 1983. "Hispanic Women: Schooling for Conformity in Public Education." *Hispanic Journal of Behavorial Sciences* 5.1 (1983): 45–63.

Moore, Joan and Pachon, Harry. 1985. *Hispanics in the United States*. Englewood Cliffs, N.J.: Prentice Hall.

Ogbu, John. 1978. *Minority Education and Caste: the American System in Cross-Cultural Perspective*. New York: Academic Press.

Ogbu, John. 1982. "Equalization of Educational Opportunity and Racial/Ethnic Inequality." In P. Altbach, R. Arnove, and G. Kelly (eds.), *Comparative Education*. New York: Macmillan.

Ogbu, John. 1988. "Class Stratification, Racial Stratification, and Schooling." In L. Weis (ed.), *Class, Race and Gender in American Education*. Albany: State University of New York Press.

Ogbu, John. 1989. "The Individual in Collective Adaptation: A Framework for Focusing on Academic Underperformance and Dropping Out among Involuntary Minority Students." In L. Weis, E. Farrar, and H. Petrie (eds.), *Dropouts From Schools: Issues, Dilemmas and Solutions*. Albany: State University of New York Press.

Ogbu, John. 1994. "Racial Stratification and Education in the United States: Why Inequality Persists." *Teachers College Record* 96.2 (Winter 1994): 264–298.

Omi, Michael and Winant, Howard. 1993. "On the Theoretical Concept of Race." In C. McCarthy and W. Crichlow (eds.), *Race, Identity, and Representation in Education*. New York: Routledge.

Ortiz, Vilma and Cooney, Rosemary Santana. 1982. "Sex-Role Attitudes and Labor Force Participation among Young Hispanic Females and Non-Hispanic White Females." Paper presented at the American Sociological Association, San Francisco.

Ortiz, Vilma. 1994. "Women of Color: A Demographic Overview." In M. B. Zinn and B. T. Dill (eds.), *Women of Color in U.S. Society*. Philadelphia: Temple University Press.

Palmer, Marynick P. 1983. "White Women/Black Women: The Dualism of Female Identity and Experience in the United States." *Feminist Studies* 9.1 (Spring 1983): 151–170.

Pessar, Patricia. 1984. "The Linkage Between the Household and Workplace of Dominican Women in the United States." *International Migration Review* 18.4 (Winter 1984): 1188–1211.

Pessar, Patricia. 1987. "The Dominicans: Women in the Household and the Garment Industry." In Nancy Foner (ed.), *New Immigrants in New York City*. New York: Columbia University Press.

Pessar, Patricia. 1990. "Dominican International Migration: The Role of Households and Social Networks." In R. Palmer (ed.), *In Search of a Better Life: Perspectives on Migration From the Caribbean*. New York: Praeger.

Phoenix, Ann. 1987. "Theories of Gender and Black Families." In G. Weiner and M. Arnot (eds.), *Gender under Scrutiny*. London: Hutchinson and the Open University Press.

Pinar, William. 1993. "Notes on Understanding Curriculum as a Racial Text." In C. McCarthy and W. Crichlow (eds.), *Race, Identity, and Representation in Education*. New York: Routledge.

Portes, Alejandro. 1996. "Introduction: Immigration and its Aftermath." In A. Portes (ed.), *The New Second Generation*. New York: Russell Sage.

Raissiguier, Catherine. 1993. "Negotiating Work, Identity, and Desire: The Adolescent Dilemmas of Working-Class Girls of French and Algerian Descent in a Vocational High School." C. McCarthy and W. Crichlow (eds.), *Race, Identity, and Representation in Education*. New York: Routledge.

Raissiguier, Catherine. 1994. *Becoming Women, Becoming Workers: Identity Formation in a French Vocational School*. Albany: State University of New York Press.

Reid, E. 1989. "Black Girls Talking." *Gender and Education*, Special Issue: "Race, Gender and Education" 1.3 (1989): 295–300.

Rich, Adrienne. 1980. "Compulsory Heterosexuality and Lesbian Existence." *Signs* 5.4 (1980): 631–660.

Riddell, Sheila. 1992. *Gender and the Politics of the Curriculum*. London and New York: Routledge.

Riley, Kathryn. 1985. "Black Girls Speak for Themselves." In G. Weiner (ed.), *Just a Bunch of Girls: Feminist Approaches to School*. Milton Keynes and Philadelphia: Open University Press.

Rivera-Batiz, Francisco. 1993. *The Multicultural Population of New York City: Set of Tables for Presentation*. October 26, 1993. Unpublished.

Rivera-Batiz, Francisco. 1994. "The Multicultural Population of New York City: A Socioeconomic Profile of the Mosaic." In F. Rivera-Batiz (ed.), *Reinventing Urban Education: Multiculturalism and the Social Context of Schooling*. New York: Institute for Urban and Minority Education Press.

Rodríguez, Clara E. 1989. *Puerto Ricans Born in the U.S.A.* Boston: Unwin Hyman.

Rodríguez, C., Korrol, V., and Alers, J. (eds.) 1984. *The Puerto Rican Struggle: Essays on Survival in the United States*. Maplewood, N.J.: Waterfront Press.

Roman, Leslie. 1976. "Intimacy, Labor, and Class: Ideologies of Feminine Sexuality in the Punk Slam Dance." In L. Roman, L. Christian-Smith, and E. Ellsworth (eds.), *Becoming Feminine: The Politics of Popular Culture*. London and Philadelphia: The Falmer Press.

Roman, L., Christian-Smith, L., and Ellsworth, E. (eds.). 1988. *Becoming Feminine: The Politics of Popular Culture*. London and Philadelphia: The Falmer Press.

Rubin, L. 1976. *Worlds of Pain*. New York: Basic Books.

Sadovnik, Alan (ed.) 1995. *Knowledge and Pedagogy: The Sociology of Basil Bernstein*. Norwood, N.J.: Ablex.

Sarup, Madan. 1986. *The Politics of Multi-racial Education*. London: Routledge and Kegan Paul.

Schofield, Janet W. 1995. *Computers and Classroom Culture.* Cambridge and New York: Cambridge University Press.

Scott-Jones, Diane, and Clark, Maxine. 1986. "The School Experiences of Black Girls: The Interaction of Gender, Race, and Socioeconomic Status." *Phi Delta Kappan* 67 (March 1986): 520–526.

Semel, Susan. 1995. "Basil Bernstein's Theory of Pedagogic Practice and the History of American Progressive Education: Three Case Studies." In A. Sadovnik (ed.), *Knowledge and Pedagogy: The Sociology of Basil Bernstein.* Norwood, N.J.: Ablex.

Sharen, S. (ed.). 1990. *Cooperative Learning: Theory and Research.* New York: Praeger.

Sharp, R. and Green, A. 1976. *Education and Social Control.* London: Routledge and Kegan Paul.

Sharpe, Sue. 1987. *Just Like a Girl: How Girls Learn to be Women.* Harmondsworth, England: Penguin.

Sidel, Ruth. 1990. *On Her Own: Growing Up in the Shadow of the American Dream.* New York: Penguin.

Simms, Margaret. 1988. "The Choices that Young Black Women Make: Education, Employment, and Family Formation." Working Paper No. 190. Wellesley College Center for Research on Women, Wellesley, Mass.

Simon, Roger. 1987. "Work Experience." In D. Livingstone (ed.), *Critical Pedagogy and Cultural Power.* South Hadley, Mass.: Bergin and Garvey.

Simon, W. and Gagnon, J. 1971. "Psychosexual Development." In D. L. Grummon and A. M. Barclay (eds.), *Sexuality: A Search for Perspectives.* New York: Van Nostrand Reinhold.

Skeggs, Beverly. 1991. "Challenging Masculinity and Using Sexuality." *British Journal of Sociology of Education* 12.2 (1991): 127–139.

Slavin, Robert. 1985. "Cooperative Learning: Applying Contact Theory in Desegregated Schools." *Journal of Social Issues* 41.3 (1985): 45–60.

Sleeter, Christine. 1993. "How White Teachers Construct Race." In C. McCarthy and W. Crichlow (eds.), *Race, Identity, and Representation in Education.* New York: Routledge.

Smith, Dorothy. 1987a. *The Everyday World as Problematic: A Feminist Sociology.* Boston: Northeastern University Press.

Smith, Dorothy. 1987b. "Women's Perspective as a Radical Critique of Sociology." In S. Harding (ed.), *Feminism and Methodology.* Bloomington: Indiana University Press and Milton Keynes, England: Open University Press.

Smith, Dorothy. 1977. "A Sociology for Women." In J. Sherman and E. Torton Beck (eds.), *The Prism of Sex: Essays in the Sociology of Knowledge.* Madison: The University of Wisconsin Press.

Smith, Elsie, 1988. "The Career Development of Young Black Females: The Forgotten Group." *Youth and Society* 12.3 (March 1981): 277–312.

Solomon, R. Patrick. 1992. *Black Resistance in High School: Forging a Separatist Culture.* Albany: State University of New York Press.

Spelman, Elizabeth. 1988. *Inessential Woman: Problems of Exclusion in Feminist Thought.* Boston: Beacon Press.

Spindler, George. 1963. *Education and Culture: Anthropological Approaches.* New York: Holt, Rinehart and Winston. Cited in L. Valli, "Becoming Clerical Workers."

Spindler, George (ed.). 1982. *Doing the Ethnography of Schooling: Educational Anthropology in Action.* New York: Holt, Rinehart and Winston.

Stafford, Ann. 1991. *Trying to Work.* Edinburgh: University Press.

Stanley, J. 1986. "Sex and the Quiet Schoolgirl." *British Journal of Sociology of Education* 7.3 (1986): 275–286.

Stanley, Liz and Wise, Sue. 1983. *Breaking Out: Feminist Consciousness and Feminist Research.* London and Boston: Routledge and Kegan Paul.

Syron, Lisa. 1987. *Discarded Minds: How Gender, Race and Class Biases Prevent Young Women from Obtaining and Adequate Math and Science Education in New York City Public Schools.* New York: The Center for Public Advocacy Research.

Tancer, Shoshana. 1973. "La Quisqueyana: The Dominican Women, 1940–1970." In A. Pescatello (ed.), *The Female and Male in Latin America: Essays.* Pittsburgh: University of Pittsburgh Press.

Taylor, Jill McLean, Gilligan, Carol, and Sullivan, Amy. 1995. *Between Voice and Silence: Women and Girls, Race and Relationship.* Cambridge: Harvard University Press.

Taylor, Sandra. 1986. "Teenage Girls and Economic Recession in Australia: Some Cultural and Educational Implications." *British Journal of the Sociology of Education* 7.4 (1986): 379–395.

Taylor, Sandra. 1989. "Empowering Girls and Young Women: The Challenge of the Gender-Inclusive Curriculum." *Journal of Curriculum Studies* 21.5 (September–October 1989): 441–456.

Thompson, Sharon. 1995. *Going All the Way: Teenage Girls' Tales of Sex, Romance, and Pregnancy.* New York: Hill and Wang.

Thorne, Barrie. 1993. *Gender Play: Girls and Boys in School.* New Brunswick, N.J.: Rutgers University Press.

Tienda, Marta and Angel, Ronald. 1982. "Headship and Household Composition among Blacks, Hispanics, and Other Whites." *Social Forces* 61.2 (December 1982): 508–531.

Thomas, Claire. 1980. *Girls and Counter-School Culture.* Melbourne: Melbourne Working Papers. Cited in K. Weiler, *Women Teaching for Change.* South Hadley, Mass.: Bergin and Garvey, 1988.

Touraine, Alain. 1981. *The Voice and the Eye: An Analysis of Social Movements.* New York: Cambridge University Press.

U.S. Bureau of the Census. 1984a. Current Population Reports, Series P-20, No. 401. *Fertility of American Women.* Washington, D.C.: U.S. Government Printing Office.

U.S. Bureau of the Census. 1984b. Current Population Reports, Series P-23, No. 146. *Women in the American Economy.* Washington, D.C.: U.S. Government Printing Office.

U.S. Bureau of the Census. 1989. Current Population Reports, Series P-20, No. 438. *The Hispanic Population of the United States: March 1988.* Washington, D.C.: U.S. Government Printing Office.

U.S. Department of Education. 1992. *The Condition of Education, 1992.* Washington, D.C.: National Center for Education Statistics.

U.S. Department of Education. 1997. *Digest of Education Statistics: 1997.* Washington, D.C.: National Center for Education Statistics.

Valli, Linda. 1983. "Becoming Clerical Workers: Business Education and the Culture of Femininity." In M. Apple and L. Weis (eds.), *Ideology and Practice in Schooling.* Philadelphia: Temple University Press.

Valli, Linda. 1986. *Becoming Clerical Workers.* Boston: Routledge and Kegan Paul.

Vazquez-Nuttall, Ena. 1987. "Sex Roles and Perceptions of Femininity and Masculintity of Hispanic Women: A Review of the Literature." *Psychology of Women Quarterly* 11.4 (December 1987): 409–425).

Waldman, Elizabeth. 1985. "Today's Girls in Tomorrow's Labor Force: Projecting Their Participation and Occupations." *Youth and Society* 16.3 (March 1985): 375–392.

Walsh, Catherine. 1991. *Pedagogy and the Struggle for Voice: Issues of Language, Power, and Schooling for Puerto Ricans.* New York: Bergin and Garvey.

Weedon, Chris. 1987. *Feminist Practice and Poststructuralist Theory.* Oxford: Basil Blackwell.

Weiler, Kathleen. 1988. *Women Teaching for Change: Gender, Class and Power.* South Hadley, Mass.: Bergin and Garvey.

Weiner, Gaby (ed.). 1985. *Just a Bunch of Girls: Feminist Approaches to Schooling.* London: Open University Press.

Weiner, Gaby and Arnot, Madeline (eds.). 1987. *Gender under Scrutiny.* London: Hutchinson and the Open University Press.

Weis, Lois. 1985a. "Without Dependence on Welfare for Life: Black Women in the Community College." *Urban Review* 17.4 (1985): 178–199.

Weis, Lois. 1985b. *Between Two Worlds: Black Students in an Urban Community College.* London: Routledge and Kegan Paul.

Weis, Lois (ed.). 1988a. *Class, Race and Gender in American Education.* Albany: State University of New York Press.

Weis, Lois. 1988b. "High School Girls in a Deindustrializing Economy." In L. Weis (ed.), *Class, Race and Gender in American Education.* Albany: State University of New York Press.

Weis, Lois. 1990. *Working-Class without Work: High School Students in a Deindustrializing Economy.* New York and Oxford: Routledge and Kegan Paul.

Weis, Lois and Fine, Michelle. 1993. *Beyond Silenced Voices.* Albany: State University of New York Press.

Weis, L., Fine, M., Proweller, A., and Bertram, C. 1998. "I've Slept in Clothes Long Enough: Excavating the Sounds of Domestic Violence among Women in the White Working-Class." *Urban Review* 30.1 (March 1998): 1–28.

Wexler, Philip. 1987. *Social Analysis of Education: After the New Sociology.* London: Routledge and Kegan Paul. Cited in Catherine Raissiquier, 1994. *Becoming Women, Becoming Workers: Identity Formation in a French Vocational High School.* Albany: State University of New York Press.

Wexler, Philip. 1992. *Becoming Somebody: Toward a Psychology of School.* London: The Falmer Press.

Wexler, Philip and Whitson, Tony. 1982. "Hegemony and Education." *Psychology and Social Theory* 3 (1982): 31–42.

Whyte, William Foote. 1973. *Street Corner Society: The Social Structure of an Italian Slum*. Chicago: University of Chicago Press.

Wilkerson, M. B. 1987. "A Report on the Educational Status of Black Women during the UN Decade of Women: 1976–85." In M. Simms and J. Malveaux (eds), *Slipping through the Cracks: The Status of Black Women*. New Brunswick, N.J.: Transaction Books.

Willis, Paul. 1977. *Learning to Labour: How Working-Class Kids Get Working-Class Jobs*. London: Saxon House Books.

Willis, Paul. 1983. "The Class Significance of School Counter-Culture." In J. Purvis and M. Hales (eds.), *Achievement and Inequality in Education*. London: Routledge and Kegan Paul.

Wilson, Deirdre. 1978. "Sexual Codes and Conduct: A Study of Teenage Girls." In C. Smart and B. Smart (eds.), *Women, Sexuality and Social Control*. London: Routledge and Kegan Paul.

Wolpe, Ann Marie. 1978. "Education and the Sexual Division of Labor." In A. Kuhn and A. Wolpe (eds.), *Feminism and Materialism*. London: Routledge and Kegan Paul.

Wolpe, Ann Marie. 1988. "Experience as an Analytical Framework: Does It Account for Girls' Education?" In M. Cole (ed.), *Bowles and Gintis Revisited: Correspondence and Contradiction in Educational Theory*. London: The Falmer Press.

Wolpe, Ann Marie. 1989. *Within School Walls*. London and New York: Routledge.

Wood, J. 1984. "Groping toward Sexism: Boys' Sex Talk." In A. McRobbie and M. Nava (eds.), *Gender and Generation*. London: Macmillan.

Wright, Erik Olin. 1985. *Classes*. London and New York: Verso.

Young, Michael (ed.). 1971. *Knowledge and Control*. London: Collier Macmillan.

Zambrana, Ruth. 1988. "Toward Understanding the Educational Trajectory and Socialization of Latina Women." In T. McKenna and F. Ortiz (eds.), *The Broken Web*. Claremont, Calif.: The Tomas Rivera Center and Floricanto Press.

Zambrana, Ruth E. 1994. "Puerto Rican Families and Social Well-Being." In M. Baca Zinn and B. Thornton Dill (eds.), *Women of Color in U.S. Society*. Philadelphia: Temple University Press.

Zinn, Maxine Baca. 1987. "Structural Transformation and Minority Families." In L. Beneria and C. Stimpson (eds.), *Women, Households, and the Economy*. New Brunswick, N.J.: Rutgers University Press.

Zinn, Maxine Baca. 1994. "Feminist Rethinking from Racial-Ethnic Families." In M. B. Zinn and B. T. Dill (eds.), *Women of Color in U.S. Society*. Philadelphia: Temple University Press.

Zinn, Maxine Baca and Dill, Bonnie Thornton. 1994. *Women of Color in U.S. Society*. Philadelphia: Temple University Press.

Zinn, Maxine Baca and Dill, Bonnie Thornton. 1996. "Theorizing Difference from Multiracial Feminism." *Feminist Studies* 22.2 (Summer 1996): 321–331.

INDEX

Africa, 154–158, 229n. 3, 9, 10
Alternative High School: description of, 9, 10, 131–132, 147–150, 225n. 4, 225–226n. 5, 229n. 11; ethos of, 136–140, 150, 198 199; follow-up study by, 206; reasons girls attend, 132–136
Althusser, Louis, 15
Amott, Teresa and Matthaei, Julie, 81, 227n. 4
Anyon, J., 17, 154, 167, 228n. 1
Apple, Michael and Weis, Lois, 21, 22
Arnot, Madeleine, 5, 15, 17, 169, 177

Barrett, Michele, 16
Bernstein, Basil, 16, 17, 145–146, 153, 166, 169, 182, 199, 202, 228–229n. 2, 229n. 5
Bourdieu, Pierre, 16
Bowles, S. and Gintis, H., 15
boyfriends (romance), 18, 66–71, 92–97, 122–129, 188–190, 197, 227n. 9, 10

capitalism, 15, 160
child-rearing, 52–54, 57, 65, 79–86, 97, 104–110
China, 158–159
classification. See curriculum
Collins, Patricia Hill: matrix of domination, 23, 80, 89
communism, 157–160
community college, 25, 41–42
cooperative learning, 148, 150–152, 156
curriculum: at A.H.S., 153–163, 166–167, 198, 199; and notion of

classification, 146; as social process, 158, 199; recommendations, 207–208

domestic labor, 53, 61–66, 83, 89–92, 116–122, 207
dropout rates, 40, 41, 61, 227n. 4

ethnography, 8

family: composition of, 37–40; influence on girls' beliefs, hopes, plans, 83–85, 89–90, 96, 98, 110–111, 113, 115–116, 118–119, 122–126, 128, 198; as site of resistance, 22; wage, 59, 204
femininity; domestic labor and, 66, 117; oppositional, 17, 19, 23–24, 174, 175–177; social constructions of, 17–19, 24–27, 49, 55, 61, 68, 73, 92, 171, 175, 179–181, 190, 195, 197, 208
feminist research and theory, 7, 16–19, 22–28, 200
Fine, Michelle, 2, 87, 131, 140–141, 153, 160, 202, 205, 226n. 7, 230n. 6
Fine, Michelle and Weis, Lois, 225n. 3
Fordham, Signithia, 3, 203
frame (framing). See pedagogy
Fuller, Mary, 174, 178, 191

gender code, 5, 6, 72, 98, 128, 169, 177, 195, 196, 197, 202
gender oppression, 16, 26
Giroux, Henry, 16, 140
Griffen, Christine, 18, 90

247